The Great Texas
Social Studies Textbook
War of 1961–1962

Number Forty-Nine

Elma Dill Russell Spencer Series
in the West and Southwest

Historian J. Evetts Haley and folklorist J. Frank Dobie having a private conversation during a public hearing of the Texas House of Representatives Textbook Investigating Committee, January 31, 1962. (Courtesy of the *Austin American Statesman*.)

The Great Texas Social Studies Textbook War of 1961–1962

Allan O. Kownslar

TEXAS A&M UNIVERSITY PRESS
COLLEGE STATION

Copyright © 2020 by Allan O. Kownslar
All rights reserved
First edition

This paper meets the requirements of ANSI/NISO Z39.48–1992
(Permanence of Paper).
Binding materials have been chosen for durability.
Manufactured in the United States of America

Library of Congress Cataloging-in-Publication Data
Names: Kownslar, Allan O., author.
Title: The great Texas social studies textbook war of 1961–1962 / Allan O. Kownslar.
Other titles: Elma Dill Russell Spencer series in the West and Southwest; no. 49.
Description: First edition. | College Station: Texas A&M University Press, [2020]
  | Series: Elma Dill Russell Spencer series in the West and Southwest; Number Forty-Nine | Includes bibliographical references and index. | Summary: "The Great Texas Social Studies War of 1961–1962 was among the most extensive social studies textbook confrontations in the nation's history, certainly the most extensive in the Lone Star State. What was unique was that this was the first time it brought forth such a widespread confrontation between Texas conservatives and Texas liberals over what should appear in social studies programs. The monumental confrontation between those Texas conservatives and liberals brought out a star-studded cast of rather colorful spokespersons concerned with the content of social studies textbooks. Whether conservative or liberal, what they had to say in their public testimonies showed they spoke with sincerity, conviction, and passion. Equally important their public testimonies are every bit as relevant today as they were in 1961–1962"— Provided by publisher.
Identifiers: LCCN 2019034349 (print) | LCCN 2019034350 (ebook) | ISBN 9781623498375 (hardcover) | ISBN 9781623498382 (ebook)
Subjects: LCSH: Texas. State Textbook Committee—History—20th century. | Social sciences—Texas—Textbooks. | Textbooks—Censorship. | Textbook bias—Political aspects—Texas. | Social sciences—Study and teaching—Texas—History—20th century. | Social sciences—Study and teaching—United States.
Classification: LCC LB3047.5.T4 K68 2020 (print) | LCC LB3047.5.T4 (ebook) | DDC 300—dc23
LC record available at https://lccn.loc.gov/2019034349
LC ebook record available at https://lccn.loc.gov/2019034350

The stressing of both sides of a controversy only confuses the young and encourages them to make snap judgments based on insufficient evidence. Until they are old enough to understand both sides of a question, they should be taught only the American side. . . . If this struggle meant anything, it is the perpetuation of the Christian ethnic. There is no freedom except under the Christian ethnic as enshrined in the Constitution and the Bill of Rights.

—J. Evetts Haley (public testimony before the Texas House Textbook Investigating Committee, January 17, 1962)

Censorship . . . is never to let people know but always to keep them in ignorance. Never to enlighten but always to darken. It is easier to appeal to prejudice than to reason, to ignorance than to enlightenment. That is the way of the demagogue. . . . No use kidding ourselves—school children aren't fools. They don't live in vacuums. They're not going to be much influenced by some dull piece of propaganda, tale-twisting, and flag waving put into a textbook. . . . It goes over them just like water goes over a duck's back.

—J. Frank Dobie (public testimony before the Texas House Textbook Investigating Committee, January 31, 1962)

Contents

Preface ix

Acknowledgments xvii

Introduction 1

Chapter 1. A Nation Divided: Political and Social
Conflicts in the United States, 1945–1961 11

Chapter 2. The Lone Star: Political, Social, and
Educational Conflicts in Texas, 1945–1961 31

Chapter 3. Trouble Brewing: Setting the Stage for
the Texas Textbook Controversy of 1961–1962 45

Chapter 4. A Call to Arms: The Texas State Textbook
Committee Hearings, September 14, 1961 74

Chapter 5. The Verdict Is In: The Recommendations
of the Texas State Textbook Committee 91

Chapter 6. Historian versus Historian: J. Evetts Haley
Battles Paul F. Boller Jr. 104

Chapter 7. At War with the System: J. Evetts Haley
and the Texas State Board of Education 118

Chapter 8. The Conflict Escalates: The Texas Legislative
Hearings on American History Textbooks 126

Chapter 9. Fighting in the Library: The Texas House
Hearings and Literary Censorship 140

viii Contents

Chapter 10. Liberals versus Conservatives: The Texas
Institute of Letters and Texans for America 152

Chapter 11. Conservative Uprising: Mel and
Norma Gabler Join the Fray 178

Chapter 12. Disorder in the Court: The Contrasting
Texas Legislative Reports 197

Chapter 13. Unfinished Business: A Civil Lawsuit for
Slander and Accusations of Legislative Wrongdoing 212

Chapter 14. A Last Meeting but Far from a Conclusion 221

Epilogue 225

Appendix A. The Texas State Textbook Committee's
1961 List of Recommended Changes 241

Appendix B. American Groups or Individuals
Voicing Concerns about Social Studies Textbooks
(Reconstruction to the Present) 251

Appendix C. Point-Counterpoint Dialogue about the
Content in Social Studies Programs 255

Appendix D. Recommended Readings on the
Topic of History Education 261

Appendix E. Recommended Readings on the Development
of American Social Studies and Textbook Wars 265

Appendix F. State-Adopted History Textbooks for 1961 277

Notes 281

Selected Bibliography. The Cold War, the American
Communist Party, Joseph McCarthy, the McCarthy Era,
Darwinism, and Creationism 301

Index 309

Preface

WHILE AT THE University of Massachusetts at Amherst, I took an advanced graduate-level history seminar where I did a study of protests of history textbooks written by a who's who of the American Historical Association. My project focused on American strategies and philosophies in textbook protests from the 1890s through the 1930s. The protests, which received widespread publicity, primarily came from veteran organizations such as the Grand Army of the Republic and the United Confederate Veterans, with each wanting either their northern or southern versions of the Civil War to appear in American history textbooks, as well as patriotic, fraternal, nativist, ethnic, religious, business, labor, isolationist, prohibitionist, state legislative, and municipal governmental groups. An examination of the values of the individuals involved in those early textbook protests reflects many of the period's tensions. The United States was experiencing a rapid transition, becoming an industrialized and urbanized-immigrant society. Many people had to adjust to a time of international isolationism, as well as the defeat of Progressive idealism and America's failure at the Treaty of Versailles, which ended World War I. The generally accepted theme became not experimentation but stability. At the time, major protests of history books involved the promotion of sectionalism, ethnic pride, nativism, Anglo-Saxonism, Roman Catholicism, neo-Confederate devotion, racism, societal stability, isolationism, Protestantism, Anglophobia, American exceptionalism or nationalism, and antiradicalism. In many instances, those criticizing the books had not read them, and widespread distortion of material by protesters was common. When those textbook protests occurred, the American Historical Association mounted a very vigorous and for the most part extremely successful defense. As a result, sales of the most controversial American history texts remained extensive.

Nevertheless, those protests would serve as models for future American social studies textbook controversies, which have continued to the present, commencing with successful protests by some conservative business groups of social studies programs by progressive authors, especially during the 1930s to the end of World War II, with their particular target of Harold Rugg and his *Problems of Democracy* series. That was followed by sporadic conservative protests, in such places as Georgia and the Houston Independent School District (ISD), banning Dr. Frank A. Magruder's *American Government* for not being patriotic enough. Even so, at the time, Magruder's political science program remained the most widely used high school civics book in the United States. With that, a temporary lull of any major-extensive American protests of social studies textbooks would not occur again until the very late 1950s and into 1961–62.

After completing my graduate work in history, I returned to Texas, my native state, where I received a teaching position. Soon afterward, while I was doing research at the State Capitol Library in Austin, an archivist friend asked me if I had seen a copy of a 1962 Texas legislative report about the content of American history textbooks. I told him I had not seen it. He had some extra copies, and he gave me a one. I took the report to my office and filed it next to my history seminar paper, thinking I might eventually get around to using it for a research project.

A little later, during the 1970s and 1980s, some of the inquiry-oriented and point-counterpoint history and political science programs I did with Terry Smart were adopted for use in the Texas public schools and were accompanied by protests from both conservative and liberal groups. This made me realize I was experiencing firsthand some of the techniques I learned from my previous research on textbook criticisms.

Then, beginning in 2012, came a series of recent works with differing interpretations about current historiographical trends and the controversy surrounding the 2010 conservative-oriented history standards adopted by the Texas State Board of Education—the latter a direct

Preface

descendant of the great Texas social studies war of 1961–62, receiving much national and international attention. One interpretation of those 2010 standards came from Keith Erekson, editor of *Politics and the History Curriculum: The Struggle over Standards in Texas and the Nation* (Palgrave Macmillan, 2012). Erekson explores how the culture war politics that produced the formation of those standards reveal a greatly polarized society with differences over such topics as abortion, multiculturalism, gun control, gay marriage, evolution, and the care of the physical environment. Erekson goes on to explore how the Texas situation features such opposing groups as the liberal Texas Freedom Network and Mexican American Legislative Caucus versus the conservative Liberty Institute, Texas Conservative Coalition, and Christian Conservatives on a State Board of Education majority. According to Erekson, these conservative successfully rewrote the state's curricula according to their own beliefs, with little regard for students doing any worthwhile problem solving, analysis, or historical reasoning. Instead, emphasis is placed on the three Cs of American history in Texas: Christians, Confederates, and conservatives.

In contrast, Bill Ames, who helped develop the Texas Social Studies Standards of 2010, answered with *Texas Trounces the Left's War on History: How a Few Texas Conservatives Prevented Liberals' Negative Portrayal of American History* (Taylor Publishing, 2012). Ames maintains that liberal historians have rewrote a history that stresses, among other things, US imperialism, multiculturalism, and anti-Christian values. Ames argues that conservatives think the good is more prevalent than the bad in American history, which he claimed was founded on the Judeo-Christian heritage, a love of country, a free enterprise capitalistic economic system, and American exceptionalism. His book also includes numerous samples of comments from both liberals and conservatives before the Texas State Board of Education and what that conservatively dominated board ultimately approved in 2010.

In the same year as Erekson and Ames, Gail Collins published *As Texas Goes . . . How the Lone Star State Hijacked the American Agenda* (Liveright Publishing, 2012). Collins argues the Texas Social Studies Standards of 2010 were advised by a panel of so-called experts, including a member of the Minutemen Militia, another who claimed that only the white race was responsible for advancing civil rights for minorities in America, and yet another who felt that the federal income tax was against the teaching of the Bible. Collins's thesis is that since the 1960s, the public school textbook selection in Texas had been a target of the religious Right, which claimed their children were being exposed to a form of godless secularism and an overload regarding the benefits of federal governmental policies. Collins felt that the conservative majority on the Texas State Board of Education had placed in the standards their own favorite topics, such as replacing "democracy" with "constitutional republic" and adding such conservative historical figures as Phyllis Schlafly of the Eagle Forum and groups such as the Moral Majority, Contract with America, the Heritage Foundation, and the National Rifle Association.

Those books were followed by others, including David O'Donald Cullen and Kyle G. Wilkison (eds.), *The Texas Right: The Radical Roots of Lone Star Conservativism* (Texas A&M University Press, 2014). Cullen and Wilkison, along with seven other scholars, present a history of the origins of the Texas Right, from Reconstruction to 2014, arguing that right-wing Texans have historically responded to suspected movements that they felt cast doubt on the democratic process, instead emphasizing "liberty" over equality and economic individualism over community interests, without a fully thought-out philosophy. Among other things, the authors discuss right-wing Texans' negative reactions to labor unions, the United Nations, Jews, welfare, socialism, communism, civil rights, immigration, budget deficits, taxation, government regulation of business, and social security. Along with such Lone Star State conservative political activists as the Texas Regulars, Jeffersonian Democrats, Dixiecrats, John Birch Society, and Minute Women of America, the authors also feature such individuals as conservative governors Allan Shivers and Price Daniels, Christian evangelist J. Frank Norris, radio commentator Dan Smoot, US Army retired general Edwin Walker, and textbook critics J. Evetts Haley and Mel and Norma Gabler, with the latter five individuals among those who in one way or another played major roles in the great Texas social studies textbook war of 1961–62.

Fritz Fischer, with *The Memory Hole: The United States History Curriculum under Siege* (Information Age Publishing, 2014), then examines what he calls the radical Right and the radical Left and how their values affect contemporary history textbook content, with special consideration of how the two groups have dealt with textbook content about the founding fathers, Robber Barons, American exceptionalism, the New Deal, Joseph McCarthy, the "Golden Age" of the 1950s, and the presidency of Ronald Reagan. He charges the Far Right and the Far Left with forcing their preferred versions of history onto students, instead fostering a careful, analytical mind-set in the study of history. He covers textbook attacks from the late twentieth century to 2012, including the Texas situation of 2010, and concludes that all such educators seem to ignore that the discipline of history should engage students in an analytical process of inquiry, with an emphasis on *how* to think and not *what* to think.

Last but not least is Robert Wuthnow's *Rough Country: How Texas Became America's Most Powerful Bible-Belt State* (Princeton University Press, 2014). Wuthnow, the Gerhard R. Anderson Professor of Social Sciences and director of the Center for the Study of Religion at Princeton University, with his in-depth survey of religious history in the Lone Star State, focuses on events from Reconstruction to the early twenty-first century by considering how religion in Texas was influenced by slavery and the harsh frontier lifestyle. He explores how the founding of religious schools increased religion's role in both denominational and partisan politics, especially in regard to racial and ethnic problems and public morality. Wuthnow argues that within that background, many white conservative Christians were influenced in one way or another, with the result that beginning with the Prohibition movement, many of them gradually became more involved in the political scene. They became involved in textbook selection in the 1920s over the topic of evolution and increased their presence regarding issues such as social studies content, abortion, and LGBTQ issues into the early twenty-first century, led by such individuals as Texas governor Rick Perry and opposed to adversaries like the Texas Freedom Network. Wuthnow concludes that this "Rough Country" mentality made Texas the nation's strongest Bible Belt state, which carried over into such areas as social studies textbook selection.

It has also long been known that nationally, since Reconstruction and well into the twenty-first century, there have been American criticisms or disagreements among protestors and academics regarding the evolution of American historiography and the inclusion of such groups as minorities in social studies content, particularly in the area of history. This has been evident, for example, in survey studies of social studies battles such as the following: Joseph Moreau *Schoolbook Nation: Conflicts over American History Textbooks from the Civil War to the Present* (University of Michigan Press, 2003); O. L. Davis Jr. and Howard D. Mehlinger (eds.), *The Social Studies: Eightieth Yearbook of the National Society for the Study of Education* (University of Chicago Press, 1981); and Ronald W. Evans, *The Social Studies Wars: What Should We Teach the Children?* (Teachers College Press, Columbia University, 2004), *This Happened in America: Harold Rugg and the Censure of Social Studies* (Information Age Publishing, 2007), *The Hope for American School Reform: The Cold War Pursuit of Inquiry Learning in Social Studies* (Palgrave Macmillan, 2011), and *The Tragedy of American School Reform: How Curriculum Politics and Entrenched Dilemmas Have Diverted Us from Democracy* (Palgrave Macmillan, 2011).

This book seeks to add to this tradition of inquiry, exploring one of the most lively textbook controversies of our time. The resonance of Texas' great social studies textbook war of 1961–62 continues to be felt in the present day as history continues to unfold before our very eyes.

History is always changing and evolving. Likewise, when thinking about this unusual episode in Texas history, it's tempting but unreasonable to assume the people who gave public testimony never changed their opinions about what they said in the 1961–62 public textbook hearings. Emotions ran extremely high, especially during public hearings before the House Textbook Investigating Committee, when press, radio, and television reporters were present. The hearings were crowded with people anxious to testify, sometimes at length, and often important and well-known participants were present, all of which added to the excitement.

During the late 1970s, I had the good fortune to get to know on a first-name basis a friend who had testified during those 1962 House hearings. I had read his testimony—a fact I never mentioned to him. It was with considerable embarrassment that he recalled the event. "I can't remember why we were all so furious," he said, "and now it's humiliating to repeat some of the ridiculous things we said." He said he had testified at length, mostly about the importance of being diligent to prevent Communist influences in public schools and had especially attacked two books, *East of Eden* and *The Grapes of Wrath* by John Steinbeck, although he had never read either novel. Later, his high school daughter took him to task for his performance, which she, with all the assurance of an adolescent, had pronounced "just plain dumb!" "I think she was right," he told me. "I should have kept my mouth shut." I seriously doubt that he was the only one testifying to later change his mind, whether conservative or liberal.

While writing this book to depict a particular episode in Texas history, I *especially* had in mind all of the nation's social studies teachers and their colleagues, public school librarians and all other librarians, as well as college/university students preparing to teach social studies, along with their social studies methods teachers. Social studies teachers and public school librarians are and will continue to be the warriors on the front lines if during their professional careers they encounter a complaint about something they said in class or used in a textbook, a handout, a computer program, a PowerPoint presentation, or a video—or if they recommend a certain library book or even have it on one of their bookshelves. My hope is they will use this historical account with its numerous and very relevant point-counterpoint arguments as a resource for any possible assistance it may provide. It is likewise my intention that they or anyone else reading this volume will keep in mind the advice of nineteenth-century historian Lord John Emerich Dalberg-Acton. He maintained no one should have the right to criticize or dispute an opposing view until one can express that view not only as well as but better than its proponents can.

Acknowledgments

I WANT TO express my very special thanks to Eunice Herrington, my administrative assistant, for assisting me with scanning original sources and doing newspaper research. To my sons Donald and Edward Kownslar, for helping me with my computer problems and making known some valuable research sources. To Brandy Flores, our history department's academic office administrator, for keeping my endnotes intact, as well as Tom Shelton at the Institute of Texan Cultures—all for their most valuable help in locating some necessary original sources and audio recordings. To Jason Hardin of the Trinity University Library, for his assistance getting me some clearances regarding needed permissions, and to Mary Jane and Raymond Judd, for providing some difficult to locate biographical information.

I appreciate the continued support offered by Jay Dew of Texas A&M University Press as well as the wonderful archivists and other staff members at the Lorenzo de Zavala State Library and Archives, the Texas Legislature Reference Library, and the Texas Education Agency. I am also indebted to my anonymous critic readers.

I am grateful to have received permission to reprint excerpts from Paul F. Boller Jr., *Memoirs of an Obscure College Professor* (Texas Christian University Press, 1992), and William Martin, "The Guardians Who Slumberth Not" (*Texas Monthly*, November 1982); the photo of J. Evetts Haley and J. Frank Dobie, courtesy of the *Austin American Statesman*; and the photo of the Texas House of Representatives Textbook Investigating Committee, courtesy of the *Amarillo Globe-Times*. I owe a debt of gratitude to the Texas Education Agency, for the use of public testimonies on September 4, 1961, before the Texas State Textbook Committee; the Texas Legislative Reference Library, for the use of public testimonies

xviii   Acknowledgments

during January–April 1962, before the Texas House of Representatives Textbook Investigating Committee of the Fifty-Seventh Legislature; and the Texas State Library and Archives Commission, for the use of public testimonies on November 3, 1961, before the Texas State Board of Education.

Finally, and most importantly, I dedicate this volume to my wife, Marguerite Louise Hanicak Kownslar, without whose essential editorial assistance none of my books would even exist.

The Great Texas
Social Studies Textbook
War of 1961–1962

Pictured from left to right: William Dungan, Robert Bass, Nelson Cowles, Ronald Roberts, and John Alaniz. (Courtesy of the *Amarillo Globe-Times*, February 26, 1962.)

Introduction

WHEN COMPARED with what other surveys of American textbook battles demonstrate about content and historiography, the great Texas social studies war of 1961–62 was not all that unique, but it was among the most extensive social studies textbook confrontations in the nation's history—certainly the most extensive in the Lone Star State—and it shattered the temporary lull in major American social studies book protest battles that extended from the end of World War II into the very late 1950s.

During that time period, there were differences of opinion, primarily among academics, over the proper place, role, or emphasis history should receive in the social studies curriculum, and some local complaints about certain history content. There were also some concerns over political science programs, which some conservatives claimed were too pro–New Deal. However, overall, by the end of World War II, there was a temporary lull in protests regarding the social studies work of progressive educators. There was even a noticeable lack of criticism against Harold Rugg, who, as a result of repeated conservative attacks on his *Problems of Democracy* series, watched sales of his works fall by some 90 percent by the mid-1940s. While there were some localized conservative protests of Frank Magruder's *American Government* (discussed further in chapters 2 and 3), there were seemingly no extensive or major social studies battles during the period of 1946–60.

Education historian Ronald Evans argued that the threat of communism during 1946 to the 1950s was a major theme of the era, conveyed in schools as a threat to democracy. Within this framework, historian Joseph Moreau noted that textbooks of the immediate post–World War II era into the 1950s generally portrayed the history of the United States

2   Introduction

as a nation supporting common values and a land of economic well-being for all, with a typical family much like the Eisenhower era television version of *Father Knows Best*.

Joseph Moreau, as well as other scholars on the subject such as Evans, also noted that all this began to change when history authors and publishers began to deal with the problems of race relations, women's rights, and new ways to study American history. For example, in his *Schoolbook Nation* (University of Michigan Press, 2003), Moreau even wrote a lengthy chapter about how the story of America in school textbooks was changing, entitled "The Narrative 'Unravels,' 1961–1985," to show that by the early 1960s, the content and teaching of social studies and particularly that of American history was beginning to undergo another major transition, with publishers no longer providing dual editions of their American histories textbooks—one version for selected southern states and another version for the remainder of the nation.

Publishers by that time and into the early 1970s were also adopting new guidelines for authors, stressing greater emphasis on the inclusion of multiculturalism in their textbooks, with some conservatives opposing this. On a national scale, social studies programs by the early 1960s, along with university-level courses and programs, were being created and written by an emerging new professional group of historians, somewhat in the tradition of the older progressive ones but with more inclusive and multicultural ideas. These writers were supported by the reawaking of groups within a new emerging civil rights movement. African Americans and other minority groups were successfully able to influence content, particularly in elementary- and secondary-level American history books, in places such as Michigan, New York, and California. These somewhat liberal places were just beginning to experience their own major social studies wars, commencing during the early 1960s. In their various ways, such individuals as historian Paul F. Boller, folklorist J. Frank Dobie, and civil rights attorney Maury Maverick Jr., who opposed conservatives during the 1961–62 Texas social studies war, upheld these "new-school" ideas of what history books should include and what purposes they should serve for students.

All this occurred due to an emerging civil rights revolution and offshoots of the National Defense Acts of 1958 and 1961, which eventually federally funded programs for Project Social Studies, soon to begin in

Introduction 3

such places as Harvard University, Amherst College, Carnegie Mellon University, Ohio State University, and Colorado's Social Science Education Consortium, among others. These programs placed a major emphasis on inquiry-oriented, problem-solving, more inclusive and multicultural, and point-counterpoint approaches—the essence of the New Social Studies movement.

In the midst of all these new developments by the early 1960s, Texas issued a call for new social studies textbook programs, and the result was a social studies war never before witnessed in the Lone Star State—which was to become one of the most extensive in the nation's history. Equally significant, in 1961, Texas just happened to be in a position to be among the first of the nation's many other major social studies battles to emerge from the post–World War II era, soon followed elsewhere in the form of battles led by liberal civil rights groups. But it was the Texas battle led by some conservatives that would shatter the post–World War II temporary lull in major social studies textbook conflicts, especially on the topic of history education.

While there had been earlier disagreements in Texas about social studies content, previous battles over proposed social studies books in the Lone Star State were minor when compared with what occurred during 1961–62. Over the years, those disagreements continued to increasingly fester in Texas, until it seemed to explode with the conservative-dominated social studies standards of 2010, as explored further in the epilogue.

The Great Texas Social Studies War of 1961–1962 is thus the result of a thorough examination of the origin of this controversy, which established precedents for future Texas social studies battles well into the twenty-first century by increasing the scope and intensity of social studies adoptions in Texas for the next five and a half decades. Indeed, the Texas adoptions of social studies programs would never be the same after 1962.

The conflict began with the protestations of conservative groups such as Texans for America, the Texas Society of the Daughters of the American Revolution, the John Birch Society, and the Minute Women. Organizations that opposed these conservative groups included the Texas Institute of Letters, American Civil Liberties Union, Texas Library Association, and American Studies Association. Its members were New

Deal and Fair Deal Democrats and supporters of a civil rights revolution. The clash of values between the two Texas groups saw conservatives desperately trying to preserve the status quo while liberals fought for change, with more inclusive histories in the area of historiography. The clash brings to mind a quote stated long before by comedian Will Rogers who, paraphrasing Mark Twain, said, "The good old days ain't what they used to be and probably never was."

The Texas social studies textbook war of 1961–62 was greatly influenced by negative reactions to widespread extensions of federal authority, beginning with Pres. Franklin Roosevelt's New Deal and Pres. Harry Truman's Fair Deal domestic programs, with more and more Texas Democratic Party political leaders supporting these programs. There were also anxieties arising from the creation of the United Nations, the US Supreme Court decisions restricting the rights of states facing an emerging civil rights revolution, along with fears associated with the post–World War II Cold War era, McCarthyism with its Red Scare, a nuclear arms race with the Soviet Union, the reemergence of progressive education, and the election of ever-leaning liberal Democrats John F. Kennedy as president and Lyndon B. Johnson as vice president of the United States, carrying Texas in the process. These developments provided the spark that ignited an extensive Texas firestorm over social studies textbook content.

The monumental confrontation between those Texas conservatives and liberals brought out a star-studded cast of spokespersons concerned with the content of social studies textbooks. Whether conservative or liberal, their public testimonies exuded with sincerity, conviction, and passion. Some of those testifying obviously spent considerable time preparing what they had to say and deserve credit for that. Equally important, their public testimonies are as relevant today as they were in 1961–62.

Those testimonies so crucial to this book come from transcripts of speakers before the Texas Education Agency's Texas State Textbook Committee on September 14, 1961; transcripts of public testimonies during a November 13, 1961, meeting of the Texas State Board of Education; public testimonies in the "Report to the Texas House of Representatives to Speaker Byron Tunnell and Members of the 58th Legislature by the House Textbook Investigating Committee of the

Introduction 5

57th Legislature" (House document pursuant to HSR 736 and 205); and other public testimonies in January–April 1962, before the Texas House of Representatives Textbook Investigating Committee during its public hearings. They are referred to in the endnotes by the person giving the testimony, the date of the public testimony, and the line "public testimony before the Texas House of Representatives Textbook Investigating Committee." Those House hearings are now housed in audio recordings and transcripts at the Lorenzo de Zavala State Library and Archives Commission and the Texas Legislative Reference Library. One can obtain copies or recordings of those public testimonies from the appropriate state governmental agencies.

Parts of this volume also include word-for-word statements by the participants. For historical accuracy, the language used by the participants will be maintained and will not be edited to conform to twenty-first century standards of political correctness. Some of the public testimony or other excerpts included in this volume are lengthy. That is intentional, in order to capture the flavor, tone, and scope of the relevant arguments, crucial to what each side argued, and to make every attempt to avoid taking any speaker's comments out of context.

Indeed, this volume features what became during 1961–62 an explosion of arguments or ideas then put forth by Texas conservatives and Texas liberals in regard to social studies textbook content and the issue of censorship. The goal is to preserve the *essence* of their arguments, whether liberal or conservative, and let readers make up their own minds about this textbook controversy, in keeping with poet Robert Frost's advice that "education is the ability to listen to or consider anything without losing your temper or your self-confidence." And, no matter what the participants believed regarding the 1961–62 Texas textbook issue, the public testimonies in this volume are intended for serious readers who wish to examine objectively the various sides of this textbook issue, with the focus being on the arguments presented, which are as relevant today as they were during 1961–62.

The last paragraph in each chapter contains a transition to the following chapter. The purpose is to show how this controversy evolved as a step-by-step process gradually spread through a sequence of developments from one *interrelated* issue to another, which inevitably escalated into that great Texas social studies cultural war. What is depicted in one chapter quickly led to a related controversial issue described in the following chapter, as the issues seemingly had an unstoppable, dovetailing, and snowballing effect, with a life all their own. In essence, each chapter details a conflict that developed in a previous chapter, and is not a separate entity unto itself. This format is so as not to disturb the rhythm of events as they emerged, with the main theme throughout this volume focusing on one central question: what should public school students in a democratic society be allowed to study in a social studies course?

Chapter 1 is an overview of the post–World War II national and foreign scenes when the United States was in a Cold War with the Soviet Union and experiencing an emerging American civil rights revolution—major factors that set the stage for the 1961–62 Texas book protests.

Chapter 2 covers the predominate conservative political, economic, and social scenes in Texas, with some Cold War social studies textbook controversies, primarily over Frank A. Magruder's *American Government*, during the 1940s and 1950s—a direct prelude to the major social studies Texas 1961–62 protests, which occurred on a much wider scale.

Chapter 3 focuses on the changing Texas political scene by 1961–62 and historical explanations regarding the major concerns of conservative Texas textbook critics by that time. Those concerns dealt with Judeo-Christianity and the foundations of American civil government, Darwinian evolution, secular humanism, Communism and civil rights, and progressive education, with emphasis on the works of John Dewey, George Counts, and Harold Rugg.

Chapter 4 deals with the Texas State Textbook Committee hearings of September 14, 1961, when Texans for America and the Texas Society of the Daughters of the American Revolution expressed concerns about social studies content (especially the history programs) up for state adoption.

Chapter 5 shows the changes in the social studies programs recommended by the State Textbook Committee after its members had considered and mainly discarded complaints about the textbooks from members representing Texans for America and the Texas Society of the Daughters of the American Revolution.

Chapter 6 focuses on additional complaints about the history textbooks, carried over from Chapter 5, made by historian J. Evetts Haley of Texans for America about historian Paul F. Boller's alleged subversive conduct and content in an American history textbook he coauthored with Jean Tilford—a program highly recommended for adoption by the Texas State Textbook Committee and soon afterward approved for state adoption by the Texas State Board of Education. The chapter concludes with Boller's response to Haley's charges.

Chapter 7 shows Haley's continued concerns about the Boller-Tilford book, as well as Haley's arguments against the policies of the Texas State Board of Education. The chapter ends with Boller's further defense regarding his loyalty to the United States.

Chapter 8 depicts the immediate result when the Texas State Board of Education approved for adoption all of the history textbooks protested by Texans for America, as well as all of those protested by the Texas Society of the Daughters of the American Revolution, basically ignoring criticisms the two groups had about the books. Unsatisfied that their major concerns had not been met, the two groups then persuaded the Texas House of Representatives to conduct an investigation of history texts on the state-adopted list. That House Committee investigation, with its seven public hearings, became one of the most contentious episodes to date in state legislative history.

Chapter 9 shows the spread of the controversy from the classroom to the library, when some content about American literary writers and others noted in the approved history textbooks were considered controversial to members of Texans for America. That concern led to a motion to ban library books involving a who's who of American writers and thinkers. Those allegedly suspect authors, artists, or others included Ernest Hemingway, J. Frank Dobie, Sherwood Anderson, Stephen Vincent Benet, Aldous Huxley, Thomas Wolfe, George Orwell, McKinley Kantor, John Steinbeck, Herman Wouk, Lincoln Steffens, Ida M. Tarbell, Aaron Copland, Stephen V. Benet, Maxwell Anderson, Ralph Bunche, Theodore Dreiser, Bernard De Voto, Albert Einstein, William Faulkner, Sinclair Lewis, Upton Sinclair, Eugene O'Neill, Willa Cather, Jack London, and Carl Sandburg.

The debate over public school library books continues in chapter 10, when the House of Representatives Textbook Investigating Committee allotted time for members from the Texas Institute of Letters and Texans for America to make their opposing views known on the general issue of book censorship.

During the House textbook hearings, Mel and Norma Gabler also joined with Texans for America and the Texas Society of the Daughters of the American Revolution to make their first major public appearance, the subject of chapter 11. The Gablers would go on to become two of America's most well-known conservative textbook critics of the late twentieth century.

The results of the House Textbook Investigating Committee hearings, summarized in chapter 12, left its five House members—three conservatives and two liberals—in such disagreement that they decided to write separate reports on the appropriate content in social studies programs. Their lack of consensus reflects the wide cultural divide between opposing political views of that time.

Chapter 13 deals with further turmoil resulting from the Texas House of Representatives Textbook Investigating Committee hearings, when a private citizen insinuated that a member of that committee had a previous Communist affiliation. That House member went on to sue her for slander. Two of the members of the House Textbook Investigating Committee then accused one another of legislative wrongdoing, which led to investigations of their charges by the Texas House of Representatives and Texas Attorney General.

Chapter 14 focuses on the last meeting of the Texas House of Representatives Textbook Investigating Committee, after it ended its public hearings and received two petitions from private citizens. One petition included a call for the state legislature to approve a law eliminating from public school libraries any sources it deemed communistic of pornographic. The other petition urged the Texas House of Representatives to continue its investigation of social studies programs in the Texas public schools. By then, however, most members of the House had become so weary of the textbook controversy that they decided to ignore both petitions and end their textbook investigation.

As a classroom teacher, I always end my classes with a review of what was covered during each session with my students. Thus the epilogue serves as a review of the controversy, summarizing its effects on the present day; it ends with a list of questions for anyone to consider, especially regarding the future adoption of social studies programs.

Appendix A contains all the changes that the Texas State Textbook Committee formally recommended regarding the history programs up

Introduction 9

for state adoption in 1961—changes also approved by the Texas State Board of Education.

For further information about protests of American social studies books, appendix B contains a listing of American groups or individuals, from Reconstruction to the present, expressing concerns about the content of social studies programs.

Appendix C has a relevant point-counterpoint timeless summary dialogue on the topic of what should be included in social studies programs, with summary arguments presented by some of the more than 124 Texas conservatives and Texas liberals who offered public testimony before the Texas State Textbook Committee, the Texas State Board of Education, and/or the Texas House of Representatives Textbook Investigating Committee during the 1961–62 great Texas social studies war.

Appendices D and E contain annotated bibliographies with summaries of topics covering the period from the 1800s well into the twenty-first century. The bibliographies contain works by numerous authors, conservative and liberal, each offering particular interpretations of historiographical trends and/or nationwide social studies content battles on topics such as (1) the writing, teaching, and learning of history; (2) what has appeared and why in American history and/or social studies books to the present; and (3) major American social studies textbook wars. In addition to the works already cited by Keith Evekson, Bill Ames, Gail Collins, David O'Donald Cullen, Kyle G. Wilkison, Fred Fischer, and Robert Wuthnow, these annotations summarize the works of more than forty other writers regarding the areas of historiography, learning, and teaching of American history.

Appendix F contains state-adopted history textbooks for 1961 followed by a bibliography on such topics as the Cold War, the American Communist Party, the McCarthy era and Joseph McCarthy, Darwinism, and Creationism.

Looking back, the whole process, beginning with what should have been a routine textbook adoption in 1961, instead assumed incredible and inevitable momentum on its own to become the most controversial textbook adoptions to that time in Texas, if not one of the most extensive social studies textbook conflicts in the nation's history.

1

A Nation Divided

Political and Social Conflicts in the United States, 1945–1961

MAJOR SOCIAL STUDIES textbook protests in Texas during 1961–62 were the immediate result of events of the post–World War II era affecting the nation at large, with the emergence of McCarthyism, a Cold War with the Soviet Union, and an emerging civil rights revolution. Textbook critics debated the appropriate curriculum, with some supporting state powers over those of the federal government, free enterprise capitalism, American exceptionalism, and Protestantism, along with opposition to communism, socialism, the United Nations, the New Deal, and the Fair Deal. Reflecting the tumultuous climate of a nation in transition, Texas soon enough found itself embroiled in an all-out social studies textbook war—a conflict that ultimately found its basis in the great changes and growing pains endured by post–World War II America as a whole.

To better understand the story of this Texas social studies textbook controversy, imagine it is the fall of 1961. Many Americans were reacting with some degree of anxiety or uncertainty to the world situation as they knew it. They did not have the knowledge or hindsight people today have about the immediate post–World War II era. And, while times and people change, this is the story about what some Texans thought and did during 1961–62, and how events of that time had an immediate impact on the Texas adoption of social studies textbooks. It is important to put this era in context and to keep in mind what was occurring and why people thought and acted as they did with the knowledge they had available.

In the fall of 1961, John F. Kennedy, a Massachusetts Roman Catholic educated at Harvard University, had been president of the United States for less than seven months, and he and his vice president, Lyndon B. Johnson, who was becoming more and more liberal, both had allies in Congress and the US Supreme Court in a push for greater federal social and economic programs as further expansions of Franklin Roosevelt's New Deal and Harry Truman's Fair Deal, along with greater federal guarantees in such areas as civil rights guarantees for all citizens. They and the American public likewise faced a period of international turmoil, with an extremely dangerous nuclear arms race between the United States and the Soviet Union. Rather than allow democratic elections in Eastern European countries the Soviets controlled after World War II, Josef Stalin instead forcefully installed his own Communist governments there. In so doing, Stalin was in direct violation of the February 11, 1945, Yalta Agreement he made with British prime minister Winston Churchill and US president Franklin Delano Roosevelt. According to that agreement, Europe's restoration would "be achieved by processes which enable the liberated peoples to destroy the last vestiges of Nazism and Fascism and to create democratic institutions of their own choice." Stalin, Churchill, and Roosevelt pledged to defend "the right of all peoples to choose the form of Government under which they will live," so that "all men in all the lands may live out their lives in freedom from fear and want."

The Cold War continued in earnest when Soviet premier Nikita Khrushchev, unhappy over the 1960 U2 spy episode, began boasting that the Soviet Union would bury the United States and thwart America's goals by using the all-important veto power on the Security Council of the United Nations. Pres. Dwight D. Eisenhower responded by arguing that peace could be maintained by being so strong militarily that a nuclear war between the United States and the USSR would be unthinkable, since no country would risk "mutually assured destruction."

By 1961–62, China was also firmly under the control of Mao Tse-tung's Communists, and the Dalai Lama was in India, having fled Tibet after a failed uprising by Tibetans against Chinese rule. The Korean War had become a stalemate, and in 1961 there were more than eight thousand American military personnel still listed as missing in action or unaccounted for in that conflict with no direct evidence of death; North Korea had also failed to return about nine hundred American POWs to US authorities. American troops were still "advisers" in a festering Vietnam conflict. Moreover, just ninety miles from the shores of the United States, Fidel Castro's Communist government controlled Cuba, especially after an ill-fated CIA-trained counterrevolutionary force landed on Cuba's Bay of Pigs to overthrow the Castro regime. East Germany had just closed the border between the western and eastern parts of Berlin, and the Communist government began building the Berlin Wall. And in America's attempt to catch up to the Soviet Union in the space race, which earlier had launched Sputnik on October 4, 1957, astronaut Alan Shepherd became the first American in space aboard the *Mercury-Redstone 3*, leading President Kennedy to tell Congress, "I believe that this nation shall commit itself to achieving the goal, before this decade is out, of landing a man on the moon and returning him safely to the earth."

On the domestic front, the Red Scare of the post–World War II era caused an anti-Communist movement, which increased in intensity when evidence of Communist subversion within the United States arose during the late 1940s and early 1950s. The Smith Act of 1940 made it illegal for anyone to advocate or teach about the overthrow of the American government by force and prohibited anyone in the United States to be a member of any organization that supported such views. While not enforced during World War II due to the US alliance with the Soviet Union, the federal government applied the Smith Act after the war to imprison some leaders of the American Communist Party. The Communists appealed their case to the US Supreme Court in *Dennis v. United States* but lost in 1951. The court majority used a version of the "clear and present danger" doctrine of the *Schenck* case of 1919 as its rationale. The clear and present danger issue related to the Smith Act resurfaced in 1957 with the case of *Yates v. United States*. Again, American leaders of the Communist Party were involved. This time, the court overturned their convictions, as well as the Communist Control Act of 1954, signed into law by Pres. Dwight D. Eisenhower, which virtually outlawed the Communist Party in the United States. The Supreme Court held that no one could be punished simply for advocating communism, which was within the right of freedom of speech. What could be punished, the court said, was speech that incited others to specific actions while trying to overthrow the government by force.

There were some American Communists or Communist sympathizers who wanted to help the Soviet Union by spying for it. They included at least several hundred US citizens, beginning during World War II. That was also when US governmental personnel intercepted all transmissions the Soviets sent to America. By the late 1940s, authorities found a method, called *Verona*, to decipher those coded messages without Soviet knowledge. Their messages revealed how some Americans spied for the Soviet Union. One spy was physicist Theodore Hall, who worked at Los Alamos developing the atomic bomb. Hall actually gave the Soviets most of the key essentials for building the atomic bomb. He had help from another idealistic American Communist, Saville Sax. Since the FBI could not let the Soviets know about the existence of its decipher operations, the two men were never brought to trial. Some of the other American officials spying for the Soviets, about one hundred of the three hundred identified from the decodes, were in the OSS (forerunner to the CIA), and the Justice, State, Treasury, and Defense departments. All those suspected remained free for the same reason as Hall and Sacs—to prevent the Soviets from knowing about Verona. More spies could have been identified, except that William A. Weis, one of those familiar with the decipher operation, told the Soviets about it in 1948. They immediately changed their code systems. Weis was charged with contempt of court, but he, too, could not be convicted publicly without revealing the secret existence of the spying operation and endangering America's national security.

Some of the more well-known examples of espionage in the United States included an admitted Communist spy, Whittaker Chambers, who in 1948 charged former Department of State official Alger Hiss of spying for the Soviet Union. His accusation against Hiss dominated the nation's headlines for months. Hiss sued Chambers for libel and lost, and federal authorities in 1950 convicted Hiss on two counts of perjury.

The most famous spy case of the era involved Julius and Ethel Rosenberg. They received the death penalty for conspiracy to commit espionage and were executed in June of 1953. Ethel was executed

A Nation Divided 15

primarily on the testimony of her brother, David Greenglass, another American spy for the Soviet Union. Later declassified documents showed that Julius gave a KGB officer some US military electronic secrets having to do with a proximity missile that could destroy a target without even hitting it directly. Greenglass later admitted he lied about Ethel being a spy, and later-released Verona documents (which the US government could not admit it had at the time) as well as KGB documents showed that although Ethel knew about her husband's espionage activities, she did not spy for the Soviet Union.

The Rosenberg case became even more significant because of an earlier case in Great Britain involving Klaus Fuchs, a German-born British physicist who had worked on the American development of an atomic bomb. He went on trial in London in 1950 and was convicted of giving the Soviets atomic secrets during 1943–47. His espionage helped the Soviets successfully detonate their first atomic bomb in September of 1949—probably three years before they could have done so without Fuchs's help. Shortly afterward, three British officials spying for the Soviet Union—David McClean, Guy Burgess, and Kim Philby—fled to Russia to avoid prosecution from British authorities.

As the hunt for Red spies accelerated, many American civilian groups began to help law enforcement agencies seek out alleged Communists or their sympathizers. Those suspected of being Communists or Communist sympathizers could be put on a blacklist. Some blacklisted individuals refused to sign the newly required loyalty oaths, maintaining that the oaths violated basic civil rights. Most people, however, went along with the trend and signed the oaths. To do otherwise could get them accused of being soft on communism.

What developed was a climate of fear that began as far back as 1938, when the US House of Representatives formed the House Un-American Activities Committee. This was an anti-Fascist, anti–New Deal, and anti–labor union effort, but later included anti-Communist goals. US Representative Martin Dies Jr. of Texas, chair of the House Un-American Activities Committee, warned: "Never participate in anything without consulting the American Legion or your local Chamber of Commerce." Dies did learn of some Soviet espionage in the United States but was basically ignored when the country entered World War II with the Soviet Union as an ally. After the war, Dies renewed his work with great zeal.

16   Chapter 1

With help from J. Edgar Hoover and the FBI, the goal of the House Un-American Activities Committee during the post–World War II era and until its demise in the 1970s was to search out and identify individuals suspected of being Communists, radicals, or nonconformists—including homosexuals, who some feared could be subject to blackmail. These individuals were lumped in a group some of the House Un-American Activities Committee members deemed unpatriotic or disloyal to the United States. The influence of such activities by the House Un-American Activities Committee damaged the careers of many teachers; librarians; writers; actors; singers; employees in federal, state, and local governments; reporters; and others who either had refused to testify before local, state, and federal Communist-hunting committees or were "tainted" by having to testify or knowing others who did. Many lost their jobs.

Working in conjunction with the House Un-American Activities Committee by 1951 was Republican Joseph Raymond McCarthy's Permanent Subcommittee on Investigations at the Senate Committee on Government Operations. McCarthy, who was not informed of the existence of Verona, used his political power as chairman of the Senate subcommittee to investigate federal civil servants and held televised hearings in regard to possible Communist influences in the US Army. McCarthy violated an agreement with Joseph Nye Welch, the army's special counsel, not to mention that a young Republican attorney in Welch's law firm was at one time a member of the National Lawyers' Guild, who defended the Rosenbergs and others in the entertainment field accused of being Communists. When McCarthy did that in a televised army hearing, Welch countered to McCarthy: "Have you no sense of decency, sir? At long last, have you left no sense of decency?" It was one of the most devastating things ever said to McCarthy.

McCarthy also attacked, among others, Pres. Harry Truman; former secretary of state George C. Marshall, who had been the military general directing American and Allied fighting forces during World War II and had received the Nobel Peace Prize; and Secretary of State Dean Acheson. McCarthy called Marshall a traitor, Acheson the "Red Deal of Fashion," and Truman a drunkard who "should be impeached." McCarthy even alarmed President Eisenhower to the extent that regarding appointments to the Atomic Energy Commission, Eisenhower told James Hagerty, his press secretary: "We've got to handle this so that all of our scientists are not made out to be Reds. That goddamn McCarthy is just likely to try such a thing."

McCarthy believed American government personnel associating with Communists were unfit, just as persons known to associate with kidnappers would be ill suited to babysit children, even though a court of law had never found them guilty of a crime. McCarthy made the following comparison:

> [Consider] the case of the applicant for a job as bank cashier who travels with safe-crackers, robbers, and gamblers. Naturally, such a man would not be hired as cashier and allowed access to depositors' money. The fact that the bank president does not give him a job as cashier does not mean the job applicant has been found guilty of any crime. It merely means that the bank president, using good horse-sense, decides that his depositors are entitled to have this man kept away from their money while he has associates who are bank robbers and safe-crackers. Certainly in dealing with the lives of countless sons of American mothers and the liberty of the American people, we should be using the same good common horse-sense that the bank president uses.[1]

A defense of McCarthy came from Roy Marcus Cohn, McCarthy's chief of staff, who later became a successful lawyer in New York City and president of the American Jewish League against Communism. Cohn regarded McCarthy as a man of very simple tastes who was sometimes "impatient, overly aggressive, overly dramatic," acted on impulse, would sensationalize evidence to show its seriousness, and sometimes did not do his homework well, but "he was right in the essentials," since the US government had within it "enough Communist sympathizers and pro-Soviet advisers to twist and pervert American foreign policy for close to two decades. . . . [Attacks on McCarthy's methods] suffer from a credibility gap because of the double standard of many critics, particularly the press, radio, and television."[2]

Nevertheless, McCarthy's tactics had become a concern of members of the US Senate, particularly Republican Margaret Chase Smith of Maine as well as CBS journalist Edward R. Murrow and former first lady Eleanor Roosevelt. A US Senate subcommittee headed by anti-Communist and Maryland Democrat Millard Tydings finally concluded McCarthy had carried out "a fraud and a hoax" in claiming that Owen Lattimore, a Far Eastern policy specialist, was a Communist spy. Then, on December 2, 1954, the Senate voted 67 to 22 to censure McCarthy for bringing the Senate into "dishonor and disrepute" and damaging the dignity of Congress by declaring he had "affected the honor of the Senate and . . . repeatedly abused the [Senate] subcommittee and its members who were trying to carry out assigned duties, thereby obstructing the constitutional processes of the Senate, and that this conduct of . . . McCarthy is contrary to senatorial traditions and is hereby condemned." Then US senator Lyndon B. Johnson said, "If we [do not] sanction [McCarthy's] abuse, the Senate may as well close up shop." McCarthy further lost favor when the Democrats gained control of the US Senate in 1955. It cost him chairmanship of his Senate subcommittee, and he no longer could issue subpoenas or call hearings. He gradually faded into obscurity and died of liver failure on May 2, 1957, at the age of forty-eight.

During this time, loyalty review boards also began to grow in presence and influence across the country. Their members would sometimes ask persons under scrutiny about their allegiance to the United States and would alert authorities about suspected subversives—what literature they read, what their religious beliefs were (or lack thereof), what their sexual preferences or habits were, what they thought about equal rights for women or other minorities, and whether any of their friends or associates were of a different race.

Various other federal laws assisted those in the hunt for alleged Communists. The McCarran Internal Security Act of 1950 made it illegal "to combine, conspire or agree with any other person or perform any act that would substantially contribute to the establishment . . . of totalitarian dictatorship" or for any "Communist-front organization" to fail to register with the US Attorney General. The law established a Subversive Activities Control Board to monitor the activities of Communists in America and to forbid entry into the United States for anyone who had ever been a member of any totalitarian organization. President

Truman vetoed the bill on the grounds that it would "put the government into the business of thought control." He said the act was "about as practical as requiring thieves to register with the sheriff." Congress then proceeded to override his veto. However, in 1965, the US Supreme Court ruled the McCarran Act unconstitutional on the grounds that the government could not force a person to register as a Communist because the law as written amounted to self-incrimination.

Another law, also passed over President Truman's veto, was the McCarran-Walter Immigration and Nationality Act of 1952, not rescinded until 1990. It required any foreigners who visited the United States to pass a series of very complicated loyalty checks before gaining entry into the country. Truman stated in his veto message, "Seldom has a bill exhibited the distrust evidenced here for citizens and aliens alike."

While President Truman opposed excesses of such investigations, he was not exempt from helping them along. Especially significant was his 1947 loyalty program, Executive Order 9835, which focused more on national loyalty than security. Its associated loyalty review board did not allow for full due process of law, and those accused could not confront people who testified against them. This was accompanied by the Truman administration publishing the Attorney General's List of Subversive Organizations (AGLOSO) in 1947. It listed hundreds of suspected organizations without any notice, evidence, or hearings. As a result, the list damaged the reputation of hundreds of groups, and many non-government employees lost their jobs. During 1948–51, government investigators also checked on more than 4,000,000 federal civilian employees. Charges were brought against some 12,000 employees, and 379 of them received dismissals as security risks. However, lacking sufficient evidence, none were ever indicted for espionage. Nationally, nearly 14,000,000 Americans signed loyalty oaths in order to be employed. The loyalty oaths became so prevalent that New York State even had those applying for fishing licenses sign an oath condemning communism.

President Truman had issued Executive Order 9835 to counter charges that he and the Democratic Party were soft on communism and to act against excesses of the House Un-American Activities Committee and other committees like it. But Truman came to realize that overzealous security officials had taken his order too literally, and hundreds of law-abiding Americans came to suffer greatly from his executive order. He expressed his concerns in a speech on November 14, 1947:

> We must not . . . permit employees of the federal government to be labeled as disloyal or potentially disloyal to their government when no valid basis exists for arriving at such a conclusion. . . . Hearings before the board will be conducted so as to establish all pertinent facts and to accord the suspected employee every possible opportunity to present his defense. . . . The government, as the largest employer in the United States, must be the model of a fair employer. It must guarantee that the civil rights of all employees of the government shall be protected properly and adequately. It is in this spirit that the loyalty program will be enforced.[3]

Nevertheless, when the Korean War broke out in 1950, President Truman signed a law allowing the detention of "dangerous radicals" in the event that the president declared a national emergency. That never came about, nor did he approve a 1950 recommendation by FBI director J. Edgar Hoover that he suspend the writ of habeas corpus and imprison some twelve thousand American citizens suspected of disloyalty to the United States.

President Truman became so distressed over the Red Scare witch hunt that in November of 1953, after he had left office, he said in a television appearance that McCarthyism "is the corruption of truth, the abandonment of our historical devotion to fair play. It is the abandonment of the 'due process' of law. It is the use of the big lie and the unfounded accusation against any citizen in the name of Americanism or security. It is the rise to power of the demagogue who lives on untruth; it is the spread of fear and the destruction of faith in every level of our society." In subsequent public speeches, he called the McCarthyites "smearers and slanders," "hate-mongers," and "political gangsters" who used "innuendo and smear and just plain common, ordinary lies" to hurt government employees, and declared that "character assassination is their stock and trade."

Even so, Truman's successor, President Eisenhower, issued Executive Order 10450 in 1953, which revised the federal loyalty program to make it easier to try to identify alleged security risks, which included "[a]ny deliberate misrepresentations, falsifications, or omissions of material facts. Any criminal, infamous, dishonest, immoral, or notoriously disgraceful conduct, habitual use of intoxicants to excess, drug addition, sexual perversion, or financial irresponsibility. Any facts which furnish reason to believe that the individual may be subjected to coercion, influence, or pressure which may cause him to act contrary to the best interests of the national security." Eisenhower went further and ordered that all companies doing business with the federal government get rid of any suspected homosexuals, because they could possibly be blackmailed.

The year 1953 also brought the State Secrets Privilege Surveillance Program. It forbid disclosure of data in court when "there is a reasonable danger that compulsion of the evidence will expose military matters which, in the interest of national security, should not be divulged." This meant that Americans suspecting the government of spying on them would not have legal standing to sue the government if it claimed secrecy on national security grounds.

At state and local levels during the immediate post–World War II era and into the sixties, materials for public schools and libraries remained targets of "Red hunters," including members of the anti-Communist John Birch Society and the Minute Women—with both groups also opposing anything they regarded as sympathetic to big government and creeping socialism. In many communities, for example, any praise of the United Nations in a textbook sometimes resulted in it not being adopted for classroom use. The rationale was that Communists were too influential in the United Nations.

Also on the domestic front, there was the beginning of a massive civil rights movement, which critics and Red Scare proponents linked back to communism. This was because the American Communist Party advocated the racial integration of all public facilities and schools. Additionally, as noted, for example, by Philip J. Jaffe in *The Rise and Fall of American Communism* (Horizon Press, 1975), Guenter Lewy in *The Cause That Failed: Communism in American Political Life* (Oxford University Press, 1997), and Joseph R. Starobin in *American Communism in Crisis, 1943–1957* (Harvard University Press, 1972), the Communist

22 Chapter 1

Party USA, founded in 1919 as part of the American labor union movement, among other things, was opposed to racial and ethnic discrimination not only in the workplace but in all other aspects of American life.

By the mid-1950s, however, so many FBI informants had infiltrated the American Communist Party and financed its activities that its membership was less than five thousand. This allowed J. Edgar Hoover, director of the FBI, to keep watch on the party's remaining members, who had little opportunity to commit acts of espionage against the United States.

However, during that time, one did not have to be a member of the Communist Party to spy for the Soviet Union. Americans Theodore Hall, Saville Sac, Whittaker Chambers, Ethel and Julius Rosenberg, and David Greenglass, for example, were not members of the Communist Party. Even so, for many Americans, the Communist Party USA's support of racial integration linked it with other domestic groups seeking the same goals, such as Dr. Martin Luther King's civil rights efforts.[4]

In the area of civil rights, changes began when the US Supreme Court ruled on December 12, 1938, in the case of *Gaines v. S. W. Canada* (305 U.S. 337) that the state of Missouri could not prohibit African Americans from enrolling in its University of Missouri Law School. Plaintiff Lloyd Lionel Gaines won the case, but four months later vanished, possibly due to foul play. Six years later, the US Supreme Court in *Smith v. Allwright* (321 U.S. 649, 1944) held that the Texas Democratic Party's exclusion of African Americans from the party's primary elections was a violation of the rights of African Americans. In 1946, the US Supreme Court then ruled in *Mendez v. Westminster* (161 F2d 774, 64 F Supp. 544 S.D. Calif 1946, 9th Civ.) that placing children of Mexican descent in separate, substandard, inferior public school educational facilities was also in violation of the equal protection clause of the Fourteenth Amendment. Following that, the case of *Delgado v. Bastrop ISD* (Civil No. 388 W.D. Tex. 1948) held that de facto segregation of Mexican Americans children was illegal. Finally, California became the first state to desegregate its public schools. Two years later, the US Supreme Court in *Shelley v. Kraemer* (334 U.S. 1) held that covenants prohibiting the sale of real estate to blacks or members of other racial groups were legally unenforceable, and the US Supreme Court in *Spiuel v. Board of*

Regents of the University of Oklahoma (332 U.S. 63, 1948) again ruled that states could not discriminate against law school applicants on the basis of race.

In 1948, the United Nations also made a statement about basic civil liberties and freedoms. While serving as the US ambassador to the United Nations, Eleanor Roosevelt was instrumental in the formation and ratification of the Universal Declaration of Human Rights, the most sweeping statement to date in world history, urging guarantees of civil rights in *all* areas. For three years, as chairperson of the UN Commission on Human Rights, Roosevelt argued, compromised, and fought hard for the adoption of the document, until she convinced the General Assembly to approve it on December 10, 1948. The document was revolutionary in what it proclaimed—for example, the claim that everyone (and it meant *everyone*) is entitled to all basic rights and freedoms "without distinction of any kind, such as race, color, sex, language, religion, political or other opinion, national or social origin, property, birth or other status." She agreed to the nonbinding and mainly symbolic declaration as a first step with treaties to follow at a later time. Her view of the United Nations was one of pragmatism rather than idealism. She recognized the organization was not a cure for all the world's woes, but felt it was useful as a clearinghouse for ideas and offered a means to help the less fortunate as a police force when necessary to settle international disputes. Roosevelt especially wanted the Soviet Union in the United Nations so that all countries could recognize Soviet propaganda and hypocrisy for what it was.

Also in 1948, Pres. Harry S. Truman ordered the gradual racial desegregation of all factions of the armed services. Then the US Supreme Court heard the cases of *Shelley v. Kraemer* (334 U.S. 1) and *Hurd v. Hodge* (334 U.S. 24), ruling that racial covenants in real estate deeds violated the Fourteenth Amendment and the Civil Rights Act of 1866. The court followed that in 1950 with *Henderson v. United States* (339 U.S. 816), which struck down racially segregated railroad dining cars, and *Sweatt v. Painter* (339 U.S. 629), which, as in *Gaines v. S. W. Canada*, desegregated the graduate education program at the University of Oklahoma. Herman Marion Sweatt, an African American, had applied for admission to the University of Texas Law School. The school denied Sweatt's application; instead, it set up a separate school for Afri-

24   Chapter 1

can Americans: the Texas State University Law School. Sweatt with then NAACP attorney Thurgood Marshall took his case to the US Supreme Court by suing the all-white University of Texas Law School for admission. The Supreme Court decided it was Sweatt's constitutional right to have a legal education equal to that offered by the State of Texas to students of other races. Since the education offered to Sweatt at the all-black law school would not be equal to the one offered at the all-white University of Texas Law School, he had been denied his Fourteenth Amendment constitutional rights. Unfortunately, Sweatt later withdrew from the University of Texas School of Law, to quote one federal judge, "after being subjected to racial slurs from students and professors, cross burnings, and tire slashings." Shortly thereafter, the US Supreme Court in 1953 with *District of Columbia v. John R. Thompson Company* (346 U.S. 100) unanimously ruled that restaurants in the nation's capital could not be segregated according to race, nor could restaurants refuse to serve African Americans.

Two other key cases with landmark civil rights decisions came in 1954. That year, the US Supreme Court in *Hernandez v. Texas* (347 U.S. 475) ruled that Mexican Americans could not be barred from serving on juries, a violation of the Fourteenth Amendment. The other case occurred with the unanimous US Supreme Court case of *Brown v. the Board of Education of Topeka, Kansas* (347 U.S. 483, 1954). The court overruled the 1897 case of *Plessy v. Ferguson* (163 U.S. 537) by declaring the doctrine of "separate but equal" unconstitutional. Specifically, the court ruled:

> Today, education is perhaps the most important function of state and local governments. Compulsory school attendance laws and the great expenditures for education both demonstrate our recognition of the importance of education to our democratic society. It is required in the performance of our most basic public responsibilities, even service in the armed forces. It is the very foundation of good citizenship. Today, it is a principal instrument in awakening the child to cultural values, in preparing him for later professional training, and in helping him to adjust normally to his environment. In these days, it is doubtful that any child may reasonably be expected to succeed in life if he is denied the opportunity of an education. Such an opportunity, where the state has undertaken to

provide it, is a right which must be made available to all on equal terms. . . . We conclude that in the field of public education the doctrine of "separate but equal" has no place. Separate educational facilities are inherently [by nature] unequal. Therefore, we hold that the plaintiffs are, by reason of the segregation complained of, deprived of the equal protection of the laws guaranteed by the Fourteenth Amendment. This disposition makes unnecessary any discussion whether such segregation also violates the Due Process Clause of the Fourteenth Amendment.

The court followed that in 1955 with "Brown II," maintaining such desegregation proceed with "all deliberate speed." The results were calls from racial segregationists for the impeachment of Chief Justice Earl Warren and a determination to keep public schools segregated for as long as possible.

While all this occurred, Irene Morgan, a twenty-two-year-old African American mother of two, made her own history. Morgan worked in a factory making World War II bombers. After visiting her mother during July of 1944, she boarded a Greyhound bus in Gloucester, Virginia, for Baltimore. She refused to give up her seat when she was instructed to move further back in the bus to accommodate a white couple. At the time, it was illegal in Virginia and nine other states for blacks to sit next to whites on public buses. After being arrested, she paid a $100 fine for attacking a sheriff and one of his deputies when they arrested her, but would not pay a $10 fine and $5.25 in court costs for not relinquishing her seat on the bus. NAACP attorney Thurgood Marshall took her case to the US Supreme Court and used it to have the court declare racial segregation unconstitutional in interstate transportation. The Morgan case did not outlaw segregated seating for intrastate travel, but nine years later, it did pave the way for action by Rosa Parks, a seamstress, active member of her church, secretary and youth adviser of her local NAACP, and great-granddaughter of a white plantation owner and a slave housekeeper. Parks, then age forty-two, made civil rights history when on December 1, 1955, she refused to give up her seat to a white man on a city bus in Montgomery, Alabama, the first capital of the Confederacy. Shortly after police arrested Rosa Parks, Dr. Martin Luther King Jr., then age twenty-six, a newcomer to town, and pastor of the Dexter Baptist

26   Chapter 1

Church, called a meeting to discuss the matter. With help from African American activist Jo Ann Robinson of Montgomery's Women's Political Council, African Americans agreed to boycott the city bus system on the day of Parks's December 5 trial. This was also the time of King's conversion to nonviolent civil disobedience.

Those involved in the boycott initially asked the city authorities for a desegregation plan that would reserve seats on buses for blacks. When the city refused, the bus boycott continued and eventually lasted 381 days. It resulted in a November 13, 1956, US Supreme Court victory in *Browder v. Gayle* (142 F. Supp. 707), with the court declaring all bus segregation unconstitutional. The Montgomery boycott leaders then ended their bus stoppage on December 21, 1956, and Rosa Parks went on to help Dr. Martin Luther King Jr. in his civil rights efforts. As for King, he, along with Rev. Joseph Lowery and Ralph David Abernathy, would create the Southern Christian Leadership Conference in 1957.

Legal formalities aside, African Americans continued to experience prejudice and discrimination, especially in the South. Inadequate schools, lack of professional advancement, poor health services, threats, beatings, and even lynchings and other forms of violence were endured by many blacks. Additionally, at least seventeen southern states had anti-miscegenation laws, prohibiting marriage between anyone classified as "white" and those classified as "colored." A growing number of people felt all that had to change, and it did with the death of a fourteen-year-old Chicago youth named Emmett Till. During the summer of 1955, while visiting cousins in Tallahatchie County, Mississippi, Till allegedly whistled at Carolyn Bryant, a white female clerk at the local store. Shortly thereafter, he was found dead. Authorities charged two white men, Roy Bryant (husband of Carolyn) and J. W. Milan, with the murder of Till, but they were found not guilty by an all-white jury. In 1956, the two men sold their story to *Look* magazine, in which they admitted to killing Till, after seizing him at his cousin's house, severely beating him, bashing in his head, and dumping his body into a river. The murder of Till made national headlines and helped further mobilize those in the civil rights revolution.

Opposition to the civil rights movement continued when in March of 1956 ninety-six southern Congressmen issued a "Southern Manifesto." It condemned *Brown v. Topeka* as a "clear abuse of judicial power" and

A Nation Divided

a violation of "the reserved rights of the states and the people." Then, in 1957, Governor Orval Faubus of Arkansas used National Guard troops to keep nine black students—Thelma Mothershed, Minnijean Brown, Terrance Roberts, Melba Pattillo Beals, Jefferson Thomas, Gloria Ray, Elizabeth Eckford, Carlotta Walls, and Ernest Green (ages fourteen to sixteen)—from entering Central High School in Little Rock. A very reluctant Pres. Dwight David Eisenhower, who had said, "I do not believe you can change the hearts of men with laws and court decisions," finally used one thousand troops of the 101st Airborne Division to force Central High to admit the black students. A group of white students called for a walkout, but only about 60 of the 1,800 members of the student body participated. Many white students welcomed their new African American classmates, as did many white adults in Little Rock who urged for integration of the schools. Faubus then shut down the Little Rock schools for a year, but the school board reopened them, with African Americans integrated into several of the schools in the district.

By 1961, other segregationists also took action. Georgia's governor Eugene Talmadge had long successfully fought any attempts at desegregation. Governor Ross Barnett of Mississippi tried unsuccessfully to bar African American James Meredith from enrolling at the University of Mississippi—Meredith's fourth try. Theophilus Eugene "Bull" Connor of the Birmingham, Alabama, Public Safety Commission used brutal force to try to halt civil rights activists. South Carolina US senator Benjamin Ryann Tillman said, "When you educate a negro, you educate a candidate for the penitentiary or spoil a good field hand." Mississippi governor James K. Vardaman expressed, "What the North is sending down [for schools] is not money but dynamite. This education is ruining our negroes. They're demanding equality." Governor and later US senator Strom Thurmond of South Carolina launched the Dixiecrat Party in 1948. It opposed Pres. Harry Truman's 1948–49 civil rights program, a prelude to the ones of the 1960s under President Lyndon Johnson. Thurmond was adamant about keeping his state segregated, and when he and many southern segregationist Democrats bolted the Democratic Party, it almost cost Truman's reelection to the presidency in his own right,

Such moves for civil rights were also coupled with voter registration drives and civil and criminal lawsuits—all of which led to the creation

28   Chapter 1

of new laws and court decisions. For example, in 1957, Lyndon Baines Johnson, then Democratic Party Senate Leader, pushed through the first civil rights bill enacted by Congress in eighty-two years. It provided that anyone cited for contempt of court in a civil rights criminal case could receive a trial by jury. In reality, however, the trial usually would be by an all-white southern jury which was most unlikely to convict anyone of violating the voting rights of African Americans. But the new law was a breakthrough in at least bringing to trial a person accused of violating another's civil rights. Following that law was one in 1960 that allowed for federal government supervision of the registration African American voters. All these laws were a prelude to the later federal civil rights laws of the mid-1960s pushed through Congress by then president Lyndon Baines Johnson as part of his Great Society program.

The early part of 1961 also marked the ratification of the Twenty-Third Amendment to the US Constitution. This allowed the citizens of Washington, DC, to vote in presidential elections. Following that, Freedom Riders went to the South to begin voter registration drives for African Americans and attempted to extend the racial integration of all public facilities. During May of 1961, many of the Freedom Riders were beaten by whites and arrested by police in Alabama and Mississippi, prompting the federal government to send US Marshalls to Montgomery to restore order. The year 1961 was also when Harper Lee's *To Kill a Mockingbird* became a best seller. That was just after the Boston Red Sox became the last professional major league baseball team to racially integrate African Americans onto its roster.

Meanwhile, civil disobedience protests against racial segregation continued, including sit-ins at segregated lunch counters, which began on February 1, 1960, Greensboro, North Carolina, when four African American college students from the all-black Agricultural and Technical College were told by a Woolworth's waitress, "We don't serve Negroes here." As noted by Edward Rothstein of the *New York Times*:

> And when they were refused because they were black, because much of Greensboro was racially segregated and because Woodworth headquarters had decreed that the company policy was to "abide by local custom"—the four students continued to sit in

A Nation Divided

mute protest. They returned the next day and the next. Within a week, 1000 protestors and counter-protestors packed the store. By the end of March, "sit-ins" had spread to 55 cities in 13 states. By mid-April, the Student Nonviolent Coordinating Committee had been established to expand student involvement. And by the end of July when the Greensboro Woodworth's counter was desegregated, this form of nonviolent protest had become one of the central strategies of the American civil rights movement.

That sit-in was followed by violence toward the civil rights activists when Freedom Riders were attacked by whites in Anniston and Birmingham, Alabama.

General opposition to the tactics of the segregationists was gradual at first but soon spread as new leaders and new groups began to emerge. By 1961, they included those already active or those waiting in the wings ready to emerge. This involved African American singer and actor Paul Robeson; Ralph Abernathy and Jesse Jackson of the Southern Christian Leadership Conference (SCLC); John Lewis, James Forman, and Stokley Carmichael of the Student Nonviolent Coordinating Committee (SNCC); James Farmer of the Congress of Racial Equality (CORE); Malcolm Little, better known as Malcolm X, and Louis Farrakhan of the Nation of Islam; Eldridge Cleaver of the Black Panthers; Roy Wilkins of the National Association for the Advancement of Colored People (NAACP), along with the League of United Latin American Citizens (LULAC) and the American GI Forum in Texas; Cesar Chavez and the United Farm Workers Union; Betty Friedan and the National Organization of Women (NOW); and Russell Means and Dennis Banks of the American Indian Movement.

Also joining the fight for the passage of additional civil rights legislation were other organizations, which included the American Civil Liberties Union, the Americans for Democratic Action, the American Veterans Committee, and the Jewish War Veterans. Union groups included the AFL-CIO, American Newspaper Guild, Brotherhood of Sleeping Car Porters, International Ladies Garment Workers Union, National Alliance of Postal Employees, United Auto Workers, and United Steel Workers. Religious groups joining the movement included the American Jewish

Committee, American Jewish Congress, United Presbyterian Church, National Baptist Convention, National Catholic Conference for Interracial Justice, National Council of Churches, Protestant-Episcopal Church, and United Synagogues of America.

Thus the timing and tensions of the era could not have been better for a Texas confrontation between conservatives and liberals to determine the appropriate content of social studies programs adopted for use in the state's public schools. Their rehearsal for the 1961–62 episode would begin with the immediate post–World War II era, with its foreign and domestic tensions predominant.

2

The Lone Star

Political, Social, and Educational
Conflicts in Texas, 1945–1961

IT WAS AN ERA in the United States marked by increased tensions over a Cold War with the Soviet Union, McCarthyism, an emerging civil rights revolution, and an expansion of federal authority over that of the states. And Texas was no exception to the fray. During the early post–World War II period in Texas, some Texans were suspicious of the politics of Franklin D. Roosevelt's New Deal programs and those of Harry Truman's Fair Deal, the United Nations, and the push to extend civil rights guarantees, especially to ethnic minorities and women. Texas in 1961 had a population of just over nine and a half million people, with much of its leadership in state government dominated by conservative big businessmen. Texas and many other states still used a poll tax as a deterrent to keep poor people (mainly racial minorities) from voting. Texas women had only been allowed to serve on state civil or criminal court juries since 1954 and had great difficulty in acquiring access to any form of birth control. During 1961–62, women composed only 1 percent of members of the Texas legislature, and sex education in the state's public schools was virtually nonexistent. Moreover, nationally, in 1961 no women served on any of the federal benches. Additionally, Texas, along with sixteen other southern states, had a law forbidding interracial marriages between blacks and whites. In answer to the 1954 *Brown v. Topeka* decision, Texas approved a law in 1957 that allowed for public school racial integration only if a school district had enough facilities to successfully accomplish it. That was followed by a state law that allowed public school districts to close so as to avoid any federal orders for them to integrate—laws never enforced and quickly declared unconstitutional by federal courts. Nevertheless, in 1961 very few of the state's African American and Mexican American students attended racially desegregated public schools, nor were African American teachers anywhere near fully integrated into public school teacher councils. The median income for African American Texans as well as for Mexican American Texans also remained far below that of Anglo Texans. And, Texas, like the rest of the South, still had existing segregation policies in regard to equal rights for racial minorities in the areas of education, voting, working conditions, housing, health care, and public accommodations.

Additionally, much of the political leadership of Texas at that time was reflected in who served as governor. From 1947 to 1957, Democratic governor Allan Shivers dominated much of the Texas political scene. He supported antiunion right-to-work laws, organized Texas conservatives via a "Democrats for Republican Dwight D. Eisenhower" campaign in the 1952 presidential contest against Democratic nominee Adlai Stevenson, opposed the *Brown v. Topeka* school integration case, and supported the 1956 Southern Manifesto condemning that court decision, claiming many racial integration supporters were Communists. Although Shivers was never charged with fraud, he was indirectly implicated in a scandal involving the depriving of World War II African American veterans equal access to grants from the Texas Veterans Land Program.

The next Democratic governor, Price Daniel, who served from 1957 to 1963, usually wanted to preserve the status quo of the Texas political scene. Earlier, when he was attorney general of Texas, he defended the University of Texas Law School in the *Sweat v. Painter* case in its attempt to keep the school racially segregated. As a US senator from Texas, he also signed the 1956 Southern Manifesto opposing the *Brown* decision. Although he usually supported the New Deal and the Fair Deal, he was opposed to what he felt was the growing bureaucracy associated with these programs.

Two scholars in particular offer excellent overviews of this period in Texas history. They are historians George Norris Green, with *The Establishment in Texas Politics: The Primitive Years, 1938–1957* (University of Oklahoma Press, 1979), and Don E. Carleton, with his comprehensive *Red Scare! Right Wing Hysteria, Fifties Fanaticism, and Their Legacy in Texas* (Texas Monthly Press, 1985). Green focuses on Texas politics between 1938 and 1957, when the state was ruled by what he called the establishment "reflected in numerous and harsh anti-labor laws, the suppression of academic freedom, a segregationist philosophy, elections marred by demagoguery and corruptions, the devolution of the daily press, and a state government that offered its citizens, especially the minorities, very few services." He defined the conservative establishment as a loosely knit plutocracy of upper classes led mainly by wealthy Anglo businessmen, oil men, bankers, and lawyers, "dedicated to a regressive tax structure, low corporate taxes, anti-labor laws, political, social, and economic oppression of blacks and Mexican Americans, alleged states' rights and extreme reluctance to expand state services." As for federal issues, the establishment "demanded tax reduction, a balanced budget, and the relaxation of federal control over oil, gas, and water and other resources."

Carleton deals primarily with the successes of the Radical Right when attacking personnel and curriculum in the Houston public school system, formulating a case study of what he terms the "Second Red Scare" during the 1950s. He maintains the era was "characterized by a widespread series of actions by individuals and groups whose intentions were to frighten Americans 'with false and highly exaggerated charges of Communist subversion for the purpose of political, economic, and psychological profit,'" who directed their attention to the Houston public school system. Their main targets were the New Deal, the Fair Deal, racial integration, labor unions, the United Nations, progressive education, cosmopolitanism, big government, and liberal theologies. Carleton explains much of this was due to the "fear of change, disorder, and the unknown [which] is a primal instinct, a natural and ineradicable component of the human condition." Such characteristics would become evident in much of the public testimonies offered by those who opposed the history programs adopted by the State of Texas

34 Chapter 2

in 1961, as well as by the actions of some conservative Texas spokespersons prior to that time. Examples of how this type of political leadership in Texas government and certain textbook protest groups in the Lone Star State reacted to the tensions of this period are numerous. One was the Texas Communist Control Law of 1951. It required Communists and those involved in suspected Communist front groups to register with the state's Department of Public Safety (DPS) and forbid Communists from being on primary ballots or holding nonelective positions. Registrants had to list sources of income, places of all residences, past or present, any organizations of which a member, reveal names of anyone thought to be a Communist, "and any other information requested by the Department of Public Safety relevant to the purposes." Violation of the law carried a fine of $1,000 to $10,000 and a two- to ten-year prison sentence.[1]

At the urging of Gov. Allan Shivers, the Texas House of Representatives also considered a bill in 1951 to have membership in the American Communist Party punishable by the death penalty. Former World War II combat marine, civil rights attorney, New Deal Democrat, and then state representative Maury Maverick Jr. of San Antonio was responsible for killing the bill. Elected to the legislature with strong labor union, African American, and Hispanic backing, Maverick indicated: "No one will understand this today, but I once offered a left-wing amendment to have membership in the Communist Party punished by life in prison. It sounds funny now, but the McCarthyites were at the time talking about putting people in the electric chair for mere membership. We pulled stunts like that just to slow the goddamned bill down." Maverick also was only one of four House members to vote against a law outlawing the Communist Party, the law later overturned by unanimous vote of the US Supreme Court. He recalled:

> I was one of the four people who voted against outlawing the Communist Party in Texas. But, I finally realized that some conservatives weren't looking for Communists in Texas. Governor Allan Shivers knew there weren't really any Communists in Texas. What he was trying to do was keep the budget down and not tax corporations and not tax rich people, and not pay schoolteachers, and not have three meals a day that were adequate for people in insane asylums. I introduced a bill to raise daily appropriations for food

The Lone Star   35

in San Antonio's Mental State Hospital from about seventy-five
cents to a dollar and ten cents. That is a thirty-five cent increase.
And the headline in the *Dallas Morning News* said, "Liberals Run
Amok." That was after I was trying to get some poor devil to eat
three meals a day. What the hell has that go to do with being liberal
—someone having enough food to eat three meals a day?

Amazingly, a member of the Texas State Board of Education in 1954
surveyed teachers in the public schools and found only one Communist
out of sixty thousand teachers polled. The local school board fired that
teacher. [2]

Education historian Ronald Evans probably said it best not only for
the Texas situation but for the entire nation that from the end of World
War II into the late 1950s, a political "chill settled over the discussion
of controversial issues" with "the dominate theme of the era, both in
schools and out, was the struggle over communism. . . . When it was
given attention in schools, it was portrayed as a threat to democracy."
Evans especially noted that "schools, the curriculum, and social studies
in particular have frequently served as an ideological battleground and
as a site for the attempted purification of American ideology. The era of
anticommunism in schools provides strong examples of the ideological
nature of schooling and the potential impact of educators' ideological
biases and fears of subversion on schooling and on educational organizations. It offers a warning of the problems that may result from blind
patriotism in defense of our ideals and of the need for continuous effort
to preserve free thought, free inquiry, freedom to teach, and freedom to
learn."

Historian Joseph Moreau felt much the same in his sweeping survey
of major concerns about American history textbooks and the teaching
of American history from the Reconstruction to the late 1980s, arguing
that "the meter of our arguments over national character, the steady rising and falling of public interest in questions of race, class, religion, and
other markers of identity, continually echo through the hallways of our
schools." He added that this "national soul-searching has always played
out through textbooks, especially those purporting to explain the country's past. . . . Writing history is always political. It always reflects the
relations of power in the society."

Such observations became evident in the educational systems of Texas during the immediate post–World War II era, when many public school and university teachers and administrators came under suspicion for allegedly being "subversive," with some losing their jobs. One example of the hunt for "suspect" Texas teachers or administrators at the university level involved the case of Homer Rainey, president of the University of Texas at Austin, and some of his faculty. The Texas state legislature investigated Dr. Clarence Ayers, an economics professor at the University of Texas at Austin. He was among some university teachers there—four tenured economics professor and four nontenure teachers, the latter four fired by the University of Texas Board of Regents—singled out as possibly "subversive" for, among other things, supporting the New Deal. In class, Ayers had discussed what he thought were shortcomings in capitalism. Upon looking into the matter, a University of Texas committee decided Ayres was most certainly not a Communist, as some legislators had suspected. Instead, he was a "classical-modern economist" who had his students carefully consider all sides of an issue.

The controversy over the economics professors cost Rainey his job for defending them and offering a dramatic defense of academic freedom and opposition to book censorship. Among those who staunchly supported Rainey was Jane Legette Yelvington McCallum, one of the individuals responsible for getting women the right to vote in public elections in Texas and the first female to serve as Texas secretary of state. When the Regents fired Rainey in 1944, the American Association of University Professors responded by placing the University of Texas on probation until 1953. Rainey would go on to have a distinguished career at the University of Colorado. All along, Representative Maverick had argued that Rainey, Ayres, and the other economics professors were not Communists, and in the process, Maverick managed to successfully filibuster a bill for the Texas House to establish its own Texas Un-American Activities Committee.[3]

The area of public school education in Texas also came under special state scrutiny. As early as 1941, for example, a Texas law required every public school teacher in the state to sign a loyalty oath that the teachers had never openly advocated "doctrines which seek to undermine. . . . the republican and democratic forms of government in the United States." Another Texas law in 1949 required not only teachers but all school personnel, including all students, to officially disavow any membership in "subversive groups." It required signing of the loyalty oath by all state employees and all college students. State employees had to have their oaths notarized and give it to their payroll clerk before being paid. Commissioner of Education J. W. Edgar "felt that was a bit too much and notified all city and county superintendents that they were not required to make any report whatever to the Texas Education Agency nor would the Agency check on compliance to the law." By the late 1960s the US Supreme Court declared all such laws unconstitutional.[4]

Various Texas conservative groups also focused their attention and frustrations on the content of social studies books, to make certain they would stress the benefits of free enterprise capitalism, sectionalism, states' rights, limited federal government, as well as the faults of socialism, communism, and the United Nations. Examples include the emergence of the Minute Women, which became one of the most vocal anti-Communist groups in Texas and elsewhere. The Minute Women, chartered in Connecticut in 1949 by Suzanne Stevenson, was an organization that grew to more than fifty thousand members by 1952, with most membership concentrated in Texas, California, West Virginia, Maryland, and Connecticut. The Houston chapter had some five hundred members, mostly composed of white middle-class and upper-class women, usually between the ages of thirty and sixty. Stevenson's plan was for the women never to protest as a group but only as individuals, working behind the scenes through a telephone bank program—one member would call five members, who each would call five members, and so on.

The Minute Women opposed as too liberal the Public Broadcasting Service (PBS), socialized medicine, labor unions, welfare programs, and racial integration of public schools. They favored adherence to states' rights over federal rights and favored repeal of the graduated federal income tax; they opposed federal aid to public schools, as well as the UN Educational, Scientific and Cultural Organization (UNESCO), since it taught "students to think, not as citizens of America first, but as citizens of the world." The Minute Women wanted the United States to withdrawal from the United Nations, which they considered a Communist front organization. They supported free enterprise and urged the use of America's nuclear arms to deal with Communist countries rather than "effete striped-pants diplomacy," as well as the elimination of Communist or socialistic "subversion and immorality in our nation's schools."[5]

The Minute Women also felt the National Education Association was an "American Gestapo" and, according to the *Houston Chronicle*, a Communist front. This led the National Education Association (NEA), at the request of its Texas and Houston members, to investigate the charge. Of 1,918 Houston Independent School District (ISD) teachers polled, it found "258 teachers who had been pressured to support a political candidate or to slant courses to a certain political belief, 259 who had been asked not to support the Houston Teacher's Association, and 844 who feared that they might be fired because of their social and political beliefs. All told, 1,112 teachers had personally experienced 'unwarranted pressure.' The leading pressure sources were principals, board members, and school administrators along with such outside forces as the Minute Women, the American Legion, and *Houston Chronicle*."[6]

Additionally, the Minute Women also wanted books removed from public schools and libraries if the books were by authors they deemed "subversive," such as Albert Einstein, Louis Untermeyer, Thomas Mann, D. H. Lawrence, as well as materials about sculpture, the mentally ill, alcoholism, child care, architecture, and even mystery novels. Such actions created a controversy in San Antonio, where the Minute Women met opposition first from Thomas Pape, associate editor of the *Alamo Register*, the official paper of San Antonio's Roman Catholic Archdiocese. According to George Norris Green:

> Pape evaluated the Minute Women's program, as outlined by Stevenson who was visiting the city, and pointed out that her sales tax—the poor man, having less to spend, pays less—overlooked the fact that many Americans must spend their entire salaries to support their families, but the rich do not have to. Stevenson, a Catholic, also called for total free enterprise, which, the editor noted, "reached its peak with ninety-six hour workweeks in the last century" and which was also contrary to an encyclical issued by Pope Pius XI. Another Minute Women's plank was states' rights, which was set forth in such a way that it meant opposition to fed-

The Lone Star 39

eral civil-rights legislation. Pape declared that the states' rights champions had no valid opposition to civil rights if they did not try to persuade their own state legislatures to pass civil-rights laws. The editor added that the teachings of the [Roman Catholic] church regarding the brotherhood of all men were too well known to repeat. The Minute Women were opposed to socialism and communism, which Pape thought was commendable except that they suffered from the delusion that Truman's Fair Deal program was socialism, even though some of the legislation proposed had been called for by the American bishops as far back as 1919.[7]

When San Antonio mayor Jack White, whose wife was a Minute Woman, and the city council had their own people put on the city library board, things changed greatly for a while. The library board abolished audiovisual services, since PBS was considered too liberal, and "House Un-American Activities Committee reports were required to be taken out of the obscure government documents library and placed in the main library, and they had to be bound, prominently displayed, and advertised by ten by twelve inch signs."[8]

The reaction to this was quick, especially from hundreds of San Antonio citizens and even William Randolph Hearst's *San Antonio Light*. Former New Deal US congressman and San Antonio mayor Maury Maverick Sr. was among those most outspoken about actions of the Minute Woman and their supporters, and was instrumental in eventually ridding the city of their influence when he told them their tactics and those of US Senator Joseph McCarthy and the House Un-American Activities Committee were nothing more than "civil persecution, fear, malice." He went so far as to tell an audience in 1954 that "the urge to persecute, to make inquisitions, to punish, to make people squirm, to find out everybody else's business or sex life, and to humiliate, may seem strange, but it is strong in some." He asked, "Do women and men have to be brought before legislative committees to give affidavits as to whether they slept with certain people . . . whether you were drunk and disorderly on a certain night? . . . This sounds ridiculous, of course, but Congress has such rights, so have other bodies within their own spheres." Maverick felt the federal Bill of Rights allowed people protection from what he called "illegal punishment by legislative committees

40   Chapter 2

... or unfair newspaper publicity or the remarks of bulldozing Senators or Congressmen."[9]

The Minute Women's attempt to change public education on a statewide level began in 1953, when the group wanted to eliminate from high school world history textbooks any mention of the United Nations Declaration of Human Rights or any interpretation. The only body which could do that was the State Board of Education. At the board meeting, member and attorney Jack Binion frustrated the Minute Women when he made a motion to leave the declaration in the textbooks but omit any editorial comments about it. Binion's motion carried by a 9–6 vote, much to the displeasure of the Minute Women. The Minute Women also suffered another major defeat in 1953 when they ran a candidate for president of the Texas Parent-Teacher Association, who lost by a vote of 3,218 to 608.[10]

Not to be outdone, the Minute Women at the local level in 1953 were successful in the firing of Houston ISD Deputy Superintendent George Ebey. Hired a year earlier from Portland, Oregon, Ebey supported the First Amendment of free speech but thought the Communist Party was "to be abhorred." A team of ex-FBI employees investigated Ebey and concluded he was not disloyal to the United States. Nevertheless, the Minute Women charged him with being soft on communism and nonsupportive of white supremacy. Especially disturbing to the Minute Women was that Ebey, while a curriculum director in Portland, had enrolled Asian American children in classes with Anglo American children and hired an African American teacher to teach at the same school. Attorney Jack Binion, a member of the Texas State Board of Education, represented Ebey pro bono, since Binion felt Ebey needed a lawyer. No matter, the Houston ISD School Board by a vote of 4–3 fired Ebey. One woman accused Ebey of "race-mixing," and the evening he was fired, one spectator yelled "nigger lover" at him. His firing set off a national outrage, expressed in such publications as *Time* magazine, the *Nation*, the *Christian Century*, and the *Oregonian*, among many others, calling the incident a major setback for academic freedom in American education. Ebey and his family moved to California, where he became a senior staff member at the Stanford University Research Institute and was awarded federal security clearance to work on government defense contracts. Ebey was later quoted as declaring, "I find it a bit ironic . . .

The Lone Star

that probably my most significant contribution in education came from being lynched professionally by savages in a community where I was a relative stranger."[11]

Other social studies textbooks also came under fire from the Minute Women and the Texas Society of the Daughters of the American Revolution prior to 1961. Both groups were concerned about Dr. Frank A. Magruder's *American Government*, the most widely used high school civics book in the United States. In 1949, the Daughters of the American Revolution declared the book's patriotism suspect. Their newsletter, *Editorial Reviewer*, had a critique of the book, but one scholar said the Daughters of the American Revolution critique had "glaring inaccuracies," and few people even bothered to read the book. Even so, the report attracted national publicity and caught the attention of members of the Houston ISD school board, especially when Georgia's State Board of Education banned the book's use in all the public schools in Georgia.[12]

During that the same year as the Daughters of the American Revolution's report on the book, two conservative members of the Houston ISD, Ewing Werlein and Dr. Henry Peterson, led a successful effort voicing the objections from many teachers to ban further use of Magruder's *American Government*. The book, adopted by the state in 1928 and used by the Houston district since 1933, had one particular paragraph that offended Werlein. According to Don E. Carleton:

> A fine-print footnote referred to the postal system, federal electric power projects, and progressive taxation as "bits of socialism" and said, "Public free education and old age assistance are examples of communism . . . to each according to his need." Since the book held that the public school system and postal system were worthwhile, Werlein feared this might mislead children into thinking socialism and communism were beneficial. "I haven't read the rest of the book," Werlein admitted, "but to me the one paragraph cited plants an insidious seed in the minds of students." Hubert Mewhinney, a *Post* columnist who sometimes exhibited views at variance with his newspaper's editorials, commented that "[i]f so shrewd and experienced a man as Ewing Werlein took ten years to catch on to the meaning of that paragraph, the guileless little high school students never caught on at all."

Carleton noted how Werlein "explained to the teachers that this is a matter beyond their competence. School teachers often are idealistic theorists. They are often duped and misled. They are sheltered in a classroom and are not often exposed to the chicanery of the outside world." Despite the Houston board's action, the Texas State Board of Education readopted the book for a new six-year period as the sole state-approved civics text. The Houston ISD thus had to pay for a substitute textbook out of its own funds if it refused to use the Magruder text. Unfortunately, because of an already inadequate budget, the school board could afford to buy only one set per classroom of an allegedly more patriotic civics book, which resulted in only one book for every five students. When the board again refused the teachers' request to re-adopt the book, the district civics teachers went without a government text for five years, until 1954.[13]

Protests also came from Bertie Maughmer, a prominent leader of the Minute Women. She was a member of the Houston ISD Houston School Board and wife of a policeman. Before being elected to the school board in 1957, she had been head of the Houston Police Officers' Wives Association and parliamentarian of the Houston area Parent-Teacher Association's Council. In her campaign for the school board, Maughmer campaigned for the continued racial segregation of the public schools, maintained "race mixing" was anti-Christian, and said she would "rather go to jail than see my kids go to school with niggers."[14] Once elected to the school board, Maughmer had it ban *Geography and World Affairs* and *Geography and the World*, arguing that both books showed favoritism toward the United Nations and "one-worldism." She also was most critical of *Applied Economics* as well as *Economics and You*, textbooks preferred by more than 90 percent of the state's economic teachers. She opposed one of the economic books for stating that sometimes people can save money by buying goods through cooperatives (that was socialism or communism) and the other book for being what she claimed was "too objective" in its treatment of capitalism. Maughmer also objected to a recommended reading list that included noted and award-winning historian Allan Nevins of Columbia University and famous novelist Edna Ferber, both of whom Maughmer called "fellow travelers." Superintendent of Schools

The Lone Star 43

Bill Moreland, growing increasingly irritated with the book censors, told board members the publishers of those texts represented the very best examples of the American capitalist and free enterprise system.[15]

With that action and the board's plan to select as deputy superintendent G. C. Scarborough, leader of a White Citizens Council, Moreland had had enough and resigned as superintendent. The board then made Scarborough interim superintendent. He quickly moved world history and world geography to the tenth grade (from the eighth grade), so that students would not be exposed to Karl Marx and the Russian Revolution of 1917 or any possible communist "propaganda" until later in their high school career. When the board members had to decide whether to make Scarborough permanent superintendent, Maughmer, unhappy with his denial of her request to ban other textbooks as well as fire some teachers who had, for example, supported her opponent in the last school board election, voted (along with another conservative and some liberals) not to promote Scarborough. As a result, Scarborough asked for and received early retirement. The board then hired as Superintendent Dr. John McFarland, a middle-of-the-roader on political issues and former head of the Amarillo schools.[16]

As for Maughmer, her departure from the school board in 1960 was one she probably never could have imagined. She and her husband, Earl, had serious marital problems and had discussed divorce. One evening, they had a bitter argument about his going on a boat ride without her. As he was dressing to go to work for his night shift at the county jail, Maughmer shot Earl with his .357 magnum pistol, with the bullet going from his right elbow into his stomach. He managed to take the gun from her and then collapsed. Maughmer, realizing what she had done, called for an ambulance. Earl told police he had shot himself by accident, but when he recovered nine days later, he told the police the truth. They arrested Maughmer for shooting Earl, but the Harris County grand jury, at the urging of Earl and considering her status as a civil leader and letters urging leniency from other prominent Houston citizens, refused to indict her. Shortly thereafter, she and Earl divorced, she resigned from the Houston School Board, and she faded from public view.[17]

Thus the tumultuous period following World War II through the decade of the fifties saw many social, political, and particularly education conflicts regarding the content of state-adopted social studies programs. Yet it was far from the end of the conflict over the content of Texas social studies books; the era was only a prelude of what was to occur during 1961–62, when a cultural war between conservatives and liberals escalated to a degree never before seen in Texas concerning the state adoption of social studies programs.

3

Trouble Brewing

Setting the Stage for the Texas Textbook Controversy of 1961–1962

BY 1961 THERE was a temporary transition within the Texas political scene—one geared toward more acceptance within the population, marking the dawn of a more liberal political agenda. This was evident in 1961 with Roman Catholic, Massachusetts Democrat, and former US senator John F. Kennedy and Lyndon B. Johnson, previously a US senator from Texas and among the last of the prominent New Deal Democrats, in 1961 becoming president and vice president of the United States, respectively, carrying Texas in that election. The pair had a very comfortable majority of their fellow political party members in both houses of Congress, as well as a liberal-leaning US Supreme Court. In the process, Texas also had one of the nation's most progressive liberals, Ralph Yarborough, representing it in the US Senate during 1957 to 1971, joined by fellow Texan Sam Rayburn as speaker of the US House of Representatives. Johnson, Yarborough, and Rayburn had already waged many political battles with conservative Allan Shivers when he was governor. Yarborough also was a leader of the progressive-liberal wing of the Democratic Party, who fought for a GI Bill for veterans and what later became part of Johnson's Great Society program, with its Medicare and Medicaid, the War on Poverty, the Endangered Species Act, greater guarantees of labor union rights, and more federal funding for universities and students. Like Sam Rayburn, Johnson, and Kennedy,

Yarborough had actively supported Franklin Roosevelt's New Deal and Harry Truman's Fair Deal. Unlike Governor Price Daniel when he was in the US Congress, Rayburn, Johnson, and Yarborough had refused to sign the 1956 Southern Manifesto opposing the *Brown v. Topeka* school desegregation decision.

For some conservative Texans, there was also another issue with the ever-leaning liberal Lyndon Johnson, who, when Democratic Party Senate Leader in 1957, pushed through the first civil rights bill enacted by Congress in eighty-two years. As noted previously, it provided that anyone cited for contempt of court in a civil rights criminal case could receive a trial by jury. In reality, however, the trial usually would be by an all-white southern jury, which was most unlikely to convict anyone of violating the voting rights of African Americans. But the new law was a breakthrough in at least bringing to trial a person accused of violating another's civil rights. Following that law was one under Johnson's leadership in 1960, which allowed for federal government supervision of the registration African American voters, which was a prelude to the later more significant federal civil rights laws of the mid-1960s pushed through Congress by then president Johnson as part of his Great Society program.

Meanwhile, just prior to 1960, some Texas Anglo, Hispanic, and African American civil right activists and public school teachers in San Antonio and Houston, in opposition to racial segregation and wanting a greater voice in curriculum and the selection of textbooks, had organized racially integrated affiliates of the American Federation of Teachers (AFT), which soon became the chief bargaining agent for teachers in those public school districts and set the example for other Texas public school districts to soon do the same. Shortly thereafter was also when Henry B. Gonzales, with great support from Lyndon Johnson, became the first Texan of Mexican ancestry to serve in the US House of Representatives. African Americans Garlington J. Sutton and Hattie Mae White had likewise recently broken racial barriers by being the first African Americans elected to public office in Texas since Reconstruction—Sutton to the governing board of a San Antonio junior college district and White to a seat on the Houston ISD school board. Additionally, Lone Star State conservatives had already lost in federal courts involving such Texas cases as restrictions on ethnic minorities being a violation of the Fourteenth Amendment, with *Smith v. Allwright, Delgado v. Bastrop, Sweatt v. Painter,* and *Hernandez v. Texas.* Some Texas conservatives could only ask what might come next.

What did come next was a Texas battle never seen before between conservatives and liberals over social studies programs, when publishers in 1961 submitted their books for adoption before the Texas State Textbook Committee and the Texas State Board of Education. It ushered in a major new Texas conservative textbook protest group replacing the Minute Women, but it was just as concerned about what appeared in social studies textbooks for the public schools. This group was called Texans for America, joined by the Texas Society of the Daughters of the American Revolution.

This beginning of a temporary swing to the left in the Texas political pendulum slightly away from a dominate conservative agenda was more than enough to stir some Texas conservatives to action, especially from Texans for America and the Texas Society of the Daughters of the American Revolution, by seeking to gain acceptance of their political agenda via the content of social studies programs used in the public schools of Texas. In this regard, some historical background is necessary to explain the Texas textbook adoption process and also provide explanations for certain views expressed by the protestors.

In 1961, Texas was one of twenty-five states in the elementary field and nineteen on the high school level that required the state adoption of textbooks for use in public schools. And Texas, with one of the nation's largest public school enrollments, by its state-approved adoptions could dominate much of the content that public schools elsewhere had available. This was because publishers earned greater profits from issuing just one edition per textbook for much of the country. As noted by journalist and editor Hillel Black, the "only way a publisher can hope to partake of the largest state-controlled market in the country is to win approval of the state's officials. And if approval hinges on a firm's willingness to revise the text, the publisher usually bows to the textbook authorities' demands."[1]

This made Texas a national leader in textbook sales for the public schools, mainly because of its process of adopting books. In 1961 terms, the textbooks for Texas public schools were selected through a process involving the State Textbook Committee, the Commissioner of Education, the State Board of Education, and the local public school districts. State Senator A. M. Aikin, the chief architect of the 1949 Gilmer-Aikin Law, which established the process of adoption of textbooks in Texas, said, as a legislator, "I came here thinking a child ought to get an equal educational opportunity whether he was born in the middle of an oil field or the middle of a cotton field."

The law Aikin coauthored set up a process that by 1961 had established a State Board of Education elected by the people. That year, Board of Education members in turn appointed a Commissioner of Education who recommended to the State Board a fifteen-member Textbook Committee composed of school personnel, a majority of whom had to be classroom teachers. The Textbook Committee members each could have advisees from both the public schools and outsiders to advise them on whether the submitted books met the standards or guidelines, called "Adherence to the Proclamation," set by the State Board of Education and hear protests of submitted textbooks. The Textbook Committee recommended which books, to a maximum of five per subject area, the committee wished to recommend to the Commissioner of Education, who could delete books from the list but needed to leave at least two on it. The commissioner then made a recommendation to the State Board of Education, which could accept or refuse his recommendation but could not add any books to the list.[2]

The textbook adoption process began in May of 1961, when the State Board of Education issued a textbook proclamation, listing its required standards and inviting publishers to present sealed bids on which subjects they would be submitting for approval that year. In July, the publishers presented their textbooks to be considered for adoption and allowed citizens concerned about the books to examine copies. In 1961, this was a problem for many textbook critics or protestors, called "petitioners," since the books had to be borrowed from superintendents of schools or from the publishers, and any concerns protestors had about the books had to be submitted to the Texas Commissioner of Education a month later. (The short time schedule was remedied somewhat in 1970 when copies of the submitted books were also placed in the state's twenty Regional Service Centers. Later, by 2011, the textbooks submitted for state adoption could be viewed online and publishers could market their programs directly to school districts.)

In 1961, critics of textbook programs had to file a Bill of Particulars with the Commissioner of Education regarding any textbook program they found objectionable before the Textbook Committee, which held its hearing in September. Protestors could appear before the Textbook Committee and voice their concerns. In October, the Textbook Committee made its decisions about which books to recommend to the Commissioner of Education. The commissioner then worked with the staff at the Texas Education Agency, which could also recommend changes from publishers with the approval of the commissioner. The commissioner in turn would make recommendations to the State Board of Education, which had the final say in November, after hearing from any remaining textbook protests.

According to rules governing the Texas Textbook Committee hearings in 1961, critics of the textbooks were the only ones permitted to have outside experts testify on their behalf. Of course, authors of the textbooks and their publishers could also respond to any criticisms before the State Textbook Committee or State Board of Education. (It was not until 1982–83 that others could respond to the protestors or offer support for any of the textbooks submitted for adoption before the State Textbook Committee or State Board of Education.[3])

There was one another unique requirement of anyone submitting curricular materials for state adoption in Texas in 1961, as well as a requirement for all those appearing to protest textbooks. This was the textbook loyalty oath, with Texas being the only state to require such an oath from textbook authors and protestors. Beginning in 1953, all authors of books submitted for Texas adoption and those publicly protesting them had to sign an oath swearing that they had never been a member of the Communist Party or any group on the US Attorney General's list of subversive organizations for the previous five years. If the author was deceased, the publisher had to swear for that person. J. B. Golden, director of the textbook division at the Texas Education Agency, said, "The Loyalty Oath is just a chance for every good citizen to go up and pledge allegiance. It is also a trap for Communists. If we lay enough of those traps around the country, we are going to get them sooner or later. . . . I think a Communist will sign anything. Whenever a citizen accuses an author at a textbook hearing, we run right out to the state Public Safety Department to see if they have a file on him."[4]

50   Chapter 3

Fortunately for the textbook authors, none ever appeared on the Public Safety Department lists. As will be obvious from the 1961–62 Texas textbook hearings, the loyalty oath requirement, however, did not deter textbook critics from making charges or assumptions questioning the loyalty of some textbook authors, authors in the recommended reading lists, or other materials included in the works of the textbook authors.[5]

Within this setting during 1961–62 were conservative Texas citizens, particularly those from Texans for America, the Daughters of the American Revolution, as well as Mel and Norma Gabler, who felt they were losing a cultural, social, economic, and political war with liberals, and had concerns about content in the social studies books submitted for state adoption. Their main concerns, as well as those who differed from them, are delineated into seven major areas as follows. More extensive elaborations of those topics can also be found within sources in the selected bibliography.

Concern One: Judeo-Christian Foundations of American Government

Reacting to the threat of communism during hearings about textbooks before the 1961 Texas State Textbook Committee as well as before the 1962 Texas House of Representatives Textbook Investigating Committee, conservatives claimed that the social studies books did not make special note that the culture of the United States was founded on Judeo-Christian principles, with the Ten Commandments as the major foundation of American law.

It is true that some of the early history of the United States was influenced by the Christian tradition, such as the Pilgrims' Mayflower Compact of 1620 or the Fundamental Orders of Connecticut of 1639. The Pilgrims or Separatists seeking religious freedom for themselves, for example, left the established Church of England and received an economic charter from King James I so they could settle on the London Company's territory in Virginia. Their ship, the *Mayflower*, was blown off course, and the Pilgrims landed near Cape Cod in Massachusetts. Because the Pilgrims had no charter to establish a colony on that land or make laws under the King's grant, they drew up their own agreement—the Mayflower Compact—which gave them the power of representative government to legislate as servants of King James I. Forty-one of the *Mayflower* passengers signed that social compact or contract, establishing a religious "civil body politic" with some separation of church and state (for example, allowing only civil marriages) and including the wording "Having undertaken for the glory of God, and the advancement of the Christian faith, and the honour of our King and country, a voyage to plant the first colony in the Northern parts of Virginia [Massachusetts Bay to] frame such just and equal laws . . . for the general good of the Colony," with the consent of the governed always supreme. The Fundamental Orders of Connecticut, in effect until Connecticut received a royal charter in 1662, provided for freemen to elect a representative assembly, officers of the assembly, a governor, and judges with no suffrage test for voting, all "to maintain and preserve the liberty and purity of the gospel of our Lord Jesus which we now profess as also." The ideas for such compacts were forerunners to later American ones establishing a concept of self-government—the US Constitution being a secular/civil document, not a religious one.

Part of the Christian tradition in American history is also evident in the Maryland Toleration Act, which, like the Pilgrims in Massachusetts and the Puritans in Connecticut, created a form of representative government. Maryland was established as a haven for Roman Catholics who had suffered from persecution from some Protestant groups. In 1649, Maryland's representative assembly approved an act "for the more quiet and peaceable government of this Province, and the better to preserve mutuall Love and amity amongst the inhabitants thereof." It went on to declare "that noe person or persons whatever within this Province thereunto belonging professing to believe in Jesus Christ, shall from henceforth bee any wales troubled, Molested or discountenanced for or in respect of his or her religion nor in the free exercise thereof within this Province."

On a similar note, some conservative Christian fundamentalists quote the 1892 US Supreme Court case of *Church of the Holy Trinity v. United States* (143 U.S. 457). US Supreme Court Associate Justice David Josiah Brewer, writing for the court in his opinion, noted an 1885 federal statute, the Alien Contract Labor Law. It prohibited "the importation and migration of foreigners and aliens under contract or agreement to perform labor or service of any kind in the United States, its territories, and the District of Columbia." The court held that a minister was not a foreign laborer under the statute, even though he was a foreigner. The minister was a British Anglican priest hired by the church to work in the United States. Brewer, as an aside to this in his decision, wrote, "These, and many other matters which might be noticed, add a volume of unofficial declarations to the mass of organic utterances that this is a Christian nation."

When questioned about the "Christian Nation" statement by many people, Justice Brewer answered with his book *The United States: A Christian Nation* (John C. Winston, 1905, digitized in 2006, New York Public Library). He gave his answer as part of the Haverford Library Lecture Series. In his lecture, he noted:

> But in what sense can [the United States] be called a Christian nation? Not in the sense that Christianity is the established religion or the people are compelled in any manner to support it. On the contrary, the Constitution specifically provides that "Congress shall make no law respecting an establishment of religion or prohibiting the free exercise thereof." Neither is it Christian in the sense that all its citizens are either in fact or in name Christians. On the contrary, all religions have free scope within its borders. Numbers of our people profess other religions, and many reject all. . . . Nor is it Christian in the sense that a profession of Christianity is a condition of holding office or otherwise engaging in public service, or essential to recognition either politically or socially. In fact, the government as a legal organization is independent of all religions.

He added:

> I could go on indefinitely pointing out . . . illustrations [of Christian practices] both official and non-official, public and private; such as the annual Thanksgiving proclamations, with their following day of worship and feasting; announcements of days of fasting and prayer; the universal celebration of Christmas; the gathering of millions of our children in Sunday Schools, and the countless volumes of Christian literature, both prose and poetry. But I have said enough to show that Christianity came to this country with the first colonists [such as with the Pilgrims and their Mayflower

Compact of 1620] and has been powerfully identified with its rapid development, colonial and national, and to-day exists as a mighty factor in the life of the republic. This is a Christian nation.

Yet, Thomas Jefferson, the author of the Bill for Establishing Religious Freedom in Virginia in 1786, a law he regarded as his second greatest accomplishment after the Declaration of Independence, provided that no one "shall be compelled to frequent or support any religious worship, place, or ministry whatsoever, not shall be enforced, restrained, molested, or burthened in his body or goods, or shall otherwise suffer, on account of his religious opinions or beliefs; but that all men shall be free to profess, and by argument to maintain, their opinions in matters of religion, and that the same shall in no wise diminish, enlarge, or affect their civil capacities." Jefferson especially opposed those who he felt sought "dominion over the faith of others, setting up their own opinions and modes of thinking as . . . true and infallible [and] endeavored to impose them on others." That 1786 Virginia law was supported by such prominent Virginians as George Mason, called the father of the later enacted federal Bill of Rights, and James Madison, father of the Constitution, who, like Jefferson, opposed any harassment by the Anglican Church, especially of such groups as Baptists.

Moreover, issues over the proper extent of separation of church and state, interpretation of religious freedom guaranteed by the First Amendment, and the relationship between civil government and organized religion, have continued to engage Americans in debate to the present. Examples abound: Roger Williams, Separatist Puritan minister, creator of the establishment of the colony of Rhode Island, and regarded as founder of the American Baptist Church, and Thomas Jefferson strongly supported separation of church and state, but for different reasons. Williams did so because he believed "forced worship stinks in God's nostrils" and wanted a "wall of separation between the garden of the church and the wilderness of the world" to protect religious worship from intrusion by the state. Jefferson did not want the church to corrupt the state. Both Williams's and Jefferson's attitudes were also evident in some of the early state constitutions, including those of Texas, Kentucky, New York, North Carolina, South Carolina, Georgia, Delaware,

Maryland, Kentucky, and Tennessee, which prohibited clergy from running for public office, and some of those states, such as Texas, even forbid clergy from serving on juries.

Alan Wolfe, in reviewing David L. Holmes's *The Faiths of the Founding Fathers* (Oxford University Press, 2006) and Jon Meacham's *American Gospel: God, the Founding Fathers, and the Making of a Nation* (Random House, 2006), also noted that none of the first six presidents were traditional Christians:

> All were influenced to one degree or another by Deism. . . . John Adams, a Unitarian, did not accept such Christian basics as "the trinity, the divinity of Christ, total depravity and predestination." Thomas Jefferson, James Madison and James Monroe were outright Deists [as were Thomas Paine, Benjamin Franklin, and John Quincy Adams]. George Washington never referred to Jesus in any of his writings. Men of the enlightenment, [all of] them feared what George Washington called "the horrors of spiritual tyranny." All of them doubted the divinity of Jesus. Their conception of religious liberty made room for non-Christians and even nonbelievers, and their language deliberately avoided Sectarian terminology. They were intellectual radicals, willing to push the idea of religious tolerance further than it had ever been pushed before.

Such men of the Enlightenment were familiar with early Amorite laws, Mosaic law, Athenian democracy, Roman Law, the Code of Justinian, English Common Law, including the Magna Charta, the English Petition of Rights, the English Bill of Rights, the development of Parliament as well as English cabinet government, and writings such as those by Nicholas Copernicus, Galileo Galilei, Isaac Newton, Tycho Brahe, Johannes Kepler, Frances Bacon, Rene Descartes, Hugo Grotius, Thomas Hobbs, John Locke, Baron de Montesquieu, Voltaire, William Blackstone, Jean Jacques Rousseau, and Adam Smith.

In essence, many of those founding fathers were not atheists or unschooled men but in one way or another scholarly and Enlightenment Deists who today might be called "secular humanists." Jefferson, instead of using Christianity in the Declaration of Independence, used "the laws of Nature and of Nature's God," and in the second paragraph, "that They are endowed by their Creator with certain unalienable Rights."

Trouble Brewing

James Madison especially noted that for almost 1,500 years, Christianity had shown itself to be "more or less in all phases, pride and indolence in the clergy, ignorance and servility in the laity, in both, superstition, bigotry, and persecution."

During the Constitutional Convention of 1787, the delegates also approved Article VI, Section 2, which requires all legislative, judicial, and executive officials to take an oath of allegiance to the Constitution, with the provision that in regard to the federal government and all state governments, "no religious Test shall ever be required as a Qualification to any office or public Trust under the United States." Madison even argued that government service should be "open to merit or every description, whether native or adoptive, whether young or old, and without regard to poverty or wealth, or to any particular profession of religious faith." His argument was in response to those who felt federal civilian service should be denied to pagans, Deists, or Muslims. The First Amendment to the US Constitution likewise states, "Congress shall make no law respecting an establishment of religion, or prohibiting the free exercise thereof."[6] Thus neither the US Constitution nor the Declaration of Independence makes any mention of Christianity. Nor was Christianity promoted as a plan for government during debates to establish the Articles of Confederation of 1781 or in the *Federalist Papers* by Alexander Hamilton, James Madison, and John Jay, all of which focused on the desperate need to create a secular social contract. The Christian religion issue was also not a major concern during state debates over ratification of the proposed federal constitution, especially by Patrick Henry and George Mason, who opposed ratification, or James Madison and Edmund Randolph, who supported ratification.[7]

It is likewise well to keep in mind that a 1797 American treaty with Tripoli, supported by George Washington, John Adams, and Thomas Jefferson, contained the following: "As the government of the United States of America . . . is not, in any sense founded on the Christian religion." This treaty was also approved unanimously by the US Senate.[8]

There is also no question about many of the delegates (but not all of them) of the Constitutional Convention of 1787 being Christians. However, two of the most influential movers and shakers at the meeting, James Madison and Benjamin Franklin, were not Christians, and the main goal of the delegates present at the convention was to create a

56 Chapter 3

new secular federal government based on the separation of powers with a system of checks and balances.

Some of the textbook critics referred to a June 28, 1813, letter John Adams sent to Thomas Jefferson, claiming that Adams said, "The general principle on which the fathers achieved independence were the general principles of Christianity." What Adams actually wrote concerned soldiers who fought in the American Revolution:

> There were among them Roman Catholics, English Episcopalians, Scotch and American Presbyterians, Methodists, Moravians, Anabaptists, German Lutherans, German Calvinists, Universalist, Arians, Pristleyans, Socinians, Independents, Congregationalists, House Protestants, Deists and Atheists, and Protestants . . . all educated in the general principles of Christianity, and the *general principles* of English and American liberty . . . in which all those young men united, and which had united all parties in America. . . . Now I will vow, that I then believed and now believe that those general principles of Christianity are as eternal and immutable as the existence and attributes of God. . . . In favor of these *general principles*, in philosophy, religion and government, I could fill sheets of quotations from Frederic of Prussia, from Hume, Gibbon, Bolingbroke, Rousseau, and Voltaire, as well as Newton and Locke.

Adams was speaking of Christianity as a Unitarian and not as a Christian.

Then, there is the phrase "In God We Trust" on coinage and paper money, to which many nonreligious people object. The founding fathers did not place it there. Instead, the motto appeared first on the two cent coin in 1864 due to pressure from northern religious groups during the Civil War. Pres. Theodore Roosevelt had the phrase removed from the ten dollar coin in 1907, arguing it was sacrilege to have God's name on money, but Congress put it back in 1908. Other money with the saying "In God We Trust" followed, and at the height of the McCarthy era, Congress made the phrase the national motto.

In 1892, Francis Julius Bellamy, a Socialist, a Baptist minister, and an advocate of separation of church and state, wrote what became the American Pledge of Allegiance with the words "I pledge allegiance to my Flag and to the Republic for which it stands, one nation, indivisible, with liberty and justice for all." In 1954, Congress, with urging from

Pres. Dwight D. Eisenhower, added the words "under God" to that pledge.

However, there are examples that do not correspond to complete separation of church and state. For example, churches and religious organizations have tax exemptions or are tax-exempt IRS entities, but in the past they had to abide by a federal law stating that those religious organizations would be "absolutely prohibited from directly or indirectly participating in, or intervening in, any political campaign on behalf of or in opposition to any candidate for elective office." Pres. Donald Trump in 2017 sought to relax enforcement of that law and said his order would allow pastors and churches the right to openly participate in the political realm without the IRS prosecuting them. Republicans in Congress agreed with Trump in their tax law in 2017.

Another example comes in the form of the national holidays of Thanksgiving and Christmas. In addition, Quakers and other pacifists are exempted from military service as combatants but must serve in other types of military or civic duty. Parents can use a religious exemption to avoid having their children attend public schools, and in some instances governments can help finance the bus fares of students in parochial schools, lend books to those schools, and let public school students have released time to be in religious instruction. On the frieze of the US Supreme Court building, Moses is listed as one of the world's eighteen greatest lawgivers, and the Ten Commandments appear on the floor across from the copies of the Declaration of Independence and the US Constitution in the National Archives. The United States has had a National Day of Prayer since 1952. Congress has chaplains from a variety of religious faiths, not solely Christian, to offer prayers before it, although the vast majority doing the praying are Christians, with a small minority being Jews, Muslims, or Hindus. Also, the US Armed Forces also makes officers of its chaplains who are from a variety of religious faiths, not just Christianity. Such places as prisons and police departments sometimes have chaplains from a variety of religions, whose salaries are paid by tax dollars.

In fact, in 1983, the US Supreme Court in a 6–3 ruling in *Marsh v. Chambers* (463 U.S. 783) even declared that legislative prayer is constitutional by the funding of chaplains due to the "unique history of the United States" but unconstitutional if the selection of those offering the prayers act with "impermissible motive" when choosing who would pray or if the prayers give preference to one religion over another or denigrate another religion. This allowed the Nebraska legislature to open its sessions with a prayer from a salaried Presbyterian preacher, maintaining it was a "deeply imbedded in the history and traditions of the country."

Later, in 2014, the US Supreme Court in a 5–4 decision with the case of *Town of Greece, New York v. Galloway* (572 U.S. __) held the Constitution allows towns to begin their business with sectarian prayers serving to show the solemnity of the occasion. Justice Anthony Kennedy for the majority opinion said beginning with the first sessions of Congress, there had been ceremonial prayers and went on to declare: "To hold that invocations must be nonsectarian would force the legislatures that sponsor prayers and the courts that are asked to decide these cases to act as supervisors and censors of religious speech, a rule that would involve government in religious matters to a far greater degree than is the case under the town's current practice of neither editing or approving prayers in advance nor being critical of their content after the fact." In her dissent, Justice Elena Kagan disagreed with Kennedy's decision and especially his assertion that the legislative prayer is "a practice that was accepted by the framers and has withstood the critical scrutiny of time and political change." Justice Kagan countered that such founding fathers as George Washington, Thomas Jefferson, and James Madison went to great lengths to keep sectarian language from public discourse and the "demand for neutrality among religions is not a product of 21st century 'political correctness' but of the 18th century view." She added, "No one can fairly read the prayers from Greece's town meetings as anything other than explicitly Christian—constantly and exclusively so."

Then, in 2017, in the case of *Trinity Lutheran Church of Columbia v. Comer* (582 U.S. __), the Supreme Court dealt with a church that wanted to use state funds to repurpose old tires to resurface a playground, which Missouri held violated the principle of separation of church and state. A majority of the US Supreme Court held that the state could fund the playground for the sake of public safety by narrowly deciding that "the case involves express discrimination based on religious identity with respect to playgrounds resurfacing. We do not address religious uses or funding or other forms of discrimination." Justices Sonia Sotomayor and Ruth Ginsburg dissented, writing "to hear the Court tell it, this is a simple case about recycling tires to resurface a playground. This case is about nothing less than the relationship between religious institutions and the civil government—that is, between church and state. This Court today profoundly changes that relationship by holding, for the first time, that the Constitution requires the government to provide public funds directly to a church."

Then, over the objections of Americans United for Separation of Church and State, the Trump administration in 2018, using the *Trinity Lutheran Church of Columbia v. Comer* decision, allowed religious organizations whose property had received storm damage to apply to FEMA for financial aid.

Academic tenure at public and private American colleges likewise has origins in religion. Tenure sometimes allowed one to speak more freely in the old European ecclesiastical institutions of higher learning, and academic regalia has its origins in the robes worn by Roman Catholic priests. But nowhere in all this is any official governmental endorsement of "Christianity."

However, other US Supreme Court cases have also endorsed a form of separation of church and state. For example, in *Everson v. Board of Education* (330 U.S. 1, 1947), the court used the Establishment Clause of the First Amendment by declaring that no reimbursement could be made for public transportation to a private school, while reaffirming the First Amendment's religious clause as the "wall of separation between church and state." With *McCollum v. Board of Education* (333 U.S. 203) in 1948, the justices by an 8–1 vote maintained that released time was unconstitutional for public schools in support of religious instruction classes, which violated the Establishment Clause of the First Amendment and Equal Protection Clause of the Fourteenth Amendment, especially when a state uses its public school system to aid religious faiths in dissemination of their religious doctrines. Additionally, in 1963, the case of Ellery Schempp, a Muslim student who opened a Qur'an during Bible reading time (*Abington School District v. Schempp* [374 U.S. 203]), declared Christian prayer or Bible reading to be religious exercises, and it was unconstitutional for public schools to require them. But in *Zorach v. Board of Education of the City of New York* (343 U.S. 306, 1952), the court also ruled 6–3 that "released time programs

60   Chapter 3

are acceptable to religious schools if the instruction takes place away from the public school campus for one hour per work week and with no public funding." In 1962, the US Supreme Court in *Engel v. Vital* (370 U.S. 421) overruled such cases as *Vidal v. Gipard as Executors* (1844), likewise declaring that it is unconstitutional to have public school students recite a prayer written by a school official, even though the prayer was nondenominational and students could ask to be excused from saying it. A year later in *School District Abington Township v. Schempp* (374 U.S. 203), the court struck down a state law that required Bible verses to be read in school each day as a violation of the separation of church and state. In 1975, the court in *Meek v. Pittenger* (421 U.S. 349) also held that states may not provide church-related schools with films, magazines, charts, projectors, or similar equipment, but, by earlier rulings, could provide money for secular textbooks that aid the students attending such schools, but only if that does not advance the teaching of religion. Finally, in 1980, the court in a 5–4 vote outlawed the posting of the Ten Commandments on public school walls, ruling that the Kentucky law violated the federal constitution's guarantee of religious freedom.[9]

A unique exception to separation of church and state involves four of the San Antonio, Texas, Spanish missions: Conception, San Jose, San Juan, and Espada. They have a rather unusual partnership, created by the US Congress in 1978 as part of the San Antonio Missions National Historical Park. President Jimmy Carter would not sign the bill until he was assured it preserved the separation of church and state. It is a cooperative agreement with the Roman Catholic Archdiocese of San Antonio, whereby the four mission churches continue full time as houses of worship while the National Park Service has an agreement of cooperation and management of some mission lands, along with the City of San Antonio, Bexar County, and the San Antonio Conservation Society. Mission San Juan also has a special arrangement with the National Park Service, San Antonio National Historical Park, and the San Antonio Food Bank, through which the mission's eighteenth century irrigation system and farming lands have been restored and maintained, with help from the Los Compades Society, San Antonio Conservations Society, and San Antonio River Authority. The half million pounds of fresh food grown on the mission's land will go to the San Antonio Food Bank. The four San Antonio missions, along with the Alamo, are also a World

Heritage Site established by the United Nations Educational, Scientific, and Cultural Organization.

Even so, while the federal constitution never contains the words "God" or "Christianity," the First Amendment to the US Constitution does not mention that an individual state cannot have an established religion—only that the federal government cannot. In the 1790s, about half the states had an established religion, but that tradition ended when Massachusetts in 1833 became the last state to disestablish a state religion—that of the Congressional Church. Today, the US Supreme Court would most likely use the First and Fourteenth Amendments to halt any state from establishing a state religion, relying on *Everson v. Board of Education* (330 U.S. 1, 1947), declaring that "[n]either a state nor the Federal Government can set up a church." Moreover, the Eleventh Circuit Court of appeals affirmed that the First Amendment applies not only to Congress but also to the states, which cannot establish a state religion. The US Supreme Court concurred by voiding an Alabama school prayer law, applying the Fourteenth Amendment to the states the same as it did with the First Amendment and Congress.[10]

Interestingly enough, when the Texas State Textbook Committee convened on September 14, 1961, to hear public testimony from members of Texans for America and the Texas Society of the Daughters of the American Revolution, it opened with the following Christian prayer from one of the committee's members, who also referred to the United States as a "democracy" rather than a "constitutional republic," which Texas conservatives preferred:

> Graciously Heavenly Father, we would pause at this time to give thanks to Thee for the privilege of living in this great land of ours.
>
> Father, we are thankful that we do live in a democracy where we as a free people can meet together to consider the tools of learning.
>
> Father, we pray that in this meeting that the uppermost ideas in all of our minds will be to have the best type of schools of learning perfected.
>
> Father, we pray Thou wilt forgive us our sins; that Thou will lead us, and guide us in all we attempt to do.
>
> Be with us always, Father, in all that we attempt to do, we ask in Jesus' name and for his sake. Amen.[11]

62   Chapter 3

Concern Two: Darwinian Evolution

The teaching of evolution and the work of Charles Darwin also raised issues for some Texans, even in social studies textbooks. Any claims by textbook authors of people or civilizations existing prior to 4004 BCE seemed to some in conflict with creation stories in the Bible. Creationists claim the date 4004 BCE with origin of the universe, mainly due to the work of James Ussher (1581–1656). According to Alan Ford in *James Ussher: Theology, History, and Politics in Early-Modern Ireland and England* (Oxford University Press, 2007), Bishop Ussher was a well-respected Irish scholar of the Bible, a historian, and a linguist, as well as Calvinist Archbishop of the Church of Ireland. After studying what he found available in ancient history, astronomy, the Julian calendar, and the Bible, by 1650 he hypothesized that the universe began 4000 years before the birth of Jesus in 4 BCE, or immediately before Sunday, October 23, 4004 BCE. However, Bishop Ussher felt his opinion was subject to further review by scholars as new evidence about the age of the universe became available.

Charles Darwin was not alone in his theory of evolution. Alfred Russell Wallace, an English naturalist, and English biologist and publisher Robert Chambers had also arrived at the same idea. But Darwin was the first to publish the most extensive scientific work on the subject. He did so in 1859, with *On the Origin of Species by Means of Natural Selection: Or, the Preservation of Favored Races in the Struggle for Life* and his later 1871 two-volume *The Descent of Man*. Darwin never claimed human beings descended directly from apes—only that humans and apes might have had a common ancestor. But his theory nonetheless stirred up enormous negative emotional responses.

Darwin's scientific work began in earnest when he collected data on his round-the-world voyage as a naturalist on the *HMS Beagle* during 1831–36. Furthering his work, in *On the Origin of Species*, Darwin maintained that over vast amounts of time, species changed or evolved from more primitive life-forms to newer and more complex forms. This evolution came about through natural selection of inherently random forms. Darwin suggested that a species is more likely to survive when it has some advantage, such as greater intelligence, strength, or through some form of cooperation with other species. Offspring of the spe-

Trouble Brewing   63

cies will inherit the advantageous trait. In the struggle for survival, the weaker species will perish.

Darwin's use of the term "theory" indicates an idea supported strongly by evidence as an explanation of facts assembled and verified with great care. It is a method for interpreting data in an ongoing process for seeking the truth. As Bill Allen, editor of *National Geographic*, explained in his publication's November 2004 issue: "When scientists say 'theory,' they mean a statement based on observation or experimentations that explains facets of the observable world so well that it becomes accepted as fact. They do not mean an idea created out of thin air, nor do they mean an unsubstantiated belief."

Darwin knew his theory would raise a storm of protest, and it most certainly did. The biggest outcry came from religious groups. Many Christians, for example, felt Darwin's ideas conflicted with their version of the creation accounts in the scriptures. If Darwin was correct, all creatures were not formed at one time, and the earth had to be much older than anyone thought. Moreover, they felt evolution reduced people to the status of animals, and this raised problems about human nature and the soul.

Compounding the issue was the emergence of biblical scholarship about origins of the Old Testament. Jewish and Christian scholars had learned much about when Hebrew writers had begun to compile or codify their written religious literature, some seven to eight centuries after the Amorites had arrived at their Hammurabi Code, the latter of which contains many similarities to what appears in the Ten Commandments of the Old Testament. Scholars studied the introduction of such parts of Hebrew speech as verbs into the language. They found three early main sets of writers for parts of the Old Testament: (1) the J Source (for *Judean*), probably written around 1000 BCE; (2) the E Source (for *Ephraimite*), probably written about 800 BCE, toward the end or just after the Hebrews' release from their exile in Babylonia, when they developed a new form of worship centered on the synagogue and expanded on Mosaic law, setting a much higher value on human life than the Code of Hammurabi; and (3) the P Source (for *Priestly*), probably from around 600 BCE. Once established, the scholars determined, for example, that chapter 2, verses 5–23, in Genesis came from the J Source while the creation story in chapter 1, verses 1–31, in Gen-

64 Chapter 3

esis came from the P Source. This explains the two Biblical creation accounts in Genesis, with the newer one appearing first, the older source appearing second, with the two sources containing some very major differences.

Four federal court decisions, *Susan Epperson v. Arkansas* (393 U.S. 97, 1968), *McLean v. Arkansas* (529 F. Supp. 1255, 1258–64, 1968), *Edwards v. Aguillard* (482 U.S. 578, 1987), and *Kitzmiller et al. v. Dover Area School District* (400 F. Supp. 2nd 707, 2005), have ruled that states cannot approve laws that forbid the teaching of evolution in public schools or allow scientific creationism as a religious belief to be part of a public school's science curriculum. (The bibliography in appendix F also contains numerous point-counterpoint sources on evolution and creationism.)

Concern Three: Secular Humanism

Some Texas textbook critics also would drop claims of authors being subversive, pro-Communist, or associated with such individuals, and instead focus on people regarded as secular humanists, who they regarded as atheists. To some critics, secular humanists stressed faith in human beings instead of relying primarily on faith in a supreme being and advocating such things as situation ethics ("If it feels good, do it")—none of which the critics felt should be forced upon students who disagreed with such views. Those in support of secular humanism note that humanists, in the best Renaissance tradition, stress using one's own reasoning to identify and attempt to solve problems. Humanists believe that if people are to learn by developing their knowledge and intellect, they must be allowed to debate, to differ, and to make choices. Humanists, following the footsteps of such individuals as Deists Thomas Jefferson, Benjamin Franklin, James Madison, and Thomas Paine, believe in freedom and a pluralistic democracy, as opposed to any authoritarian effort to impose any one particular viewpoint on society.

On a related note, many creationists claim(ed) that secular humanism is a religion and therefore should not be taught in the public schools. The basis for their claim comes from a footnote in each of two US Supreme Court cases: Justice Hugo Black's commentary in *Torcaso v. Watkins* (367 U.S. 488, 1961) and a later a reference footnote in *United*

States v. Seegar (380 U.S. 163, 1965). In the *Torcaso* footnote, Justice Black wrote, "Among religions in this country which do not teach what would generally be considered a belief in the existence of God are Buddhism, Taoism Ethical Culture, Secular Humanism and others." Black was referring to events when some ethicists or humanists met to share beliefs that have been granted religious types of exemptions, with the primary emphasis on "types." The footnote in the *Seegar* case was about a conscientious objector who did not want to serve in the armed forces, but he did not say he believed in a supreme being. Black did not mention secular humanism by name, but only said, "If he was an atheist, quite different problems would be present." However, the Eleventh Circuit Court of Appeals with *Smith v. Board of School Commissioners of Mobile County* (827 F. 2nd 684, 1987) declared that secular humanism is not a religion, and if it is present in a textbook, then it does not violate the First Amendment. Instead, the court ruled, "[T]he message conveyed is one of a governmental attempt to instill in Alabama public school children such values as independent thought, tolerance of diverse views, self-respect, maturity, self-reliance, and logical decision-making. This is an entirely appropriate secular effect."[12]

Concern Four: Communism and Civil Rights

Some textbook protestors, resentful of federal guarantees of civil rights for more individuals, including African Americans, or any such extensions of federal power over the rights of states, also associated the civil rights movement with the goals of communism. As noted previously, the Communist Party USA favored racial desegregation in all aspects of American life. The Communist Party USA's endorsement of racial integration was enough for some people to associate it with civil rights groups, such as those led by Dr. Martin Luther King Jr. In essence, a call for civil rights was communistic. Historian Don Carleton noted moderate Texas newspaper publisher Houston Harte, who said of the 1950s, "the word Communist at least in Texas usage has come to mean practically anybody the rest of us don't like—a regrettable perversion of the old fashioned son-of-a-bitch."[13]

On the same subject, Sean P. Cunningham concluded that at the time, the Far Right mainly differed from mainstream American conservatism in that they had "a fearful and conspiratorial paranoia that found communists and subversives lurking the dark corridors of state and national government. . . . The Far Right further differentiated itself from mainstream conservatism by yelling abut communist plots and the 'slippery slope of socialism' much more loudly than did most elected Republicans or the conservative Texas Democratic establishment." Cunningham added, "As was true in most Southern states, Anglo Texans often dismissed civil rights reform as radical social engineering, usually 'Communist-inspired.' Linking race, desegregation, and communism was a common practice among Texans throughout most of the 1950s, though by the mid-1960s most politicians running for office were tempering their segregationist rhetoric." Both Nancy E. Baker and Cunningham also noted, "To be an extremist in 1964 was almost as bad as being a communist in 1952."[14]

Concern Five: Progressive Education

Progressive educators also received their share of criticism in the Texas textbook hearings. Singled out for special consideration was the work of John Dewey (1859–1952), an American philosopher, educator, atheist, secular humanist, Socialist, civil rights advocate, and evolutionist—everything most conservatives then opposed. Dewey opposed learning by memory or rote recall under teacher lecture and testing methods. Instead, as a humanist, he felt that the search for truth was an open, ongoing affair, and that schools should employ a scientific learning process via an inquiry approach relating lessons to the interests of students and current-day problems. Dewey's idea was to have students make it a habit to determine the consequences or results for a hypothesis or proposed solution to an issue. In essence, the school would be an agent for social change. As social studies professors Edgar Wesley and Stanley Wronski have noted, Dewey stressed "the indispensable element of the inquiry approach in that it requires the student to analyze a problem in a logical and systematic fashion. . . . It argues that students should learn to test the truth of a proposed solution, or hypothesis, by noting the consequences of acting in accordance with the hypothesis."[15]

For Dewey, the best education for students should exploit their actual experiences and needs, and move from there to a study of related examples from the past. In essence, he advocated making the material that students studied relevant to their own lives—in social studies, for example, focusing or combining such disciplines as history, geography, sociology, political science, anthropology, and economics. Dewey's numerous books include *The Child and the Curriculum* (1902), *Democracy and Education* (1916), *Human Nature and Conduct* (1922), *The Public and Its Problems* (1927), and *How We Think* (1933).

Some of Dewey's progressive colleagues, especially Harold B. Rugg and George S. Counts, also were criticized by some textbook protestors. Rugg, of Teachers College, Columbia University, wrote *Problems of Democracy* social studies programs in the 1930s and early 1940s in hopes of encouraging students to think critically or analytically, rather than focusing on rote memorization of data. The most thorough study of Rugg's work appears in Ronald W. Evans's *This Happened in America: Harold Rugg and the Censure of Social Studies* (Information Age Publishing, 2007).

Rugg, a World War I veteran, was a professor of curriculum at Teachers College, Columbia University, and a supporter of Pres. Franklin D. Roosevelt's New Deal programs. Rugg was also a nationally recognized leader of progressive educators, with a focus on interdisciplinary studies as part of an inquiry-oriented study of controversial issues or current problems. His goal was to question social order, so as to foster an economy where everyone would have a better standard of living. In essence, he wanted social studies to play a dominant role in changing American society. His books include *Statistical Methods Applied to Education* (1917), *Town and City Life* (1923), *A Primer of Graphics and Statistics for Teachers* (1925), *The Child-Centered School: An Appraisal of the New Education* (1928), *A History of American Government and Culture: America's March toward Democracy* (1931), *Culture and Education in America* (1931), *The Great Technology: Social Chaos and the Public Mind* (1933), *American Life and School Curriculum* (1936), *That Men May Understand* (1951), *Foundations for American Education* (1947), and *Imagination* (1963). Additionally, Rugg was a cofounder of the National Council for the Social Studies and editor of the *Journal of Educational Psychology*.

Rugg became the most prominent target of textbook protestors during the 1930s to the end of World War II when he published his *Man and*

His Changing Society, a fourteen-volume social studies program designed for middle school. This project was centered on social problems and proposed reforms with historical precedents but sometimes did not always include contrasting readings. His social studies program nevertheless became a best seller.[16] The National Association of Manufacturers, the Advertising Federation of America, the National Council for Education, the New York Economic Council, and the American Legion accused Rugg's social studies program of being anti–free enterprise, anti-American, and socialist or pro-communist, which it was not. When the accusations became very widespread, Ginn and Company, the publisher, stopped printing the program. The sale of Rugg's programs once totaled more than five million copies to some five thousand school districts, but by 1944, sales dropped by more than 90 percent. Rugg's problem was that he did support some socialist ideas, such as civil rights for all people and government help for the needy through the New Deal programs, and he also argued that American society had strengths as well as weaknesses. That got him in trouble with spokesmen for big business and patriotic groups.[17]

George S. Counts was another advocate of the progressive education promoted by John Dewey. Counts became one of the nation's leading experts in the sociological dimension of educational research, with its emphasis on child-centered learning, and proposed that teachers help build a new democratic social order. This led Counts into the area of labor union activism and civil rights. He served as New York chairman of the American Labor Party, founded the New York Liberal Party, was an unsuccessful candidate for the US Senate, was a member of the National Committee of the American Civil Liberties Union, and served as president of the American Federation of Teachers, which he managed to rid of alleged Communist influences. In *The American Road to Culture*, Counts warned:

> Another consequence of popular control of the school is that education will be affected by those gusts of passions which from time to time sweep through the masses. . . . The foreign observer, witnessing these instances of mob behavior, comes to the conclusion that the level of culture in the United States must be ex-

Trouble Brewing

69

tremely primitive. The fact is that such manifestations are merely the natural fruit of the way in which public education in America is controlled. The intellectual classes, to whose care education is entrusted by tradition in the older countries of Europe, have but little to say about the conduct of the public school in the United States. . . . but in America those masses sit in judgment on educational policy. Thus a price must be paid for the democratization of the control of education. . . . The point to be observed is that the school must inevitably exhibit the cultural limitations as well as the ideals and purposes of the forces in control.[18]

Counts's twenty-nine books include *The New Russian Primer* (1931), *The Soviet Challenge to America* (1931), *Dare the School Build a New Social Order* (1932), *The Social Foundations of Education* (1934), *The Prospects of American Democracy* (1938), and *Education and American Civilization* (1952). Counts was also research director of the American Historical Association's "Investigation of the Social Studies in the Schools—Report of the Commission on the Social Studies," published by historian Howard K. Beale in *Are American Teachers Free?* and *A History of Freedom of Teaching in American Schools* (Charles Scribner's Sons, 1936, 1941).[19]

Dewey and those educators who agreed with him likewise got caught up in the conflict of two main schools of thought that predated World War I and bled into the post–World War II era: One school of thought, the history traditionalists, felt the core of the social studies was, according to education historian Ronald Evans, "a textbook-centered approach with a focus on development of old fashioned patriotism through filiopietistic history," emphasizing socialization and that progressive education was anti-intellectual and anti-democratic, in addition to not adhering "to any standards of knowledge." The other school of thought, the issue-oriented progressive reconstructionists, stressed "a curriculum focused on social issues, decision-making, and problems with the aim of developing a more critical version of patriotism." To accomplish that, they would make such disciplines as economics, geography, sociology, anthropology, and political science the prominent core of the social studies, even in fused courses.[20]

70   Chapter 3

In the wake of World War II there was a movement to stress patriotism and emphasize what was *right* about America, with less emphasis on the nation's faults, as depicted, for example, in Rugg's progressive reconstructionist *Problems of Democracy* courses. This led William Randolph Hearst's newspapers to publish the following editorial, which was typical of the attacks on progressive education by the mid-1940s. Entitled "Our American History," the editorial argued:

> What has happened to the American school, that they have fallen so short of their fundamental responsibility to the American people? How do subversive textbooks . . . find their way into American schools? The American people . . . have left supervision of the schools to radicals and theorists who have no respect for American history and no faith in American tradition. But the actual perversion had been accomplished by Socialistic and Communist pseudo-educators who have conspired to disparage American history and to give American children a distorted conception of the principles which inspired the founders of their country.

Given the rising criticism against their work, the FBI placed Dewey, Rugg, and Counts under its watch, suspected of sympathizing with communist ideals.[21]

The story of Rugg helps illustrate the problems faced by progressive social studies authors. Historian Diane Ravitch noted that with Rugg's "rise to prominence during the late 1930s, there was a war looming in Europe and super patriotic groups such as the Daughters of the American Revolution, American Legion, and the ultra-conservative William Randolph Hearst's newspapers launched anti-communist crusades against Americans such as college professors, novelists, or other artisans for unknowingly or knowingly helping the subversive communist cause. Rugg got caught up in that anti-radicalism movement."[22]

Historian Joseph Moreau summarized the controversies regarding Rugg's work by noting "his detractors agreed the world crisis demonstrated the need for a return to economic and educational values they believed had once bound Americans together, among them individualism, free enterprise, limited government, and an embrace of tradition for its own sake. Rugg argued, and arranged his history and civics texts to demonstrate, that America's political and economic ideology had to continue evolving to meet crises at home and the challenge of communism and fascism abroad. The welfare state would have to expand, claimed Rugg, and the government would have to take more direct control of economic development."[23]

Rugg's answer was as follows:

> [F]or minority groups to attempt to censor the citizens' world in a democratic society, and particularly in time of crisis, is a matter fraught with great danger. It is to destroy the only instrument which can make democracy work. So I say to self-appointed censors of education: Censor the schools and you convince yourselves by your very acts as the most subversive enemies of democracy. Censor education and you destroy understanding . . . you instate bias . . . you give free reign to prejudice . . . finally, you create fascism. Nothing but an education in the whole of American life will build tolerant understanding in our people and guarantee the perpetuation of democracy.[24]

Despite the protests of critics, Rugg-type issue-oriented courses continue to be used today via interactive teaching. However, this style of pedagogy appears far less than traditional standard American and world history courses dominated by teacher lectures and rote memory recall exercises.[25] Indeed, the drastic decline of the publication of Rugg's programs resulted in his work not being considered a serious issue during the temporary lull of major social studies debates from the end of World War II to the late 1950s, but the "Rugg issue" would most certainly resurface with the Texas social studies protests of 1961–62.

Concern Six: The Absence of Patriotic Historical Accounts

Some of the Texas textbook critics in 1961–62 wanted more textbook authors to write histories like those appearing in the 1885 *Barnes Primary History of the United States*. The book included very lengthy biographies of such individuals as George Washington, Nathan Hale, and Patrick Henry, without anything negative being written about such in-

72 Chapter 3

dividuals, stressing only what the protestors regarded as "good patriotism." Contrary to popular perception, no one named Barnes wrote *The Primary History of the United States*. Instead, Joel Dorman Steele, the main author, and Betsy Baker Steele, his wife, wrote it. Because Joel Steele was a scientist and neither he nor his wife were historians, the textbook was named after the publisher, A. S. Barnes Company. Few people reading the book knew Steel's professional background, nor was the book ever widely used in schools. Yet, as will be explored further in the following discussion, this unabashedly patriotic style of writing experienced a resurgence when it was espoused by critics in the Texas debates of 1961–62.[26]

Concern Seven: Korean War American POWs

Some Texas textbook critics in 1961–62 raised concerns related to the behavior of American soldiers held captive by the enemy during the Korean War. It was estimated that about one-third of American POWs in the conflict unquestioningly collaborated with the enemy when captured. Critics argued that these soldiers' waning allegiance stemmed from a lack of patriotic education—they had not been taught enough about the good side of American history.

In 1959, Eugene Kinkead wrote *In Every War but One* (W. W. Norton), which summarized the findings of the US Department of Defense's five-year study on the conduct of American servicemen held captive by the Chinese and North Korean Communists during the Korean War. The study concluded that this sociological phenomenon was due to two main factors: First, the drafted American military ranks contained many men who had limited intelligence, were not well educated, or both. Therefore, they were not well equipped to use refined critical-thinking skills, such as methods to objectively evaluate differing viewpoints in order to withstand Communist propaganda techniques. Second, many of the POWs lacked the military discipline with which to counter propaganda. The exceptions were US Marines and those in Turkey's armed forces. Not a single American marine or Turkish soldier taken prisoner ever collaborated with the enemy. The marines and Turks had a "Band of Brothers" mentality that made collaboration with the enemy absolutely unacceptable. In essence, it was posited that military discipline

Trouble Brewing
73

preserved military cohesion and instilled greater allegiance to the flag. Hugh M. Milton III, undersecretary of the US Army, told Kinkead:

> [When taken prisoner] our men may be deprived of sleep, food, and medical attention in a prison camp. They should expect this and still have the will to live while these things are temporarily lacking. They should also acquire a familiarity with first aid, nutrition, and preventative medicine—all substantial helps under such conditions. On the spiritual aide, esprit de corps and a feeling of comradeship are great aids to morale. So are faith in democracy and an adherence to religious beliefs. Many repatriates [from the Korean War] told me that in the prison camps religious and ethical intangibles were of greater help and comfort to them than anything else.[27]

With this in mind, critics of social studies programs in Texas in 1961–62 cited the need for increased patriotic education and educational reforms to foster increased military allegiance and discipline in times of crisis.

Citing the aforementioned concerns, during August of 1961, members from Texans for America and Texas Society of the Daughters of the American Revolution submitted to the Texas Education Agency specific objections, called Bills of Particulars, regarding the social studies books submitted for state adoption. The conservative groups were especially disturbed by works being written by an emerging new professional group of historians, who they deemed unfit and, at times, unpatriotic. The public hearings on September 14, 1961, allowed the conservative groups to raise their criticisms of the specific textbooks they found most objectionable. Joined by some members of the John Birch Society, the Minute Women, and the American Legion, they would later repeat their concerns during public hearings held by the Texas House of Representatives Textbook Investigating Committee in 1962. At the public hearings held by that house committee, conservatives were opposed primarily by New Deal/Fair Deal Texas Democrats supportive of the emerging civil rights revolution. The following chapter details the hearings before the Texas State Textbook Committee on September 14, 1961, in the wake of the great social studies textbook war of 1961–62.

4

A Call to Arms

The Texas State Textbook Committee
Hearings, September 14, 1961

THE GREAT TEXAS social studies war began as a routine textbook hearing before the Texas State Textbook Committee at the Texas Education Agency on September 14, 1961. Among some of the first Texas "formal hearings," which continue to the present, the September 1961 textbook hearings were conducted by the fifteen-member State Textbook Committee. J. B. Golden, director of the Texas Education Agency's Textbook Division, allotted historian J. Evetts Haley and his Texans for America three and a half hours to make their morning presentations. Veteran social studies teacher A. A. Forester spent the afternoon session voicing the concerns of the Texas Society of the Daughters of the American Revolution. Those two groups were the only ones that fall to formally protest books before the State Textbook Committee. However, some members of both groups were also members of the anti-Communist John Birch Society, the Minute Women, and the American Legion. Newspaper and media coverage of the September 14 hearing, as well as the November 13, 1961, Texas State Board of Education meeting to adopt books for the public schools, was extremely scant. Fortunately, transcripts, minutes, and other documents of those hearings are available and provide an abundance of information.[1]

Even with limited press and media coverage of those 1961 meetings, Haley and his Texans for America, along with Forester, still managed to

A Call to Arms   75

have their say, with Haley dominating the hearings. His paternal grandfather was a Mississippi physician and planter who fought for the Confederacy during the Civil War. His maternal great-grandfather fought in Sam Houston's army at the April 21, 1836, battle at San Jacinto, and his maternal grandfather fought for the Confederacy. As a result, Haley was a member of the Sons of the Republic of Texas and the Sons of Confederate Veterans. In that regard, Haley felt Texas should not have joined the United States in 1845. His parents operated a hotel in Midland, Texas, and owned ranches nearby, and his father also served as a mayor of Midland. Haley was class president at Midland High School and captain of the football team in 1920. He recalled of that time: "The least of my ambitions was to be adjudged sane—my greatest ambition was to be a real hand—a top cowboy, filled with that fierce pride and intoxication for adventure that would keep me riding with lose rein, wildly with the leaders when the going was the worst." Over the years, Haley's ambition to be a cowboy resulted in a broken leg five times, a broken jaw three times, a broken collarbone three times, and numerous broken ribs.[2]

Haley worked at his family's ranches and others nearby before graduating from what is now West Texas A&M University and earned a master's degree in history from the University of Texas at Austin. He also was a field secretary for the Panhandle Plains Historical Society, where he did oral interviews with West Texas pioneers and gathered artifacts and archival materials for the society. In 1929, the University of Texas employed Haley on a federally funded contract to help create its archival field program and lead the Texas Historical Records Survey. When Haley became an outspoken critic of Pres. Franklin Roosevelt and head of the Jefferson Democrats to oppose Roosevelt's New Deal, the University of Texas, citing budget problems, did not renew Haley's contract. Haley claimed he was "fired because of my vigorous fight against the insidious invasion of socialistic federal power." Reporters for the *Texas Observer* "checked with the payroll department of the University of Texas to find out when Haley was at U. T. and if he was fired, as he said in his . . . testimony [before the Texas House of Representatives Textbook Investigating Committee on January 31, 1962]. The payroll department says he was not on the staff as a teacher but as a 'collector.'" *The Observer* explained that "this meant he went around the state soliciting manuscripts for the university's historical collection [from 1931 to 1935].

The payroll department does not record his having been fired. Some of the older professors at the university say they had not heard of the 'firing' until several years after he left when Haley himself first publicly described his exit in this way. They said it was their opinion the funds just ran out, that being the bottom of the depression."[3]

Haley, the rugged individualistic and states' rights advocate, opposed every aspect of Roosevelt's domestic program, thinking it violated private property rights, tended toward communism, interfered with employee-employer relations, offered needless welfare, and otherwise was a wasteful spending of federal monies. To counteract this, Haley organized the Texas Jefferson Democrats to support the Republican candidate, Alf Landon, for president in 1936. Haley's effort proved futile when Roosevelt carried 253 of the 254 counties in Texas. Haley then managed several ranches, owned his own ranch, was director of the Institute of Americanism, became president of the Panhandle Plains Historical Society, persuaded the Texas legislature to require six credit hours of American history for all students attending state colleges and universities, and was a member of the Texas Tech University Board of Regents. In 1956, he unsuccessfully ran for governor of Texas. By then, he was more vocal in his opposition to racial integration, which he thought would bring the white race a "biological decline," and wanted members of the US Supreme Court removed from office because of their unanimous decision in *Brown v. Topeka* (1954), which desegregated public schools. He urged repeal of the federal income tax and federal agricultural subsidies; wanted increased emphasis on the heritage of the United States as founded on a Christian-Judeo tradition; opposed the United Nations, foreign aid to other countries, labor unions, and the minimum wage; and favored state rights over federal rights.[4]

The 1956 governor's contest was between Price Daniel, then liberal judge Ralph Yarborough, former Texas governor W. Lee "Pappy" O'Daniel, and Haley. O'Daniel and Haley favored states' right and opposed the civil rights movement, federal price controls on natural gas (Haley had some natural gas wells on his property), and labor unions—all with a strong anti-Communist emphasis. On the issue of states' rights and public school integration, Haley supported the Doctrine of Interposition, describing it as follows:

A Call to Arms 77

[The] most critical issue in our national existence. . . . It is the destruction of the Constitution and the American Republic through the complete disregard of the 9th and 10th Amendments that reserved all undelegated powers to the States. . . . In cases of "palpable deliberate . . . and dangerous" destruction of the rights and liberties of the people—as James Madison and Thomas Jefferson, the principal authors of the Constitution and the Declaration of Independence pointed out—it is "not only the right but the bounded duty of the state" to interpose its authority and say it will not comply.

Daniel won the 1956 governor's race with a vote of 628,941 to Yarborough's 463,400; O'Daniel's 347,750; and Haley's 88,772. Haley also lost another race to become Texas commissioner of agriculture.[5]

Bill Modisett, author of *J. Evetts Haley: A True Texas Legend*, recalled the following about Haley:

If a school board in the state refused to integrate—even after a suit was filed by the [NAACP] and an order to do was issued by a federal judge who also sent a marshal to arrest the [school] board—as governor, [Haley] would counter that threat with the Doctrine of Interposition. "The minute that comes," said Haley, "I will expect the sheriff of that county to arrest the marshal. And, of course, as Governor of Texas, should I be fortunate enough to be elected, I will expect to back up that sheriff, I will send a Texas Ranger to meet that marshal and arrest him and throw him in the hooscow. That, my friends, is interposition. I expect to interpose."[6]

Speaking before the National Indignation Convention in Houston in 1962, Haley was introduced by Tom Anderson, a member of the National Council of the John Birch Society. Haley stated, "I'm a newcomer to the ranks of the book burners. I'm called a witch hunter. Well, I'm not so worried 'bout witches, but I sure am worried about some these sons of witches. . . . Tom Anderson here has turned moderate. All he wants to do is impeach [Earl] Warren [Chief Justice of the US Supreme Court]. I'm for hanging him."[7]

During that time, Haley and his son were charged and fined $506 with violating the Agricultural Adjustment Act of 1936 by exceeding a wheat crop allotment by forty-three acres on their Oklahoma ranch. The issue reached the US Supreme Court, which ruled against the Haleys, although they had never taken an agricultural subsidy. Haley remarked, "If I can't make it as a rancher, I ought to do something else."[8]

After losing his bid to become governor, Haley, with support from the anti-Communist John Birch Society and the Daughters of the American Revolution, founded the group Texans for America, with two hundred members. As Haley told a Texas House of Representatives hearing, "[I]f this struggle [for the minds of youth] means anything, it is the perpetuation of the Christian ethic. There is no freedom except under the Christian ethic as enshrined in the Constitution and Bill of Rights." One of the Texans for America's main concerns was the content of school textbooks. The Texans for America opposed the textbooks' positive take on federal rights over states, the League of Nations or the United Nations, UNESCO, social security, socialism, federal subsidies to public education or to farmers, the federal income tax, the Tennessee Valley Authority (socialism), and progressive education. They also opposed any authors involved (past or present) in the civil rights movement—writers such as Ernest Hemmingway, Sinclair Lewis, William Faulkner, Jack London, Pearl Buck, historians Charles Beard and Henry Steele Commager, scientist Albert Einstein, composer Aaron Copeland, folklorist J. Frank Dobie, and progressive educator John Dewey. Haley's ultimate solution to the state's textbook adoption process was for it to be abolished and in its place to have the parents of each child select the textbooks their children would use in school. That, of course, could create problems for any teacher potentially confronting a class of students in which each child used a different textbook.[9]

When Lyndon B. Johnson ran for president in 1964, Haley may have gone too far with his dislike of Johnson's domestic policies, especially the Great Society program. After being refused by several publishers, Haley self-published (at his own expense) *A Texan Looks at Lyndon: A Study in Illegitimate Power* (Palo Duro Press, 1964). It was well received by many conservatives but roundly condemned by nearly everyone else. Johnson simply ignored the book. Perhaps the most damaging review of the book came from novelist A. C. Green, editorial page editor of the

A Call to Arms 79

Dallas Times Herald. Green wrote, "Haley is a historian with some excellent writing to his credit, but he deserts historical principles and takes up personal hatred as his guide for *A Texan Looks at Lyndon.*" Green accused Haley of too often claiming "rumor, presumption and suspicion" as valid: "[he] then goes on to base further assumptions on the scrap heap, offering time after time, a colossally shocking inference—but never reminding the reader that the whole foundation was questionable." Green concluded that Haley's book was "a case of unhospitalized paranoia." In response, Haley called Green a "journalistic prostitute." Regardless, putting their past differences aside, in 1982 Green listed Haley's book on Charles Goodnight the best biography ever written about a rancher.[10]

Haley died on October 9, 1995. By then he had settled in Midland, and in honor of his first wife who died in 1958, he founded the Nita Stewart Haley Memorial Library and History Center to preserve the Western heritage. The library has continued to house Haley's books and papers.

The award-winning Haley was the author of articles in such publications as the *Southwestern Historical Quarterly, Southwest Review, Ranch Romances, Nature, Cattlemen,* and the *Panhandle Plains Historical Review,* as well as numerous newspaper columns. His books include *The Alamo Mission Bell* (1974), *Earl Vandale on the Trail of Texas Books* (1965), *Men of Fiber* (1963), *F. Reaugh: Man and Artist* (1960), *Erle P. Halliburton: Genius with Cement* (1959), *Story of the Shamrock* (1954), *Fort Concho and the Texas Frontier* (1952), *Life on the Texas Range* (1952), *The Heraldry of the Range: Some Southwestern Brands* (1949), *Jeff Milton: A Good Man with a Gun* (1948), *Charles Schreiner: General Merchandise—The Story of a Country Store* (1944), *George W. Littlefield: Texan* (1943), *Charles Goodnight: Cowman and Rancher* (1936), and *The XIT Ranch of Texas and the Early Days of the Llano Estacado* (1929).

A collection of Haley's essays from 1927 to 1989 appears in *On His Native Heath . . . In His Natural Element* (Nita Steward Haley Memorial Library, 1992). Other books in appreciation of Haley include Bill Modisett's *J. Evetts Haley: A True Texas Legend* (Staked Plains Press, 1996); editor Evetts Haley Jr.'s *What a World of Wonder! An Appreciation of J. Evetts Haley, Cowman, Historian, American* (Nita Stewart Haley

Memorial Library, 1990); and editor Chandler A. Robinson's *J. Evetts Haley and the Passing of the Old West* (Jenkins Publishing Company, 1978).

Haley's honors include a writing award from the Texas Institute of Letters, investiture in the Knights of the Order of San Jacinto, the Award of Merit from the American Association of State and Local History, induction into the National Cowboy Hall of Fame of the State Fair of Texas, an honorary doctorate of Humane Letters from Hillsdale College (Michigan), and the Award of Merit for "distinguished and continuing contributions to the knowledge, understanding and appreciation of Texas history" from the American Association for State and Local History, Williamsburg, Virginia.

Haley would have been especially pleased when the Alumni Association of West Texas A&M University in 2013 posthumously honored him as one of its three recipients for the Distinguished Alumnus Award, citing:

> History was his passion. . . . [H]e received a bachelor's degree from WTAMU in the subject he loved so much. He worked as the field secretary for the Panhandle-Plains Historical Society and interviewed area pioneers for a lasting legacy and archive of the Texas Panhandle region. His work led directly to the creation of the Panhandle-Plains Historical Museum. Haley, a rancher, historian, author and political activist, wrote more than twenty books as well as numerous articles about the American West and is probably best known for his book *Charles Goodnight Cowman and Plainsman*. . . . [The Haley Center] continues today to provide unparalleled research resources for students, researchers, writers, and . . . the Haley Scholars. His role in preserving the history of Texas is remarkable and marks him as a Distinguished Alumnus of WTAMU.

Folklorist J. Frank Dobie, an adversary of Haley on the book censorship issue, may have paid Haley the supreme compliment when he said, "Evetts is sometimes a mean fighter. He'll kick you in the b—s. But I'll say this, if he thinks he's right, he'll stand there alone, in the blizzard, and the rain, and fight for what he believes in."[11]

A Call to Arms 81

In the early days of the organization, Haley's Texans for America held a rehearsal for its criticisms of public school textbooks. Their rehearsal began slowly in 1960 when the group, led by Haley and Dr. Don Riddle, a Paris, Texas, veterinarian and textbook chairman of the organization, expressed concerns about some elementary history, English, and vocational agricultural textbooks proposed for state adoption in Texas. Although unsuccessful in their challenges, they claimed some books had authors with an un-American "ideological bent and reliance on Communist sources." They especially questioned the "moral ramifications" of books including material about a New Deal federal farm program of the Commodity Credit Corporation or allowing farmers to be eligible for federal conservation training and financial aid—allegedly a socialistic idea. Dr. Riddle claimed, "A textbook can be [98 percent] correct, but if you have these ideas, these ideologies in two percent, you can implant in a child's mind ideas completely contrary to the American free enterprise system." When Dr. Riddle was asked how a farmer was to learn the best way to utilize up-to-date conservation methods, he replied, "I've had to resort to the old-fashioned method of digging it out of books myself." Haley went further and said, "Our basic opposition to the promotion of this farm program [a New Deal one] is a moral one." Discussing a proposed English textbook, Haley asked, "Are we willing for Communists and Communist sympathizers to choose the literature our children read in the public schools?"[12]

All this was a prelude for the way Texans for America approached the Texas adoption of public school programs in 1961, most of which involved American history for grade eight, American history for high school, and world history for the high school level. Haley and Dr. Riddle organized testifying members of Texans for America in such a way as to dominate those textbook hearings. They were joined by the equally well-organized A. A. Forester for the Texas Society of the Daughters of the American Revolution.

Haley and Dr. Riddle had members of Texans for America focus on only one or two books each when speaking before the Texas State Textbook Committee on September 4, 1961. Their overall goal was to stress "the perpetuation of the Christian civilization of which America is the outstanding example of history."[13]

82   Chapter 4

Forester, chair of the Textbook Committee of the Texas Society of the Daughters of the American Revolution, and a thirty-one-year veteran high school social studies teacher at Texas High School in the Texarkana, Texas, ISD, served as spokesperson for the Daughters of the American Revolution. The Daughters of the American Revolution, founded in 1890, received a charter from Congress in 1896. Its membership is made up of women who are descended from persons who achieved American independence from Great Britain. Prior to the end of World War I, the Daughters of the American Revolution's main emphasis was to promote love of country and good citizenship by inculcating respect for patriotic symbols and interest in American history. After World War I, the organization began to associate nationalism with patriotism and to evaluate whether history textbooks fulfilled those goals. By 1928 it started releasing a list of textbooks which did or did not meet its criteria of acceptable books for school use and acted on their list to urge only the adoption of books it felt suitable for school children. [14]

In the following, Haley and Forester offer their overall critiques before the Texas State Textbook Committee in regard to the history books considered for adoption by Texas in 1961. Their critiques especially focused on what they felt was wrong with the books being submitted by an emerging new group of liberal historians, with Haley's public testimony going first, speaking for Texans for America.

Haley stated that he and members of his group were not testifying "as experts":

> [B]ut we are here as concerned citizens and as parents—citizens of the State of Texas and parents of youthful Texans who are in the schools, and hence we are quite concerned with their education. [We] are interested in the perpetuation of the Christian civilization of which America is the outstanding example of history. So, humbly we come before you. not only as a matter of duty, but as a matter of duty under law as passed and conferred upon us and upon you by the Legislature of the State of Texas. We therefore contend that the thing that should be considered least in our presentation is that we pretend to be expert.

He stressed the Texans' Committee for Education "represents a statewide group of over 200 people who have been active, all on a voluntary basis. in the preparation of these Bills of Particulars [the detained listing of concerns], and as you so well know, we can appear here only as adversary, not as advocates under the Texas law. There are many books we would like to say that we are for, but we cannot appear here in that capacity. So, well realizing that may in the public mind place us in a somewhat unfortunate position, we are nevertheless restricted to that." Haley added, "We have been bewildered somewhat, and perplexed, and concerned to find that we have by some been considered intruders into this field, but we are here simply to try to be of help in view of certain criteria and principles that we hold. We have had, as you so well know, difficulty within the time limitations, we think unfortunately imposed by the State Board of Education within the time limitations of getting these books, of reading them. It has handicapped us greatly; otherwise, we would have a much more finished, logical, and detailed presentation."

He then concluded by declaring, "[W]e believe the primary purpose of basic education is, first, to teach our children how to read, write and use numbers. Second, to transmit facts concerning our heritage, our history and our culture. Third, to develop intelligence and stimulate creative, wholesome thinking. And fourth, provide an atmosphere of moral affirmation without which education is reduced to mere animal training. To the extent a book succeeds or fails on these four points, we think these four points of consideration, on that consideration, will be rated good, fair, poor, or bad."[15]

Overall, by 1961, the National Daughters of the American Revolution Textbook Committee nationwide found 170 of the 220 social studies textbooks it examined to be "subversive." The Daughters of the American Revolution Committee stated, "Unfortunately, there is a perceivable pattern of 'economic determinism' running through the unsatisfactory texts on all subjects. History books and economic texts [for example] contain uncomplimentary pictures of slum areas or long lines of unemployed during the great depression."[16] None of the textbooks submitted by publishers in 1961 for consideration by the Texas State Textbook Committee or approved by the Texas State Board of Education were sanctioned by the Texas Society of the Daughters of the American Revolution. Forester actually made her case twice: once before the before the Texas State Textbook Committee in September of 1961 and again before

84 Chapter 4

the Texas House of Representatives Textbook Investigating Committee during the spring of 1962. The latter of her public testimony presentations is described as follows, and it is basically the same as her previous address before the State Textbook Committee.

In her public testimony before the State Textbook Committee, Forester offered reasons for her concerns about the content and omissions of state-approved social studies books, arguing, "Many surveys of high school seniors being made today reveal that too large a percentage of these students believe that the profit motive can be eliminated without hurting the American free enterprise system, or that most people are incapable of deciding what is best for themselves that the government should make the decisions." For her, this was because "many factors have contributed to these startling facts, and that one of these factors, perhaps the most important factor, has been the textbooks in use in our high schools, particularly in the so-called 'social studies' field." She continued:

> America, today, is engaged in a devastating war, a war declared a hundred years ago by Karl Marx. A half century later, Nikolai Lenin reaffirmed the declaration of war when he stated that communism and capitalism cannot exist in the world together. Now the man in the Kremlin, [Soviet premier] Nikita Khrushchev, speaking to the Congress of Communist Parties meeting in Moscow, reaffirmed that declaration of war. The enemy has not resorted to the traditional weapons of warfare, probably because he is doing just fine without them. Instead he has elected to use subversion and the infiltration of our free institutions. Thus, our fight has become a battle of words to prevent communist control of the minds of all men. Our most precious weapons is truth, the whole truth about our history and the competing ideologies of the day.

That "battle of words" she felt was

> where the textbooks which are studied by the American youth play a very important part in helping win this war. Thus, it is the duty as well as the right of all loyal American citizens, to evaluate these books selected for use in our public schools and public school libraries, to see that not one student in a group of high

school seniors has been indoctrinated with the idea that the profit motive can be eliminated without hurting the American free enterprise system, or that most people are incapable of deciding what is best for themselves, that the government should make the decisions. This is socialism, a system completely opposite to the free enterprise system established by the founders of the American economy, an economy which has made the United States the greatest nation in the entire world.

She quoted something J. Edgar Hoover, director of the FBI, told the US House of Representatives Un-American Activities Committee on March 27, 1947: "I confess to a real apprehension so long as school boards and parents tolerate conditions whereby Communists and fellow travelers, under the guise of academic freedom, can teach our youth a way of life that eventually will destroy the sanctity of the home, that will undermine their faith in God, that causes them to scorn respect for constituted authority, and sabotage our revered constitution."

Forester also noted that Major William E. Mayer, a US Army psychiatrist, said how about one-third of American POWs during the Korean War, in one way or another, helped the enemy while in captivity: "The behavior of many Americans in Korean prison camps appears to raise serious questions about American character and about the education of Americans. Each POW told Major Mayer that he had never learned what it meant to be an American citizen—he had never been taught true patriotism, and thus could not refute any statement made by the Chinese Communists about his country."

Coupled with the Hoover and Mayer statements, Forester also used "The Great Pretense," House Report No. 2189, which she summarized as "our lack of political and intellectual sophistication, our lack of realistic thinking, our spongy education on the nature of collectivism and the true nature of American principles as set up by the Founding Fathers, we are today losing the cold war. School Superintendents, principals, and teachers, are in a position of crucial responsibility: theirs is a 'captive audience.' The child is compelled to listen to what they teach and to read the text they select."

She went on to add that "[t]he Society of the Daughters of the American Revolution does not attack textbooks. It evaluates them—the good and the bad. These are then placed on the proper list: satisfactory or un-satisfactory."

Forester then listed nine criteria for evaluating textbook programs. In her opinion, most of the social studies textbooks up for adoption in Texas in 1961 did not meet those Daughters of the American Revolution requirements. She specifically asked the following:

Does the text present a fair and well-balanced treatment of the subject matter?

Is the exposition of the subject it is intended to cover interesting, clear and thorough? Or is it superficial and inadequate?

Is sufficient or equal attention given to all the rights of the American citizen, or does the text give a great deal of attention to "civil liberties" and very little or no attention to the right to acquire and hold property, the right to work, the right to engage in free enterprise, the right of a free society to protect itself against subversion, etc.?

How does the textbook treat socialism, communism, and capitalism? Does it use selective material to discredit capitalism and to develop an attitude of mind favorable to socialism and communism?

Is the material used a true and complete record of our free enterprise system, or is it selective material so as to develop a particular attitude of mind?

Does the text instill in the student a pride in the achievements and accomplishments of our free enterprise system?

Are illustrations such as photographs, drawings, cartoons, charts or tables given in a fair and balanced way, or is one side of, the picture presented?

Are the supplemental reading lists fair and well-balanced to give the student a well-rounded and accurate knowledge of the subject?

Does the text help prepare the malleable mind of an American high school student to take his place in a society based on constitutional government and a free enterprise economy?

She further argued that she did not think only teachers should be allowed to evaluate textbooks, for the following reasons: "(1) This violates the right of free speech and a redress of grievances. (2) It would violate the Texas law setting up the adoption of textbooks which states that any person may protest the adoption of textbooks. (3) It would certainly reflect on our educational system to admit that the product of that system is not capable of judging the qualities of a good textbook."

As for the role a textbook plays in a curriculum, she quoted Arthur S. Trace, author of *What Ivan Knows That Johnny Doesn't*, who argued: "If the textbook is bad, the teacher no matter how good he may be, is severely handicapped. It is primarily textbooks which determine the organization and presentation of the material and the thoroughness with which the basic subjects are studied. Furthermore, students discuss textbook material in class, they are asked questions about it, they take tests on it, their homework assignments are usually based on it, and whatever else they do, they are expected to master it."

Forester also felt that the Texas Commissioner of Education had too much authority in recommending books for adoption and that the Texas State Board of Education was limited in what textbooks the state could approve for adoption. As a solution, she recommended the following:

> [If] it is not feasible to get the State Board of Education to have more responsibility in the selection of textbooks, then a State Textbook Committee of 23 lay members (not engaged in teaching at that time) should be elected every 2 years, one from each congressional district, to serve separately, with same powers and rights as the state Textbook Committee composed of 23 members of teachers and administrators, one from each Congressional District. Each committee would make its own report on the selection of the multiple lists for each subject, after hearing the protests to the adoption of any book from any citizen at a joint session of the two committees.[17]

In 1962, State Representative Bob Bass proposed a bill to the Texas legislature to enact the essence of the changes recommended by Forester. However, the legislature refused to act on his request.

88   Chapter 4

The Texas State Board of Education adopted the content recommended by the State Textbook Committee on November 13, 1961. The concerns presented by Texans for America and the Texas Society of the Daughters of the American Revolution surrounding this decision came in the wake of yet another shift in the continuing evolution of American historiography. These groups, along with other Texas conservatives, protested this shift via their criticisms the New Deal, the Fair Deal, the United Nations, "suspect" authors, progressive educators such as John Dewey, and secular humanism. Their other concerns included the following:

1. Coverage in social studies books was considered slanted, especially after 1933, in support of the New Deal and Fair Deal, encouraging students to accept "[s]ocialistic and world-involvement trends" and public welfare programs.

2. Some textbook authors classified the American government as a "republic," but in all, critics alleged there was too much emphasis on the American government as a "democracy"—which sometimes translated to mob rule. Earlier in US history, most presidents prior to Woodrow Wilson did not use the term "democracy," with the exception of Grover Cleveland and Theodore Roosevelt. Regardless of this criticism, State Textbook Committee member T. W. Ogg used the term "democracy" to describe the US form of government during his opening prayer before the September 14, 1961, hearings of the State Textbook Committee.

3. Critics alleged that many of the recommended reading lists in the textbooks contained titles by "authors, writers, and artists whose loyalties have been called into question" and could be subversives or pro-Communists. (Later textbook critics substituted "secular humanists" for "subversives" or "pro-Communists.")

4. In one book, *Rise of the American Nation* (Harcourt, Brace and World), the phrase "For ye Glory of and advancement of Ye Christian Faith" was left out of the Mayflower Compact. Critics alleged that the "phrase was the foundation of America," citing the United States as "a Christian Nation"

founded on the Judeo-Christian ethic, emphasizing that the separation of church and state is not in the US Constitution.

5. Some textbooks included the philosophy of progressive educator and secular humanist John Dewey, whom critics felt "has brought such havoc to our educational process" by making material too relevant to students' lives by combining such elements or disciplines as history, geography, economics, sociology, and anthropology in social studies courses. Moreover, critics claimed that students were too young and inexperienced to effectively deal with point-counterpoint presentations.

6. Critics felt that textbook authors spent too much time discussing the problems with American society, such as lynching, Jim Crow and racial segregation, the role of the Muckrakers of the Progressive era, massive unemployment during the Great Depression, or the denial of rights to racial minorities. This could create a bad impression of the United States or foster racial hatred in students, instead of emphasizing the positive aspects of US society. Critics alleged this negative perspective contributed to US POWs succumbing to Communist brainwashing during the Korean War.

7. Textbook critics also claimed that textbooks were too critical of the free enterprise system and placed too much emphasis on federal power over state power. They wanted textbooks to emphasize the Ninth and Tenth Amendments to the US Constitution, rather than something like Clause 18, Section 1, known as the "Elastic Clause."

8. Critics claimed that textbooks placed too much emphasis on the United Nations, which they felt was dominated by Soviet Communists. The charter of the United Nations was also considered to be the work of Communists. Critics felt the United Nations or any of its agencies should not be explored in depth in any American school textbook.

9. In addition, critics felt that the UN Educational, Scientific and Cultural Organization (UNESCO) only trained American schoolchildren to be "citizens of the world" through the "desires of the idealistic International Congress by Soviet espionage."

10. As one textbook critic argued, "While the Communist Party U.S.A. now has a small number of members, some of its most active supporters were not members, were prohibited from being so. So I don't think the contention that the total number of Communists in relation to the total population of the United States will force us to the conclusion that it is not important. I think we must realize the importance of the activities in the dedication of these people and place it in the proper perspective."

11. "Too many of our history books do not make American girls and boys proud of the fact that they are American citizens." Critics rallied for the inclusion of biographies and sayings of such individuals as Patrick Henry, Nathan Hale, Ethan Allen, Anthony Wayne, John Paul Jones, Betsy Ross, Commodore John Barry, Light Horse Harry Lee, or Mollie Pitcher. They cited books such as Rev. Mason Locke Weems's *The Life of George Washington* (detailing the cherry tree episode) and Barnes's 1885 *The Primary History of the United States* (which also included stories about historic individuals).

12. Critics alleged that "[t]oo little attention is given to property rights. Most of the space is given to civil liberties and not the other rights of citizens."[18]

The war was on. The conflict was brewing. And the pot had only begun to boil over. The following chapter details the changes recommended by the Texas State Textbook Committee to the Texas State Commissioner of Education, along with the history programs adopted by the Texas State Board of Education, in 1961. The Texans for America and the Texas Society of the Daughters of the American Revolution would be far from satisfied with these decisions and would consequently rally in the face of their loss. The great Texas social studies war of 1961–62 raged on.

5

The Verdict Is In

The Recommendations of the Texas State Textbook Committee

AFTER A SERIES of deliberations, the Texas State Textbook Committee presented its recommendations to the Texas State Commissioner of Education and Texas State Board of Education on November 13, 1961. The decisions presented by the committee would spark further controversy and debate as part of the great Texas social studies textbook war of 1961–62. This chapter details the decisions of the committee in regard to a variety of academic disciplines, both within and outside the realm of social studies, inspiring further debate among conservatives and liberals alike.

While history programs had dominated the attention of the Texas State Textbook Committee in 1961, it had concerns about other educational programs as well.[1] While not an issue of great controversy to members of the committee, it recommended five geography texts each for grades 4, 5, and 6. It wanted those adopted geography books to have updated maps of Africa to show new nations and their capital cities, with all political maps dated, and also wanted geography books by Allyn and Bacon to contain "standard color symbols for elevation—symbols that [the student] will see on the wall maps in the classroom and on other maps that [the student] will be using."[2]

The State Textbook Committee also called for changes in Silver Burdett's *The American Continents*, a geography book for grade five, requiring more emphasis on the need for the United States to stand as a beacon of freedom for the rest of the world and emphasizing that the US government "through its representatives, has taken a leading part in the activities in the United Nations." That alteration would appear in the 1962 and 1964 editions of the book and was changed from the previous text, "But we must keep on trying to find agreement for the good of all. This is one important reason why the United States takes part in the United Nations." Other changes in *The American Continents* included the following:

> *Original version*: Today, other countries help us in protecting our land against possible attack. Radar listening posts . . .
>
> *Changed to*: With radar we can quickly detect the approach of enemy aircraft or missiles.
>
> *Original version*: Because it needs to trade, and because it needs military help, the United States needs the friendship of countries throughout the world. But, to keep its friends, a country must help them, too.
>
> *Changed to*: The United States trades with countries in all parts of the world. We are also providing military help to many nations. In addition, the United States aids many countries in other ways.
>
> *Original version: Getting Along with One Another*. It is often hard for people of different countries to understand each other. They come from different backgrounds. They eat different foods, wear different clothes, speak different languages. The United States sometimes finds it difficult to agree with its neighbors in all things. Nor do other countries always agree with us.
>
> *Changed to: Different Ways of Living*. It is often hard for people of different countries to understand each other. They come from different backgrounds, wear different clothes, speak different languages. The people of some nations have forms of government different from ours. Often they do not enjoy the same freedom and opportunity as our people.[3]

The Verdict Is In 93

Although they had been recommended for adoption by the State Textbook Committee, Commissioner of Education J. W. Edgar removed from the list four geography books: one for grade four, *Living in Our Country and Other Lands* (Macmillan Publishing); two for grade five, *Living in the Americas* (Macmillan Publishing) and *Your Country and Mine* (Ginn Publishing); and one for grade six, *Your World and Mine* (Ginn Publishing). Dr. Edgar argued that he removed the books because, according to the textbook proclamation, they were interdisciplinary or "fused or combination texts in other social sciences, such as history, economics, and government." The guideline for adoption stated, "Any book or books offered in this adoption that treat concurrently and completely the subjects of geography and history, more commonly known as fused books, will not meet the requirement of this Proclamation." The State Board of Education agreed, and their decision left a remaining four geography books for grade four, three for grade five, and four for grade six.[4]

Edgar removed the four geography books after hearing the arguments of the Texas Society of the Daughters of the American Revolution and Texans for America, which opposed "fused disciplines," a John Dewey–inspired approach to progressive education. According to the Daughters of the American Revolution:

> [The Dewey approach espoused by] progressive educationists is now promoted by dozens of their disciplines under the slogan "The Fused Disciplines." By this dazzling flight into semantics, the propagandists in our educational system have coined a meaningless term designed to obscure. Basically a discipline exists as an organic whole. To "fuse" it is to blur it making the subject less clear. In the fused disciplines, therefore, we come upon a mixture of history, geography, civics, and personal guidance that prevents the student from acquiring a clear concept of national boundaries, or of the great and cumulative differences of one civilization over another—for example, the differences between the achievements of the Igorots and of the Greeks . . . [one] instance of a (con)"fusion text" is a book on eastern lands, listing in its index "western," "northern" and "southern" lands as well, and ending with a chapter "Looking Backwards and Forwards"—which would have been a good title for the book itself. Such treatment is a travesty [for] education and a terrible waste of the student's time and energy.[5]

In addition to making changes to geography and social studies textbooks, the Texas State Commissioner of Education also evaluated the readoption of some high school economic texts. Previously, in 1957, the Texas State Board of Education had adopted five textbook programs for the economics elective courses available in public high schools: *Allied Economics, Economics for Our Times, Economics and You, Understanding Our Free Economy*, and *Economic Problems of Today*. The textbooks *Applied Economics, Economics for Our Times*, and *Economics and You* (in that order) were the three most popular programs preferred by teachers —accounting for more than 90 percent of the economics texts then used in Texas schools. *Economic Problems of Today* was the book least preferred, used by only 4 percent of high school teachers.[6]

These three widely used economics books were also the target of protests from such groups such as the Minute Women, Texans for America, the John Birch Society, and the Texas Society of the Daughters of the American Revolution. Some of those protests began in 1957 when Minute Woman Berti Maughmer wanted to ban from use in the Houston ISD *Applied Economics* and *Economics and You*. Maughmer felt the former was offensive for stating that sometimes people can save money by purchasing goods through cooperatives, which were deemed communistic by Maughmer. The other book, Maughmer argued, was "too objective in its treatment of capitalism," with a recommended reading list that included works by prize-winning and noted American historian Allan Nevins and famous novelist Edna Ferber, both of whom Maughmer called "fellow travelers."[7]

Then, at the May 7, 1962, meeting of the Texas State Board of Education, J. W. Edgar had planned, as a money-saving device, to recommend to the Texas State Board of Education the readoption of the five high school economics textbooks approved earlier on the 1957 listing, for a two-year renewal period. That changed as a result of earlier protests from individuals such as A. A. Forester of the Texas Society of the Daughters of the American Revolution. She had expressed concern about some of the economic textbooks during her testimony before the State Textbook Committee and a House of Representatives committee investigating the content of social studies textbooks. One of the texts she especially singled out for criticism was *Economics for Our Times*, the second most preferred book among the economics teachers

The Verdict Is In 95

of Texas. Disturbed by a number of things in the book, she faulted the authors for not listing all the provisions restricting labor unions in the Labor-Management Act of 1947 and the Landrum-Griffin Act of 1959. Her concerns about the overall suitability of the book for Texas public school students were also shared by members of Texans for America, the John Birch Society, and the East Texas Chamber of Commerce.

In essence, Forester, speaking for such conservative groups, argued for texts that greatly stressed the positive aspects of a free enterprise capitalistic economic system and patriotism:

> We, of the Daughters of the American Revolution, do not want our students indoctrinated in any type of Socialism, Liberal, Fabian, or Communism, in a small dose or a large one . . . [and] are puzzled as to why such statements as the following are not included in [any texts for our schools]. [Liberal socialism does not nationalize all industries or means of production but only selected ones. Fabian socialism is gradual socialism.] America, through only six generations, has produced more and achieved a higher standard of living than all the nations of the world in six thousand years [and] with six percent of the world's population and seven percent of the world's land, America produces 44 percent of the world's goods.[8]

During the Texas State Board of Education meetings of March and May 1962, every member of the board participated in a study of those economic books currently in use in the state's public schools. For the first time in the history of the Texas State Board of Education, its members unanimously refused a request from Texas Commission of Education Edgar regarding the adoption of some textbooks. Instead, the board unanimously recommended that the state "not readopt the present [economic] textbooks in high school economics." Instead, it called for the adoption of new economic textbooks for use in the state's public schools, beginning with the 1965 school year. Publishers of those economic textbooks did not have the opportunity to respond in an official manner to the State Board of Education.[9]

State Representative Nelson Cowles summarized the feelings of Forester and others who agreed with her, as well as the State Board of Education. In Representative Cowles's 1962 interim report on the House of Representatives Textbook Committee investigation, he noted that from "past adoptions of economic textbooks we found in content in many instances a criticism of our present free enterprise system, without a fair comparison with other economic systems. A definite effort is made to point out the flaws of capitalism without giving credit to the good merits of such a system. With some texts we found the basic philosophy of an author who would advocate complete government control of all means of production. This being completely contrary to the free enterprise system." For Cowles, "An economics text should be as positive as possible presenting our basic principles and functions of the American economy, so that our young people will understand better our way of life. Every textbook used in our schools should be prejudiced and biased in favor of individual freedom, freedom of enterprise and our Republican form of government."

As a review, Cowles noted that a "year ago practically no one would have believed that the State Board of Education would ever reject any textbooks recommended by the Commissioner of Education. Yet on May 7 1962, this Board voted unanimously to NOT re-adopt the current economics books but instead call for a new selection." Representative Cowles added that action by the State Board of Education "was the result of objections raised because three of the five economics books do not present our free economy in a favorable light. The one book of the five [*Economic Problems of Today*] which is most highly commended by Foundation for Economic Education (FEE), America's Future, etc. [pro-free enterprise groups] was not selected by [96 percent schools of the state's teachers of economics] because it seemed that many educators find this book objectionable because it goes to the other extreme and presents our Free Enterprise System as being too good compared to other systems."[10]

Soon afterward, the state legislature in 1963 held hearings on a proposal by Representative William Dungan to require a public school course on the merits of a free enterprise economic system. It was to be a course on "capitalism versus communism" for the high school curriculum. Among those giving testimony before the House Education Committee in support of the proposal was Richard Harvey, vice president of Tyler Pipe and Foundry Company, who said that since 1961 he had "become very concerned about the advance of communism throughout the world." Norma Gabler, an ally of the Daughters of the American Revolution, Texans for America, the John Birch Society, and the Minute Women, spoke at the hearings and added that such a requirement was needed "to push a book on free enterprise. It's not fair for my son to learn only the evils of capitalism." When Representative Ronald Roberts asked her, "Do you believe in a lot of government control?," she replied, "No." In contrast, El Paso Representative Maude Isaacs, a former teacher, said she did not know how such a required course could be implemented in an already overcrowded and required curriculum. Instead, she felt the solution was to simply let the economics teachers phase such material into their courses. The outcome was that the proposal by Representative Dungan did not become law.[11]

When the economics textbooks came up for adoption in 1965, one of the submitted books was the ever popular among teachers *Economics for Our Times*. It was protested by State Board of Education member Dr. B. E. Masters, president emeritus of Kilgore Junior College, as well as by the Texas Society of the Daughters of the American Revolution and Norma and Mel Gabler, the latter couple relatively newcomers among conservatives protesting books submitted for state adoption. Dr. Masters said, "I hate to see our children taught the same kind of economy that the Russians have." But again, the State Board of Education, with only Dr. Masters and two others members opposed, approved the book for adoption by a vote of eighteen to three.[12]

There was also a later issue with the 1961 state-adopted *Men and Nations*, a world history text published by Harcourt, Brace and World. It was one of the first world history books recommended by the Texas State Textbook Committee with only a few changes, even after Texans for America and the Texas Society of the Daughters of the American Revolution had protested some of the book's content. The changes recommended by the State Textbook Committee included correcting some errors in dates, substituting "probably appeared on earth" for "Men appeared on the earth" (possibly to satisfy the creationists), and adding a paragraph to show the weaknesses of communism. The changes were implemented and the text became among the most widely used world history text not only in Texas but throughout the nation as well. Then, in 1963, some Texas members of the Church of Christ claimed the book promoted "Roman Catholic doctrine" for identifying Peter as the founder of the Christian church at Rome. The critics claimed that was popular legend "but is not historical fact." After the Texas State Board of Education had a committee investigate the matter, the publisher finally eliminated a painting of Peter holding "the Gospels and the keys to heaven" and substituted one by Rembrandt depicting Paul in a Jerusalem prison. Harcourt also cut any references to Peter as the leader of the Apostles and his service as first Bishop of Rome. Those changes remained in the new 1964 edition of the book.[13]

In all, the proposed geography and economic textbooks took their biggest blows not from the State Textbook Committee but from the Commissioner of Education and the State Board of Education. Considering that the vast majority of protests in 1961 (well over 90 percent of them) involved American and world history texts, an examination of the State Textbook Committee's October 1961 report to the Texas Commissioner of Education shows the vast majority of the changes it recommended in the history books were rather lengthy but were not necessarily major alterations. Most recommended changes involved such issues as corrections to maps and historical errors, such as "Jackson" for "Johnson," or "overwhelming" for "almost unanimous," or the wrong date for an event, or updates to indicate that the Union of South Africa was no longer a member of the British Commonwealth. The State Textbook Committee also required all publishers of American history texts to include the recent ratification of the Twenty-Third Amendment to the US Constitution, granting the District of Columbia the right to vote for representatives in the Electoral College.[14]

The following is summary of the board's specific recommended changes. History book publishers were obliged to make these changes if they wanted their programs adopted.

Grade Eight, *Freedom's Frontier* (Lyons and Carnahan Publishing)

Texans for America charged that this book contained references to seven persons whose loyalty to the US had been questioned. The publisher retorted that if the charges against said persons could be proven true, those names would be deleted. Texans for America was unable to verify the accuracy of their claim, leading the publisher to conclude, "The names need not be deleted unless the committee finds more adequate evidence to indicate the necessity for such deletion."

Grade Eleven, *American History* (Ginn Publishing)

The board requested Ginn Publishing to omit civil rights activist Vera M. Dean from the text for being "on a list of persons who are extremely well-listed as to their communist and communist front affiliations by various investigative committees."

Grade Eleven, *Rise of the American Nation* (Harcourt, Brace and World Publishing)

The board requested changes to a section about the 1863 January Uprising in Poland, along with alterations to a section on the Soviet Union's atomic program: "The impression that Poland gained freedom of speech, press, religion should be corrected since the Soviet Union soon seized control of the country. Discussion should be included on the manner in which the Soviet Union acquired the atomic bomb."

Graded Eleven, *History of a Free People* (Macmillan Publishing)

The board made the following requests:

Page 435, column 2, paragraph 1—the only objection to socialism in this country seems to be that "Americans were on the whole too prosperous to want violent change."

Page 686, in "American Foreign Policy and Communism," column 2, paragraph 1, line 9, we find, "The United States can offer no pat substitute for Marxism, since by the nature of a free society, we disagree among ourselves about how to promote the good life." In that one sentence the authors seem to condemn the entire system of free enterprise and the worth of the individual.

Page 42, paragraph 2, "In these circumstances the radicals, the men who led the resistance . . ." (Substitute *patriot* for *radical*.)

High School World History, *Story of Nations*
(Holt, Rinehart and Winston Publishing)

The board asked Holt, Rinehart and Winston to "[g]ive a fuller explanation of capitalism, bringing out free enterprise, etc."

High School World History, *Men and Nations*
(Harcourt, Brace and World Publishing)

The board asked Harcourt, Brace and World to change "Men appeared on the earth" to "probably appeared on earth," possibly to satisfy the creationists. They also asked the publisher to "[i]nclude a paragraph to show weaknesses of Communism."

Grade Eight, *This Is America's Story*
(Houghton Mifflin Publishing)

This social studies text received more requests for changes than any of the others under consideration. The board requested the following:

> Page 606—Russia establishes a new society. "In 1917, while World War I was still going on, the Russians revolted against their government. They overthrew their ruler, called the Czar." "Then they set up a government in which the country was controlled by the members of one party, called the Communist Party." Could it be rephrased this way? "Before a stable government could be established, the Bolshevists, a Militant Minority, coerced the Russian people and set up a government by which the country was controlled by the members on one party, the Communist."

> Page 549, paragraph 2—The sentence: "For better or worse, the United States now had overseas possessions to govern and to defend." The publisher has agreed to substitute the following sentence for the one quoted above: "The United States now had overseas possessions to govern and to defend."

> Page 552–553—Referring to the topic, "The Puerto Ricans Are Aided," the publishers have stated that they are introducing new material to provide a more balanced treatment. This is a desirable change.

Grade Eight, Our *United States History* (Laidlaw Brothers Publishing)

The board asked Laidlaw Brothers to eliminate Marion Bauer, Ann Sterne, and Dorothy Canfield Fisher from the bibliography for allegedly being subversive. The majority of the recommended changes for this book involved updates on topics such as American transportation, communication, industry, agriculture, merchandizing, petroleum production, inventions, entertainment, music, and American capitalistic product in general.

When making their recommendations for the history books in question, the State Textbook Committee focused primarily on conforming to the social studies standards set forth by the Texas State Board of Education. Those standards stressed (1) a free enterprise–capitalistic economic system; (2) anticommunism, antisocialism, and antiradicalism; (3) American exceptionalism or US power and moral leadership among the world's nations; (4) patriotism; (5) "positive aspects of the United states and its heritage"; and (6) excluding "works which encourage or condone civil disorder, social strife or disregard for the law" or those that "undermine authority." (One wonders if the latter standard applied to the American Revolution of 1776, the Texas Revolution of 1835–36, or the American Civil War of 1861–1865.) Appendix A details the full list of the State Textbook Committee's recommendations to the State Commissioner of Education.

In the process of their revisions, the State Textbook Committee members employed 392 subject area professionals and 389 lay persons, for a total of 781 official advisers helping them evaluate all the books submitted for state adoption. This included a minimum of 75 subject area social studies teachers and professional historians, who helped the textbook committee members evaluate the submitted history books.[15]

Publishers submitted a total of nine American history texts for grade eight, eleven American histories for grade eleven, and eleven world histories total for consideration by the Texas State Textbook Committee, which could recommend to the Commissioner of Education no more than five texts for each grade level.

Eighty percent of the five books recommended for grade-eight adoption by the State Textbook Committee were protested by Texans for America, and 100 percent were opposed by the Texas Society of the Daughters of the American Revolution. For high school American history, of the five books recommended for adoption from the Texas State Textbook Committee, 100 percent were protested by Texans for America and 100 percent were opposed by the Texas Society of the Daughters of the American Revolution. The same was true of the five world history books recommended for adoption, with 100 percent of the adopted world history textbooks opposed by both Texans for America and the Texas Society of the Daughters of the American Revolution. In other words, of the fifteen history books recommended for adoption by the Texas State Textbook Committee, a total of fourteen (more than 93 percent) were labeled unsatisfactory by Texans for America, and all fifteen (100 percent) were opposed by the Texas Society of the Daughters of the American Revolution. Despite the opposition from Texans for America and the Texas Society of the Daughters of the American Revolution, well over 70 percent of those protested books received a first- or a second-round ballot vote by the Texas State Textbook Committee. That was followed by a sizeable majority vote from the Texas State Board of Education on November 13, 1961, which approved the adoption of all fifteen history textbook programs recommended by the State Textbook Committee.[16]

Unfortunately, the sales records for those fifteen history books adopted in Texas in 1961 cannot be located and may no longer exist in the archives of the Texas Education Agency, the Lorenzo de Zavala State Library and Archives, the Texas Secretary of State, or the Texas State Board of Education.

However, two scholars reported that by making a few "alterations, the publishing companies won the state textbook committee's permission to sell their books in Texas, but this did not end their sales problems. They found many local school districts unwilling to buy a book that had been under attack—even after 'objectionable' sections had been stricken. A spokesperson from D. C. Heath and Company, for example, said that the sales volume for their high school history ran $80,000 [about $650,000 in today's money] below what sales records led them to anticipate."[17]

The same phenomenon happened with the sales of Paul Boller Jr. and Jean Tilford's *This Is Our Nation* (Webster Publishing), which required almost no changes of significance but still came under severe attacks from Texans for America. Indeed, out of all the approved history textbook programs, Boller and Tilford's received by far the most criticism from spokesman J. Evetts Haley and Texans for America. As detailed in the next chapter, the Haley-Boller fight would pit two very outspoken historians against one another as the great Texas textbook war raged on.

6

Historian versus Historian

J. Evetts Haley Battles Paul L. Boller Jr.

AT THE 1961 Texas textbook hearings, Texans for America spokesman J. Evetts Haley especially singled out for criticism history textbook *This Is Our Nation*, by Dr. Paul F. Boller Jr. and Jean Tilford. In one of his many protestations, Haley criticized the Boller-Tilford text as follows: "Texans for America say the book is friendly to the United Nations. They object to material on American Indians, whose contribution to America, they say, 'is practically nil.' They object to mention of the Salem witch hunt; calling it 'overemphasis on this one particular aspect.' They say the authors seem to have an 'affinity' for [Franklin] Roosevelt. They object to a cartoon depicting the purchase of Alaska from Russia in 1867. Texans for America say the authors are trying to prepare American students for a 'Russian America.'"

Haley's critique also indicated that Texans for America objected "to 'overemphasis' on the slavery problem. They object to mention of Crispus Attucks, a Negro who was killed during the Boston Massacre of 1770." His objection concluded with references to suspected subversives in the Boller-Tilford text, including Sherwood Anderson, Maxwell Anderson, Stephen Vincent Benet, Ralph Bunche, Aaron Copeland, Theodore Dreiser, Bernard DeVoto, Albert Einstein, William Faulkner, Ernest Hemingway, Sinclair Lewis, Eugene O'Neill, Willa Cather, and Carl Sandburg.[1]

In his September 14, 1961, public testimony before the State Textbook Committee, Haley went even further in his criticisms of the Boller-Tilford text. At the time, Boller was very active and outspoken in support of the emerging civil rights movement when it was not all that much a popular thing to do in Texas. Haley was especially critical of Boller having any dealings with such groups as the Southern Educational Conference and its related organizations. In his testimony, Haley singled out the Southern Conference for Human Welfare, the Southern Conference Education Fund, the Southern Regional Conference, the Southern Educational Conference, the Southern Educational Welfare, and the Southern Educational and Conference Fund—all civil rights organizations. (Note that none of those organization ever appeared on an official listing of subversive organizations from the US Attorney.) Haley also mentioned individuals such as Carl Braden and Anne Braden, Dr. Aubrey Willis Williams, and Dr. James A. Dombrowski. All were civil rights and labor union activists in the South who sometimes worked together on various projects to end racial segregation in all areas. They were never members of the American Communist Party, nor did they ever appear on any governmental listing of members of that party, although in their work they did on occasion associate with some card-carrying Communists. However, Haley criticized Boller's association with said individuals. In order to provide greater insight into the nature of Haley's concerns, a brief background of the Bradens, Williams, and Dombrowski is provided as follows.

Boller's civil rights activist associates included Mr. and Mrs. Carl and Anne Braden. Carl Braden was convicted of sedition and sent to jail and fined for violating a Kentucky law that made working toward racial integration an approval of communism. He was able to get out on bail after serving eight months in jail. His sedition conviction was linked to an incident where he and his wife, Anne, arranged for an African American family to own a home in a white neighborhood. At the time, the State of Kentucky considered African American home ownership in a white neighborhood an act of sedition. During the 1950s, many southern states used nullification and interposition to allow the state and not the federal government to halt the racial integration of

106   Chapter 6

their public schools and other public facilities. To violate such a state law was considered an act of sedition. The US Supreme Court in the case of *Cooper v. Aaron* (358 U.S. 1, 1965) declared such laws unconstitutional and maintained that states were bound by the Supreme Court's decision and had to enforce integration, even if they disagreed with it. Given the *Cooper* decision, any further sedition charges by Kentucky against Carl Braden were dropped. However, Braden did spend a year in jail for refusing to testify about his political beliefs before the US House Un-American Activities Committee. He thought the Bill of Rights forbid any government from demanding him to reveal his personal beliefs. In their civil rights activities, Carl and Anne Braden sometimes also worked closely with individuals such as Dr. Martin Luther King Jr., Eleanor Roosevelt, southern white civil rights activists Clifford and Virginia Durr, US Supreme Court Justice Hugo Black, as well as textbook author Paul Boller.

In addition to the Bradens, Paul Boller was also associated with Dr. Aubrey Willis Williams. Williams headed the New Deal's National Youth Administration and worked with then twenty-six-year-old Lyndon Baines Johnson, who was Williams's South Texas Director of the National Youth Administration. Willis was a civil rights activist and supported the movement for equality of African Americans.

Another one of Boller's associates, Dr. James Dombrowski, also came under fire from Haley during the textbook hearings. Dombrowski held a PhD from Columbia University, served as a US Army sergeant in France during World War I, and was a Methodist minister and cofounder with Myles Horton and Don West of the Highlander Folk School in Grundy County, Tennessee, which became a training ground for labor union activism and civil rights advocates. Some of school's pupils during the 1950s included Dr. Martin Luther King Jr., Rosa Parks, Ralph Abernathy, and Carl Lewis. Because of its civil rights activities, the State of Tennessee closed the Highlander School in 1961, claiming it was a training facility for communists—the usual claim by many of those then opposed to racial desegregation. However, the Highlander School managed to reopen a year later as the Highlander Research and Education Center in New Market, Tennessee. Dombrowski joined the Socialist Party in the early 1930s but left it (and the Highlander School) and became a Democrat. From 1942 to 1946, he was executive director of the Southern Conference for Human Welfare, and during 1948–66, he was executive director of the Southern Conference Educational Fund, where he worked closely with individuals such as Clifford and Virginia Durr; liberal Democrat, former US congressman, and San Antonio mayor Maury Maverick Sr.; Dr. King; and Rosa Parks—all while Dombrowski was editor of the pro–civil rights publication *Southern Patriot*. In 1965, he was the winning defendant in *Dombrowski v. Pfister* (380 U.S. 479), a US Supreme Court case that voided a Louisiana law allowing state officials to harass and arrest without intent to prosecute those individuals fighting to end racial segregation in the South.[2]

With Boller's "unsavory" associates in mind, Haley began his public testimony before the State Textbook Committee with the following critique of *This Is Our Nation*:

> [Texans for America] object particularly to this book, though, on the basis of its slant and bias. It is not adequate and sound history and, therefore, because of this slant and bias it is particularly dangerous as a textbook and deleterious to the character of the children reading it. In regard to that feature, we wish to call attention to . . . the fact that Paul F. Boller, Jr. of Dallas, Department of History at S. M. U., has signed a non-subversive oath of office as required by Texas law. Then the publishers add three pages, two and a-half or three pages of special pleading, quoting from the book in an alleged attempt to show that this book is sound American history which we say is further proof in itself of the fact that it is a slanted textbook.
>
> Now, in regard to whether or not Boller, as we contended in our original Bill of Particulars, is soft on left-wing philosophy or on Communism, we feel we must be called upon to offer some proof.
>
> Therefore, we revert first to the Texas law requiring this oath. In Article, covered in Articles 6252 to 57, and then the copy of the oath as provided by this Texas law which specifically says the affiant, that is the person taking this oath, is not, and, during the preceding five year period, has not been a member of any organization, association, movement, group, or combination which the Attorney General of the United States, acting pursuant to Executive Order No. 9835, has designated as totalitarian, fascist, communist or subversive, and so on. . . .

108   Chapter 6

What about the [US] Attorney General's list? Among the authorities in the field of subversion it has become almost a joke because the Attorney General's list has not been kept up by the preceding administration diligently or by the current administration of the United States. In other words, the Attorney General's list is inadequate, whether for political reasons or otherwise; we would not attempt to say, but that is a historical fact. Therefore, we find it necessary to prove the point that Boller is a member of an organization [the Southern Educational Conference Fund] that is, if not soft on Communism, then certainly unwittingly following the Communist line. Its organization is not soft.

For example, first as to Boller's views. Boller . . . in a panel discussion Boller had this to, say, the newspaper account of his comment, and this is not quoted verbatim, that if they, the panel, were going to talk about international Communism he thought they had a very big subject, but if they were going to discuss domestic Communism he wouldn't consider they had much to talk about, because the Communist Party, he said, is practically defunct in this country and is an irrelevant reference of importance. Now what does [FBI Director] J. Edgar Hoover say? He says: The size of the Party is relatively unimportant, because of the iron control under which they operate. In this connection, it might be of interest to observe in 1917 when the Communists over-threw Russia, there was one Communist for every 10, or one-tenth, and in the United States today there is one Communist for every 1814 persons in this country.

. . . Dr. Boller said he was worried about Fascism because the American Fascist was really beginning to move and wanted to liquidate all American justice, and these forces are more worthy of attention than the defunct Communists. Hoover said: Anyone who opposes the American Communist is at once branded as a disrupter, a Fascist, or Red Baiter, or Hitlerite. . . .

In further support of Boller's left-wing activities [is] a photo static copy I have from the *Southwest Review*, Autumn issue of 1960, from pages 298 to 301, a magazine sponsored under the sponsorship of Southern Methodist University at Dallas. I want to call attention to the concluding sentence of this article, the summary of Boller . . . said the former Party Members of the Communist Party . . . as a consequence forced American people to preoccupy themselves with trivialities and inanities. And, he continued the stultification of American political intelligence since World War II for which Stalin and fellow travelers are primarily responsible is conceivably the only danger that the Communist Party, U. S. A. in its four decades of existence has inflicted upon this country, the stultification of the American intelligence, former Communists notwithstanding to the contrary, Communist Party, U. S. A. is for United States today a complete irrelevance, and in these dangerous times United States no longer has any margin for irrelevance. The new Communist Party, U. S. A. is a branch of international conspiracies designed to further the downfall of America, Russia's spear point at the heart of America. . . . Further, with the views of Professor Boller, we have as a matter of history, it has been established by the Investigating Committee of the United States Senate and is a matter of record that the Southern Conference for Human Welfare was organized, conceived, financed, and organized by the Communist Party in 1938. It was definitely cited by investigating agencies as a communist front in 1947. Thereafter, however, being branded a communist in that group, and their dupes following the Communist Party line and strategy let the Southern Conference of Welfare fade out of sight. The same officers, same promoters came up under a new front, merged under a new name, Southern Conference Educational Fund, Inc., an adjunct of this old Conference for Southern Welfare. . . . now it is of interest to note that Mr. Aubrey Williams, one of the most notorious of the Communist front sympathizers and active in that field, is president of Southern Conference Educational Fund, and Dr. James A. Dombrowski is the executive director.

Now it happened that this group issued a clarion call for the Southwest Regional Conference to meet in Houston on May 17, 1955, just one year after the Supreme Court's infamous [*Brown v. Topeka*] desegregation decision. This was issued, this call was issued by a motley group, coordinated by the Southern Educational Conference; the fronters, [James] Dombrowski, the executive director of Southern Conference Educational Fund, and the president was the aforesaid Communist fronter, Aubrey Williams. . . .

Now, as a noted authority, M. G. Lowman, Methodist Church, says seldom, and I quote, has appeared in public a more blatant list of fellow travelers and dupes and those who came than the Educational Fund supporters. This was the group behind the call of the meeting at Houston which was to find a new approach, they said, because they said the South was ready for a new way of living, and prominent among that group is Dr. Paul F. Boller of Southern Methodist University. . . .

Now, it was their belief that the public imagination is ready, and I am quoting, "for the acceptance of a new and positive freedom." Quotes close. In racial relations which was complete integration in line with the Communist Party platform in 1928 and their avowed interest in breaking up the South and American unity.

. . . In 1959, December 31, this Southern Conference Educational Fund through the operations primarily of Carl Braden . . . issued that call in Washington for what he called a United States Commission on Civil Rights, and for that meeting they recruited left-wing niggers from throughout the South. And they had Dombrowski on hand, and they turned it into a sounding board for the agitation of racial equality.

Now back of that group, too, were other individuals worthy of mention. Braden was identified as a member of the Communist Party. He was prominently connected with bombing incidents in Kentucky. He was sentenced. He was sentenced again for his refusal to answer the questions for contempt. . . .

Now what does that have to do with the Southern Educational Welfare Fund? The call was issued in the name of the Welfare Fund, and Paul Boller is one of its prominent supporters, but that was in 1959. What about the current situation?

Well, Braden has a wife [Anne Braden] prominently identified with Communist front organizations, and she is the secretary as their letterhead shows of the Southern Conference Education Fund, Inc.

Aubrey Williams, with all his Communist front connections, is still the president, and Dr. James A. Dombrowski is still the executive director. And you will find on the reverse side of their letterhead that from Texas Paul F. Boller is still one, is still one of their leading sponsors and members.

Now, it has been definitely proven that the Southern Conference for Human Welfare was a Communist front organization. It has been definitely proven that by a name switch the same group with the same nefarious purposes and sinister designs took over the Southern Educational Conference Fund, and it is further obvious that Dr. Boller has been an ardent supporter of this movement from the first.

We submit that Ladies and Gentlemen, as positive proof along with the other information that Dr. Boller is soft on Communism. We do not believe that a man of his intelligence is unwittingly following the Communist Party. We contend that even though he may be clear, and obviously is clear under this provision of the Texas law for his affidavit, that the list must be attested to by the Attorney General, that he is technically clear, but we contend and we feel that the evidence positively supports the fact that he is in contempt of the spirit of that law, and as we have pointed out here by reference to the law . . . it is not only your privilege but we feel it is incumbent upon you to look into the record of this man, to call upon the agencies of government which are readily available to you in your official capacity that even a private citizen cannot reach as to the validity of our contentions that this man is a tool at least of the Communist frontiers of this country, and hence his book showing the bias and slant of the fellow traveler should be rejected forthwith.[3]

If J. Evetts Haley was looking for a liberal historian to criticize, he found an ideal target in Dr. Paul F. Boller, Jr., who not only responded to the charges made against him by Haley but in the process elaborated on some key developments during the McCarthy era in Texas. Like Haley, the outspoken Boller later became an award-winning historian. Boller received his BA degree in 1939 and a PhD in history in 1947 from Yale University. After serving in World War II as a Japanese translator for the US Navy, he taught history at Southern Methodist University, and after his 1961 dispute with Haley, Boller went on to teach at the University of Texas at Austin, Queens College in New York City, the University of Massachusetts at Boston, and finally, Texas Christian University, where he held the Lyndon Baines Johnson Chair of American History.

Some of Boller's books, many of them best sellers, include *George Washington and Religion* (1963), *Quotesmanship* (1967), *American Transcendentalism* (1974), *Freedom and Fate in American Thought: From Edwards to Dewey* (1978), *American Thought: The Impact of Evolutional Naturalism, 1865–1900* (1981), *Presidential Campaigns* (1984), *Presidential Anecdotes* (1987), *A More Perfect Union* (1988), *Presidential Wives* (1988), *Congressional Anecdotes* (1991), *Memoirs of an Obscure Professor* (1992), and *Not So! Popular Myths about America from Columbus to*

Chapter 6

Clinton (1995). After a long career teaching and writing, Boller died on March 16, 2014.[4]

Jean Tilford, Boller's coauthor in writing the controversial *This Is Our Nation*, was a graduate of the University of Cincinnati with bachelor's and master's degrees in education, specializing in social studies. After teaching at Woodrow High School in Cincinnati for eleven years, she served as supervisor of social studies for the district. In 1969, she became director of the National Council for the Social Studies and later president of the organization in 1975. She died in 2002.[5]

The work of both Boller and Tilford signified an emerging historiographical trend, as was true with many of their professional colleagues; their progressive-reconstructionist approach to their writing was somewhat in keeping with Harold Rugg. Neither Boller nor Tilford were members of the American Communist Party, and they never appeared on any governmental listing of subversives. Instead, they were New Deal–Fair Deal supporters and John Kennedy–Lyndon Johnson Democrats supportive of the emerging civil rights revolution.

In his *Memoirs of an Obscure Professor*, Boller recalled the episode with J. Evetts Haley. At the time, Boller's history text was the subject of controversy. He was very active publicly in defense of the New Deal and Harry Truman's foreign policies, criticizing the McCarthyites, and advocating greater civil rights guarantees for African Americans. Being new to his role as a young and possibly politically naïve college professor, Boller unknowingly challenged the then ultra-conservative leadership of the Dallas area, as well as others statewide. That battle would prove far more difficult than a scholarly debate within the sheltered, safe, and usually (but not always) comfortable confines of an academic/university atmosphere, as Boller would soon find out.

Boller, in self-defense against Haley's criticisms, stated the following:

> Not long after I took my doctorate at Yale and began teaching history at Southern Methodist University, the *Tribune* huffily dismissed me as "an obscure professor" in an editorial attack on an article I wrote in 1953 defending Franklin Roosevelt's [November 16, 1933] inauguration of diplomatic relations with the Soviet Union. I was already being referred to as a "junior personality" by John O. Beaty, English professor at SMU, because I had criticized

Historian versus Historian

his anti-Semitic views in a letter to the student newspaper. Soon I was to be attacked as an outright Communist by McCarthyites in Texas and even blamed for SMU's football losses one season, though, as one of my conservative senior colleagues jocularly admitted to a student who had heard I was a Communist, but thought I was nice, "Yeah, he's a nice Communist!" But Texas McCarthyites didn't think I was nice; and when a high school textbook of mine [*This Is Our Nation*] came up for adoption in 1961, they raised such a rumpus that they succeeded in killing the book sales in the Lone Star state on the ground that it was "soft on communism."

He added: "It was all very ironic. I was, in fact, an old-fashioned Norman Thomas anti-Stalinist, who knew his [George] Orwell and [Arthur] Koestler and was aware of the crimes of Stalin long before Nikita Khrushchev exposed them to his colleagues in his famous speech in 1956. It amused me at first, and then disturbed me, that people who knew nothing whatsoever about Communism talked so glibly about it. But, as Lady Bird Johnson was fond of saying, 'If you're talkin', you aren't learnin.'"[6]

While a junior professor in the history department at Southern Methodist University (SMU), Boller also discussed how he got in trouble with the McCarthyites by criticizing those who attacked Pres. Harry Truman as a "puppet of sinister forces" and "playing the Communist game." Boller was especially critical of a 1951 book *The Iron Curtain over America*, by John O. Beaty, who claimed that the Khazar Jews of Russia were guilty of trying to establish communism worldwide by causing the United States to go to war with Germany in 1917 and 1941. Beaty also claimed that the Khazar Jews had encouraged Pres. Franklin D. Roosevelt to recognize the Soviet Union in 1933 and had penetrated the influential circles of the Democratic Party. Boller wrote a letter to the SMU student newspaper, *Daily Campus*, saying that Beaty's book was "a dreary performance, full of distortions, omissions, and half-truths that shows not the slightest understanding of either modern history or the dynamics of Soviet communism."

Beaty soon after published a pamphlet on "How to Capture a University" in 1954, claiming that "a certain powerful non-Christian ele-

114   Chapter 6

ment in our population" was attempting to gain control of SMU, that B'nai B'rith was a "Jewish Gestapo" for attempting to take over the SMU school of theology, that the SMU bookstore "was an outlet for official Soviet propaganda," and that the university's *Southwest Review* had a "non-Christian and leftist slant." Boller disagreed with all that and went further. In a 1954 article for the *Southwest Review*, he specifically refuted any claims that some Jews had duped Pres. Franklin Roosevelt into recognizing the Soviet Union in 1933. He then proceeded to document how much the American business community in 1933, even including the *Dallas Morning News*, had supported the US recognition of the Soviet Union to foster better trade relations and serve as a check on Japanese aggression in China. The *Dallas Morning News* quickly responded that the Franklin Roosevelt administration in 1933 had not told the American public the whole story, and if it had, the *News* would not have approved that diplomatic recognition.[7]

Boller noted that his problems with Texans for America began after he helped form the racial integrationist Dallas Civil Liberties Union in 1960, which encouraged the city to comply with the *Brown* decision of 1954. His problems compounded when he became a member of the Southern Conference Education Fund to further promote civil rights guarantees for African Americans. In addition to his civil rights efforts, Boller also publicly maintained that the influence of communism in America through the years had been vastly exaggerated. All this caused him to evoke criticism from the *Dallas Morning News* as well as from Dan Smoot, an anti-Communist contributor to the John Birch Society's *American Opinion Magazine*, author of the "Dan Smoot Report," and host of a Sunday afternoon TV program.

Boller reflected on his experiences and the criticisms he endured:

> The timing of the controversy over Communism in America could not have been worse for me. In 1961, a high school textbook, *This Is Our Nation*, which I had written with Jean Tilford, a Cincinnati public school teacher, came up for adoption in Texas. When hearings were held before the state textbook advisory committee (made up of teachers and principals) in September, cattleman J. Evetts Haley, head of Texans for America, went to Austin to testify that *This Is Our Nation* was "dangerous as a textbook and deleterious to the character of the children reading it." He

went on to say that I was "soft on communism or short on logic and learning, or perhaps both." Harris Holmes, the hard-working Texas representative of Webster Publishing Company in St. Louis, which had published the book, made a valiant defense of my integrity before the committee. [Writer and historian] Lon Tinkle, Rabbi Levi Olan, SMU faculty friends, Allen Maxwell and Margaret Hartley at the SMU Press, and many of my students gave me their warm support. And the American Studies Association of Texas passed a resolution, written by Martin Shockley, doughty English professor at North Texas State University (who for years fought hypocrisy, humbug, and hysteria in the academic world), expressing complete confidence in me and "no confidence whatsoever" in Haley. Haley, of course, was unmoved by all this. In an article on American reactionaries about this time, *Life* referred to Haley as a "crackpot," but in Texas he was thought of as a "good ol' boy."

Boller continued:

Haley's organization had a textbook committee of its own, headed by Don Riddle, a veterinarian from Paris, Texas. Riddle made a cursory reading of all the American history texts submitted for adoption and issued criticisms of most of them. But he gave *This Is Our Nation* special attention, since I taught in Texas, and it was necessary for Wally Stees, the hard-working editor whom Webster had assigned to the book, to call an emergency meeting with Jean Tilford and me to prepare detailed replies to his long list of criticisms.

He further elaborated:

Riddle's critique was shabbily written: awkward, repetitive, and filled with errors in spelling, punctuation, and grammar. The critique was also filled with inaccuracies: it accused us of omitting vital facts about American history which we had actually included in the book. But it was harder to respond to other charges. What was one to say to the allegation that we spent too much space on the Indians and on the subject of slavery? Or that it was "sadistic" to mention the Salem witch-hunt? Or that we failed to point out that the United Nations was a world government infringing on American sovereignty?

116 Chapter 6

Responding to other criticisms of his book, Boller reflected:

> Riddle was particularly upset by a quotation from Anzia Yezierska (an immigrant from Russia who published several books in the 1920s about her life in America) appearing in the book. He kept coming back to the Yezierska quote in his critique and complaining that we could have selected "a more truly American" figure to cite. We did in fact quote Washington, Jefferson, and Franklin. But when it came to the twentieth century, we also quoted John Dewey, Lincoln Steffens, Ida Tarbell, and Upton Sinclair; and all of these people, from Riddle's point of view, were suspect. Dewey, he said, had been cited twenty-one times by [the US House Un-American Activities Committee]. He also saw something sinister in a cartoon the book contained illustrating America's purchase of Alaska from Russia in 1867. The cartoon pictured Secretary of State William Seward (who had had trouble getting the U.S. Senate to ratify the Alaska treaty) laboriously pushing a wheelbarrow, called "treaty," on which was perched a huge rock labeled "Russian America" (the name of Alaska before our purchase). "The authors," Riddle warned, "purpose [*sic*] to instill in the students [*sic*] mind a Russian America."

Boller's writing was also accused by Riddle of being too friendly toward Pres. Franklin D. Roosevelt and the New Deal. He recalled:

> [I was] faulted for not saying that FDR had tricked the United States into recognizing the Soviet Union. What bothered Riddle above all else was that in a chapter on American culture in the twentieth century we mentioned scores of people—Ralph Bunche, Aaron Copland, Charlie Chaplin, Albert Einstein, William Faulkner, Ernest Hemingway, Sinclair Lewis, Eugene O'Neill, Willa Cather, Carl Sandburg, "and many more!"—whose loyalty to the United States was in question. "Our students," lamented Riddle in the grand conclusion to his report, "are supposed to learn more of the true heritage of their country by reading the works of men who are [*sic*] government investigating committee had sighted [*sic*] as being affiliated with subversive organizations; than by studying the lives and history of the men who formed our government."

The tone of the reply we framed to Riddle was moderate and unruffled; we took up his points one by one and yielded ground on none of them.[8]

Of the eleven high school American history texts submitted for consideration by the State Textbook Committee, the one by Dr. Boller and Jean Tilford tied for second place with *American History* (published by Ginn and Company) as recommended for adoption by the State Textbook Committee. *Rise of the American Nation* (published by Harcourt, Brace and World) came in first place. Despite J. Evetts Haley's protestations, the State Textbook Committee only made the following recommendations for consideration by Boller and Tilford: "Include the 23rd Amendment of the Constitution of the United States; delete *Tales of the South Pacific* as questionable for high school reading [which, according to Boller's memoirs, he did not do]; and check the date of the Treaty of Ghent."[9]

The committee had spoken, and the controversy over Boller and Tilford's *This Is Our Nation* had seemingly subsided for the time being. Haley's criticisms of both the text itself and Boller's character had apparently fallen on deaf ears. Wounded but not defeated, he soon turned his efforts elsewhere and again picked up his fight—this time targeting the Texas State Board of Education, emboldening Texans for America and other conservative organizations with a new battle cry.

7

At War with the System

J. Evetts Haley and the Texas State Board of Education

IT WAS SHORTLY after the State Textbook Committee completed its 1961 hearings, and Texans for America spokesman J. Evetts Haley had yet to hear the committee's final decision and recommended textbook changes. Suspecting that his appeals might have failed to sway the committee, on October 9, 1961, he wrote to J. W. Edgar, Commissioner of Education, indicating, "[Texans for America] respectfully urges you and the State Board of Education to reject the recommendations of the State Textbook in regard to the following [textbooks]." Boller and Tilford's *This Is Our Nation* was first on his list.[1]

Dr. Donald I. Riddle, chairman of the Texans for America Committee for Education, had also not been able to learn of the changes recommended by the State Textbook Committee. Consequently, he wrote the following to Edgar on October 11, 1961: "It is my understanding that the State Textbook Committee in its meeting on October 5, 1961, recommended for adoption (without revision) the majority of the texts which Texans for America protested. We still feel that these books contain textual material and references which are undesirable for use by the students in Texas or any other state. We earnestly request your examination and rejection of these texts on the basis of the bills of particulars [the detailed protests] submitted."[2]

On November 3, 1961, Commissioner of Education Edgar responded to Haley and Riddle by telling them "that the textbook committee was fully aware of all protests made by Texans for America and publishers' responses to them before submitting its list of recommendations." He especially noted that the "Committee had used 392 professional people and approximately 389 lay people as advisers in its review, evaluation, and selection of books recommended." Commissioner Edgar added that in his "study of the protests, I have given full consideration to all the written materials from the protestors and from the publishers which were submitted to the State Textbook Committee." He went on to stress, "I have read and considered carefully the Transcripts of the Hearing before the State Textbook Committee in which the oral presentations of the protestants and the responses of the publishing companies are covered in full." He closed by telling Haley and Riddle, "You, as representatives of Texans for America, are respectfully advised that I am declining to remove books from the committee's list on the basis of your protests."[3]

In the meantime, and before the meeting of the State Board of Education on November 13, 1961, board member Jack Binion had requested that the board members be supplied by the Texas Education Agency with a "full account" of the "protests made by the Texans for America and the Texas Society of the Daughters of the American Revolution." Binion felt "the people who come in here and criticize these books are creating a healthy atmosphere."[4]

At the next Board of Education meeting on November 13, 1961, three representatives of Texans for America requested and received permission to speak. They were J. Evetts Haley, Dr. Donald I. Riddle, and John Slay. The comments by Riddle and Slay were not included in the minutes and procedures of the meeting, but they did appear in a newspaper account. Slay, in protesting the adoption of Merle Curti's *Rise of the American Nation* (Harcourt, Brace and World), which was the first choice of the State Textbook Committee, said the book "refers to America as a democracy. This is a seed planted in the minds of children that we have a democracy rather than a republic." He neglected to note that many US presidents, such as Theodore Roosevelt, Woodrow Wilson, Franklin D. Roosevelt, Harry Truman, Dwight D. Eisenhower, and John

F. Kennedy, had also used the term "democracy" in their speeches to describe the American government.

Dr. Riddle argued that Texans for America objected to certain books because he felt the recommended reading lists contained the names of authors regarded as subversive; he did not necessarily disagree with the content of the books.[5] As reported by the press, Haley continued his crusade and told Board of Education members that Boller and Tilford's *This Is Our Nation* "is a very subtle book in keeping with the left wing approach. It has the usual leftwing obsession with democracy . . . and it reiterates the matter of class and caste in keeping with communist dialectics and semantics."[6]

Haley's other comments appeared in the minutes of the State Board of Education as follows. He charged that the public school guidance programs approved by the State Board of Education "threaten to become a gigantic mental health program for the suppression of the individuality of every child to make him a cog in a socialistic society. . . . It is for the indoctrination of your child, into a groove selected for him in advance by hand-picked servants of the Super State."[7]

When board member Jack Binion then made a motion that the board accept all books and recommended changes suggested by the State Textbook Committee and Commissioner of Education, the following dialogue between Haley and the board occurred:

C. Ray Holbrook Jr.: "Haley, I would like to ask you a question that has been bothering me for some months. It may color my thinking this morning. Last spring you wrote a number of newsletters which attacked and condemned our guidance and counseling program. In one of those letters you said that some of the members of the Board were 'soft' on Communism. I would like to know what you have to say about this and how you expect us to respect your opinion."

Haley: "Those letters were directed directly against the guidance and counseling program under orders of this Board. There was not any innuendo thereof, implied statement, or direct statement that this Board was 'soft' on Communism."

C. Ray Holbrook Jr. said he thought this was implied and asked Haley if he would clarify.

Haley: "We are attacking this program as implied by local counsel. There was no innuendo that this Board or any member thereof is 'soft' on Communism, but there was the implication that this program might open the school program of Texas to subversive practices."

Prior to this discussion, Haley directed his remarks about the lack of time and other factors detrimental to the appellants, as follows:

Haley: "We think more time for the study of these books [up for state adoption], more time for the books to be placed in our hands, more time to file our bills of particulars, more time between the decision of the Textbook Committee and their recommendations and our appeal to this Board is absolutely essential in fairness to our case and to publishers of the books."

Jack Binion: "Other than the extension of time, do you have any further suggestions? We try to be fair and do everything we can. We think it is a good program, but if any of the citizens want to criticize it, we think they have the right to do so. I would rather you would, here and now in this open meeting, tell this Board all of your complaints and all of your suggestions with regard to this important matter rather than this afternoon."

Haley: "We would like to reserve the right to come back in detail. It seems to us that the provisions of the Texas law, as we understand them, places a handicap upon us and the State. As I understand it, we are required to adopt each year a certain number of textbooks. Our chief complaint is the downgrading of textbooks generally. We do not think they come up to high standards of discipline, sub-standard challenge to children of Texas are entitled to. You are compelled, however, to adopt from them as many as five, whether any of these is appropriate."

Paul G. Greenwood: "Are you aware of the fact that we did increase the time over what it was last year?"

Haley: "Yes, sir."

Greenwood: "You are aware of the fact that three of these dates are made by statute?"

Paul Mason: "Were you satisfied with your hearing before the Textbook Committee? Did you have the idea that they were diligent in the study of the texts?"

Haley: "Yes, sir."

Greenwood proceeded to ask Haley if he were opposed to the state's furnishing of free textbooks, and Haley said as a matter of personal policy, he thought the individual parents should buy them. Emerson Stone Sr. then asked Haley if he was familiar with the fact that some eight hundred people also assisted the Textbook Committee in making their selections, and Haley said he was aware of this.

Stone: "You are somewhat familiar with the people who participated in an advisory capacity?"

Haley: "Yes, sir."

Stone: "You know them to be patriotic, loyal Americans."

Haley: "I do not have a great extended familiarity."

Stone: "What do you consider would substitute for the large and multiple list which gives local school boards the opportunity to select the texts they want?"

Haley: "I would turn it back to the parents in the district."

Stone: "Would that be your answer to the large adoption?"

Haley: "If that could not be achieved, I think it might be improved."

Stone: "What would substitute for what the Legislature provides— that there shall be adopted a multiple list of five books in each subject and the local school district has the right to select one of the five by their faculty in the local school district? What would you substitute for that?"

Haley: "Let them choose their books."[8]

At War with the System 123

Board member Jack Binion again made a motion to accept all books recommended and changes to them from the State Textbook Committee and Commissioner of Education. Dr. B. E. Masters, president emeritus of Kilgore Junior College and a state board member, then offered an amendment to that motion, suggesting that all books and changes be accepted except the Boller-Tilford text. In his statement, Dr. Masters noted that he had read all of the history books up for adoption and felt some authors put too much of their opinions in the books, especially in the case of the Boller-Tilford one. Masters then recommended that book not be adopted, since he said there "is too much of the author's opinion and his writers listed, all of them, lean to the left as you know. When you are dealing with 16 and 17 year old boys and girls, many of those writers do not fit. They are interesting, they are good histories, but at that age we are trying to make Americans. We are not filling them full of some wild-eyed theories, and I think this fuss is going on until our book men put a stop to it."

He added, "We always enjoy socializing with those fellows, but we are trying to keep our country straight, and if it goes communistic, it will be largely through the schools." Masters felt "Not all of our school teachers are good readers. They read the textbooks, headlines in the newspapers, and they can't correct these things before the students, so I think it is good and the proper thing for us to eliminate this book because it has so many of these things. So many writers use the word 'revolutions.'" Masters concluded, "Our children shouldn't hear so much about revolution. The American war for independence was not necessarily a revolution. It was a war for independence. We are not going -to keep it unless our people learn something of our history."[9]

After T. R. Hughston seconded the proposed amendment, it failed by a vote of 15–3, with Hughston, Masters, and Paul Matthews voting for Masters's amendment. The board then approved Binion's original motion, allowing the Boller-Tilford book to be adopted for use in the public schools of Texas.[10]

Not that this did Boller any good. His book sold well in other states, but the negative Texas publicity over his book definitely hurt sales, with most school districts in Texas adopting Merle Curti and Louis Paul Todd's *Rise of the American Nation*. Upon learning of Curti's success,

Boller mused, "[P]erhaps Haley hadn't won after all; Curti and I see eye to eye on most issues, and I hold him in highest esteem."[11]

After receiving numerous hate calls and letters accusing him of being a Communist, Boller took a visiting professorship at the University of Texas at Austin during 1962–63 before returning to SMU. However, during the end of his last semester at SMU in the summer of 1966, he had one last thing to say about the issue over *This Is Our Nation*. In an essay for the *Southwest Review*, he noted:

> I am not now, nor have I ever been at any time in my life, a member of the American Communist Party or any of its front organizations. And I have never had the slightest sympathy for the ideology, methods, and tactics of the Communist movement in the United States. The Communist Party is a totalitarian organization, and I have nothing but detestation for the goals and methods of totalitarian groups, whether of the extreme left or of the extreme right. Totalitarianism, which operates by means of deceit, slander, character assassination, mendacity, and thought control, violates everything I hold most dear, and it is the exact opposite of the noble principles of liberty, justice, decency, and fair play on which this country was founded and which have made this great nation.

Boller continued:

> The ideals that animate me politically are the ideals of the Founding Fathers of this country, particularly those of Thomas Jefferson, freedom of speech, thought, inquiry, and conscience; honesty and candor in expressing one's opinions; decency and a tolerance in human relations; rationality and a fair-mindedness in considering the views of others. These are the ideals I had in mind when tracing the development of the United States in *This Is Our Nation* . . . A nation inspired by Jefferson's lofty principles, as Abraham Lincoln pointed out many years ago, is the "last, best hope of the world." I think it is still the last, best hope of the world. I wanted to convey something of this spirit to high-school students when I wrote the original manuscript of *This Is Our Nation*.[12]

As for Haley, on January 17 and 31, 1962, he basically repeated before the Texas House of Representatives Textbook Investigating Committee much of these same arguments about the Boller-Tilford book that he gave before the State Textbook Committee on September 14, 1961, and the Texas State Board of Education on November 13, 1961. A check of the word-for-word transcripts and recordings of each of the 1961 proceedings of the Texas State Textbook Committee, the 1961 proceedings of the Texas State Board of Education, and the 1962 proceedings of the Texas House of Representatives Textbook Investigating Committee showed that in each case not one individual at any of those meetings asked Haley a single question about his assertions regarding Boller's political views or associations. It was as though Haley on each occasion was addressing an empty room when he talked about Boller or the Boller-Tilford textbook. Moreover, each of the five members of the House of Representatives Textbook Investigating Committee could choose five public testimonies from those persons who appeared before their committee. Each representative did select five testimonies for inclusion in their reports, but not one included any of Haley's public testimonies. No one even mentioned him by name in their final reports.[13]

However, the Haley-Boller feud was only the beginning of an expanding controversy over the 1961 Texas adoption of social studies books. This would quickly escalate to a state legislative investigation of the content of American history textbooks and later expand to other areas. The resulting proceedings would go down in history as some of the most contentious and disruptive public hearings ever conducted in the Texas House of Representatives.

8

The Conflict Escalates

The Texas Legislative Hearings on American History Textbooks

AS NOTED PREVIOUSLY, in 1961 publishers submitted several dozen American history and world history texts for consideration by the Texas State Textbook Committee. The committee recommended fifteen of these books for statewide adoption by the Commissioner of Education. Of these fifteen books, fourteen were found unsatisfactory by conservative action group Texans for America, and all fifteen books were rejected by the Texas Society of the Daughters of the American Revolution. Nevertheless, on November 13, 1961, the Texas State Board of Education approved the adoption of all fifteen history textbook programs.[1]

When the State Board of Education approved the adoption of the history books opposed by Texans for America and the Texas Society of the Daughters of the American Revolution, A. A. Forester, chair of the Daughters of the American Revolution's Textbook Committee, raised a rallying battle cry. She and those from Texans for America had made their concerns known but had been ignored by the Texas State Textbook Committee, the Texas Education Agency, and the Texas State Board of Education. It was time to take action.

Forester convinced State Representative Bob Bass to introduce a bill creating a House Textbook Investigating Committee made up of five House members. The House approved the bill from Bass, arguing there

The Conflict Escalates 127

"is a need for the textbooks used in the public schools of Texas to contain the teaching of the traditions and the philosophy of America in order to inspire young people to revere our fundamental principles of this greatest country in all the world; now, therefore, be it Resolved, that the House of representatives of the Fifty-seventh Legislature expresses its desire that the American history courses in the public schools emphasize in the textbooks our glowing and throbbing history of and souls inspired by the wonderful American principles and traditions."[2]

Specifically, the House resolution authorized "the Speaker of the House of Representatives to appoint a special committee of five house members to study the contents of textbooks in American history courses; to report to the 58th Legislature. This resolution does not require action by the Texas Board of Education, but a letter from the Board to the chairman of the House committee should offer the cooperation of the Agency."[3]

The Speaker of the House of Representatives then appointed five members of the Fifty-Seventh State Legislature to serve on that committee: Chairman William "Bill" Taylor Dungan, a former teacher, stockman, and feed company owner from McKinney, who served in the House during 1957–67; Vice Chair Robert Wilton "Bob" Bass, a rancher from De Kalb, who served in the House during 1961–69; John C. Alaniz, an attorney from San Antonio, who served in the House during 1961–67; L. Nelson Cowles from Hallsville, who served in the House during 1961–67; and Ronald Edd Roberts, a public school teacher from Hillsboro, who served in the House during 1960–67. For that time, Alaniz and Roberts could be classified as liberals, while Dungan, Cowles, and Bass were more conservative Democrats. All five representatives were reelected to office after serving on the Textbook Investigating Committee.

While press coverage was extremely limited about the Texas Textbook Committee hearings of 1961, the very opposite was the case for the 1962 legislative textbook hearings. Coverage was statewide and very extensive. The House Textbook Investigating Committee held seven official public hearings during 1962: five in Austin (January 10, 17, 24, 31, and February 9), one in Amarillo (February 26), and one in San Antonio (April 2–3). It eliminated from the official record a hearing held in Dallas due to lack of a quorum of its members, since only Representative Dungan was present. Although hundreds of people signed up to

128   Chapter 8

testify at the public hearings, the committee could only accommodate a total of 124 witnesses.[4]

The initial purpose of the House Textbook Investigation Committee was to focus primarily on the teaching of American history in Texas public schools (pedagogical methods, content, etc.), but it soon became obvious that the hearings would take a different turn. The hearings began with members of Texans for America, the Texas Society of the Daughters of the American Revolution, and the John Birch Society, along with their supporters, protesting all fifteen of the history textbooks recommended by the Texas State Textbook Committee and approved by the Texas State Board of Education in 1961. The arguments of the protestors often centered around the same concerns raised earlier before the State Textbook Committee on September 14, 1961—concerns that had clearly fallen on deaf ears.[5] Interestingly, some of the conservatives who spoke before the House of Representatives Textbook Investigating Committee during January–April 1962 admitted they had never actually read the history books in question. Instead, they raised other, more generalized issues. Indeed, the hearings ventured into numerous other opinions about what students in Texas public schools should and should not study. The following is a brief summary of the conservative arguments presented during these 1962 hearings:

1. Textbooks authors were too supportive the New Deal/Fair Deal.

2. Authors referred to America as a "democracy," not a "republic."

3. Many of the recommended library reading lists in the textbooks contained titles by "authors, writers, and artists whose loyalties have been called into question."

4. Textbooks did not contain enough emphasis on the Judeo-Christian foundations of the United States.

5. Some textbooks included the philosophy of John Dewey, a secular humanist, who critics felt "has brought such havoc to our educational process."

6. The point-counterpoint presentations of certain texts were too elaborate for young and impressionable students.

7. Texts were too critical of American society, bordering on unpatriotic.

The Conflict Escalates 129

8. Textbooks were also too critical of the free enterprise system and placed too much emphasis on federal over state power.

9. There was too much emphasis on the United Nations, which was dominated by Soviet Communists.

10. Likewise, there was too much emphasis on the UN Educational, Scientific and Cultural Organization, which only served the "desires of the idealistic International Congress by Soviet espionage."

11. Communism was still a threat, and the educational system needed to guard young minds against the communist plight.

12. Textbooks should stress patriotism above all else.

13. Too much emphasis was placed on civil liberties and not the other rights of citizens, such as property rights.

14. Textbooks should include increased discussion of the Ninth and Tenth Amendments.

15. There should only be local and not state adoption of textbooks for public schools.

16. The theory of evolution should be barred and replaced by the Biblical creation story of Adam and Eve.

17. Secular humanism should be removed from history textbooks.

18. Textbooks should include lengthy biographies and quotes from early American heroes, such as George Washington.[6]

Opposing the conservative textbook critics before the House Textbook Investigating Committee were members from such groups as the American Civil Liberties Union, the Texas Institute of Letters, the Texas Library Association, the American Studies Association, and others, including professors from the University of Texas at Austin, along with writers, poets, and current and former politicians. Those individuals were not Communists or Socialists, but rather New Deal–Fair Deal Democrats and supporters of an emerging civil rights revolution. With the Red Scare then waning in Texas and elsewhere, more Texas liberals were ready to speak out on educational issues. These individuals provided counterpoints to the previously listed conservative criticisms.

In his testimony, Rev. Brandoch Lovely, president of the Central Texas Affiliate of the American Civil Liberties Union and pastor of the

First Unitarian Church in Austin, said: "In the truest sense of the word, we of the ACLU consider ourselves a deeply conservative organization. We work hard to conserve and preserve the right of each citizen to think and speak and worship under the law and with the freedoms bequeathed to us by our founding fathers. . . . Therefore, our schools and textbooks must not become the official source of misguided piety nor half-informed and shallow patriotism."[7]

Dr. William E. Roth of Austin testified that he felt opponents of the adopted textbooks did not even want history to be taught in public schools. He argued that the critics "count the pages devoted to the American Revolution in history textbooks of long ago and compare the number with that in present day books and conclude that the Revolutionary heroes have been deliberately ignored in modern textbooks. Indoctrination with its insistence to conformity is un-Americanism." Roth added that many of the founding fathers, such as George Washington, Ben Franklin, Thomas Jefferson, John Adams, Alexander Hamilton, and Thomas Paine, "were not ardent Christians," nor was "there any mention in the foundation of our nation—its Constitution—of either God or Christ, and the President of the United States is not, under it, declared a defender of the Christian faith." With that, Rep. Bill Dungan questioned Dr. Roth, "Then I take it you're not a believer?" Their heated debate proceeded as follows:

Roth: "That question is out of order."

Dungan: "Then I'll put it in order. Are you a believer?"

Roth: "That question is out of order."

Rep. Bob Bass: "[To Roth] You've been out of the resolution [creating the House Textbook Investigating Committee] ever since you began, and you've been out of order all the time."

Roth: "Are you investigating textbooks or are you investigating me?"

Bass: "We're supposed to be investigating texts, but I don't know how you got in."

Roth: "I sneaked in, I guess."[8]

The Conflict Escalates

The liberal counterpoints continued. In his testimony, Sen. Franklin Spears told the committee that the "function of education is not to indoctrinate our young people but to teach them to think for themselves. As great a danger to this country is communism with its totalitarian horrors are some groups, not all, who would destroy our freedoms in their well-meaning attempt to preserve them. . . . It is extremely dangerous for the future of this state and the future of the nation for a few of its number to set themselves up to decide what others in that society should and should not know and read about." He went on to argue while "no textbook is perfect or slanted to suit everyone," the current method was the best one for a "free and democratic society," adding that "[i]n this time when all Americans are concerned by the attacks on freedom made by tyrannical forms of totalitarianism, this fear if from an emotional and psychological point of view is a greater danger to our civil liberties and traditional concepts of constitutional freedom than is the very tyranny which we fear."[9]

Julius Grossenbacher Jr., a San Antonio attorney, a former political science and history professor at St. Mary's University, a PTA president, and the author of *The Texas Law Enforcement Officer*, argued:

> Often I see the super-patriots foolishly rush out . . . schooled in a single thought—that communism is lurking everywhere—find it—expose it—destroy it. . . . They are like the John Birchers, very valiant, fearing Communists everywhere, and attacking everyone, and everything in sight like the late Senator [Joseph] McCarthy, who was censored by his fellow members of the United States Senate for his vicious unreasonable tactics against friend and foe alike. The Attorney General of the United States has said of all of this: "The only Communist the John Birchers have ever uncovered is President Eisenhower."

Grossenbacher concluded:

> Once we have disclosed the true facts, I think all of us will want to end this battle of words. We will want to send our children back to school thankful that we have public education, based upon freedom of thought, rather than upon enforced political or social

132   Chapter 8

theories like the communists, and we will want to go about our business as constructive citizens rather than as witch-hunters. The Communists would take our textbooks away from us. Why should we help them by tearing out some pages?[10]

Dr. Ernest C. Mossner was a Professor of English at the University of Texas at Austin, a member of the Texas Institute of Letters, a recipient of Guggenheim and Fulbright Research Fellowships, and an editor of *Texas Studies in Language and Literature,* as well as an authority on the writings of David Hume, the Scottish philosopher and historian.[11] In his public testimony before the House Textbook Investigating Committee on January 31, 1962, Mossner defended the current method of textbook selection in Texas and, after quoting from John Milton's condemnation of censorship, went on to maintain:

People, young, middle-aged, or elderly, cannot be indoctrinated or legislated into being good citizens. The facts, the truth, must be made freely available to all. "Reason is but choosing," [John] Milton also observed. In a democracy and republic (and in our history no real distinction has been made between the two) everyone has the right to express his personal opinions; but surely few will contend that all opinions are of equal value—that the child's opinion has the same weight as the adults, the uneducated person's thought the same status as that of the educated. Consider too the amateur versus the expert, the anti-intellectual versus the intellectual or "egghead."

Mossner further argued:

Are history texts to be judged by the adolescent schoolchildren themselves? One such child condemned his present high-school text simply because it omitted a certain illustration he expected to find; he also objected that the twentieth century was given too much space at the expense of Colonial and early American history. Again, a young girl was heard to remark: "We want to learn all sides of all issues, but we also want our history book to be slanted toward Americanism." One is appalled: Can truth be slanted? Surely our country, like all others, has made its mistakes; but, just as surely, most Americans are rightly proud to stand on our records. The twentieth century is well into its second half. The historian, realizing that the understanding of the world we live in is vital to our very survival, must give ample space in his book to that world, even if it means that less space is devoted to the achievements of our Founding Fathers; the elementary text cannot afford to become obese, and inevitably dull, to the fledgling in learning. An elementary textbook must not die of malnutrition by shunning the present; it cannot afford to avoid such issues as Teapot Dome, the Great Depression, the New Deal, the Fair Deal, the New Frontier, The Alliance for Progress, or the United Nations.

He went on to add that parents

who demand that a poem, a play, a novel be suppressed because it contains what they allege to be vulgar or obscene words or incidents might well understand what would happen if this principle were to be applied to Chaucer, Shakespeare, Swift, Pope, Defoe, Fielding, Sterne, Burns, Byron, Swinburne—to name but a very few classics out of the past. Are these "classics" immune merely because they are old or relatively old? And are contemporary works, no matter how brilliant and potentially "classic," to be suppressed merely because they are new? In education, as in everything else in life, to compromise with the petty likes and dislikes of everyone can lead only to the worst sort of mediocrity. True education, on the contrary, is the development of the mind to think accurately, individually, and courageously. This is the opposite of the indoctrination of Soviet teaching, which does, however, have a certain curious parallel with the desires of some of our self-appointed censors.

Mossner concluded that there is

the tangential but related question of the anti-intellectuals versus the "eggheads." The latter are the experts, usually professors, who are so frequently sneered at by the uneducated or the semi-educated. This most egregious paradox consists of the fact that so many of those who publicly scorn the professors go to considerable expense and even sacrifice to send their children to study under these very "eggheads." With their professed antipathy to the learned, these parents should logically not wish their children to be exposed to such contamination. Yet the parents demand, and the children respond favorably to, this very exposure. The college degree has become a status symbol as well as a virtual guarantee of future emolument. Do these parents really despise those who are the only ones capable of providing such gifts to their children? Or, is there some other plausible explanation of this irrational behavior? An inferiority complex? A guilt complex? . . . If, then, the State Textbook Committee (and the Texas Education Agency and the Commissioner) became genuinely undecided about the merit of a book, let them not be harried by the self-appointed censors, frequently ignorant and always biased, let them consult with a panel of scientists, of scholars, of "eggheads," authors who are authorities in the field. The dispassionate advice of such a panel would be gladly given, and, I am certain, just as gladly received. For Chaucer's description of the scholar remains unchanged after nearly six centuries: "And gladly would he learn and gladly teach." This description should be applied today not only to the scholar, not only to the grade-school teacher, but to all educated and enlightened people, in the free give-and-take of knowledge, of truth. "And ye shall know the truth, and the truth shall make you free" (John 8:32). That is the American way.[12]

Maury Maverick Jr. was a decorated World War II combat US Marine, a three-term member of the Texas House of Representatives during 1951–57, a civil rights attorney, a member of the Board of Directors of the American Civil Liberties Union, a State Democratic Party Committeeman, a teacher of political science at St. Mary's University, and a supporter of labor unions and teacher organizations. He had recently won a pro bono case before the US Supreme Court, which declared unconstitutional Jim Crow laws in Texas that prohibited whites and African Americans from fighting one another in professional boxing matches.

Maverick testified before the House Textbook Investigating Committee in defense of the textbook *Our Widening World*. It had not been recommended for state adoption by Texans for America or the Texas Society of the Daughters of the American Revolution, who claimed the text was not harsh enough on communism. Maverick intentionally directed

The Conflict Escalates 135

his comments toward those who opposed the United Nations, and he emphasized the importance of multiculturalism in history programs.

What Maverick could not then realize was that his comments on multiculturalism within a more inclusive approach to history—and about the United States as a nation of "peoples" rather than a "people"—would resonate throughout American historiography and be repeated over the years. Yet on several occasions, boos and catcalls could be heard interrupting Maverick's public testimony.

He began by saying that he was presenting testimony behalf of the book *Our Widening World* by Dr. Ethel Ewing, asking:

> What is the book about? At page 377 it is stated, "the application of Marxist principles has resulted in poverty, forced labor, and widespread human misery." Doesn't sound very pro-Communistic to me. At page 689 efforts of the U.N. to stop Communist aggression is described this way. "The warfare in Korea in 1950 with an army under the U.N. flag opposing the advance of the Communist frontier, marked a strong stand by the United Nations." But what is the book really about? For one thing, it is not about any one nation or its heroes and wasn't intended to be. To put it in a nutshell—this book is about the Family of Man—something that we Americans should appreciate most of all with our melting pot culture. You see, gentlemen, we have a great Nation not for the reason we are all alike, but because we are trying to live together in friendship despite our differences and diversities. [US Supreme Court] Justice William O. Douglas, a man who loves the soil, put it this way, "There is room in this great and good American family for all the diversities the Creator has produced in man. Our Constitution and Bill of Rights were, indeed, written to accommodate each and every minority, regardless of color, nationality, or creed—Out of that diversity can come a unity the world has never witnessed."

Maverick then went on to claim that *Our Widening World*

> tells about the ancestral lands of the United States—about Far Eastern society, about India, and Southeast Asia, the Middle East and Moslem society—Slavic, European, Anglo-American, and Latin-American society. You will remember that Franklin Roosevelt once

told the Daughters of the American Revolution that we Americans are all descendants of revolutionaries and immigrants. The book I am testifying for is also about the United Nations and its dream for human dignity and the search for peace everywhere in the world. The "Town Hall of the World" some call it, and certainly young people ought to know about it. While I oppose the original petitioners who asked you to come here, though I think they mean well and will do harm, I also want to very carefully rise in their behalf, for if I would protect my own right to freedom of speech, I must also protect theirs. In the final analysis, then, I must rely on the Democratic processes which mean, to a great extent, we citizens must depend on you committeemen to do the right thing after you have heard all the evidence. In short, we must rely on your love of liberty, your common sense, and your faith in academic freedom.

He next focused on some history of San Antonio, saying it was an

appropriate place to talk about our widening world, to talk about freedom and liberty and I hope you will let me, an ex-member of your body, tell you briefly about my home town, a community made up of people from so many different races of our widening world. From both a historical and contemporary standpoint it isn't all good here in San Antonio. We have always had one of the highest death rates from infant diarrhea and tuberculosis. Our wage scale suffers badly by comparison with Houston or Dallas. But, St. Anthony's town is a dramatic place for the right kind of things, too; a town which can demonstrate the truth of and need for a book like, *Our Widening World*. We have been at it a long time, here in San Antonio—we know something about our widening world. Evidence indicates that Domingo DeTran, the first Governor of Texas, viewed this area in 1691. Here the Franciscans came and built their missions. Here to what was then called the "New Philippines" came the Canary Islanders—and before them the Apaches and Comanches watered their horses at San Pedro Springs, not far from here. Most anthropologists contend, by the way, that the American Indian is the descendant of Mongoloid groups, his ancestors having crossed the Bering Straits more than 30,000 years ago. To San Antonio, the Anglo-Saxon began to migrate—pushing his way through East Texas not so very long after George Washing-

The Conflict Escalates

ton left the office of President. Here a young West Point graduate, Lt. A. W. Magee, joined together with Bernardo Gutierrez in a joint Anglo-Mexican effort against the Spanish Crown. Gutierrez was one of Father Hidalgo's men and on the streets and plazas of San Antonio men talked about liberty and died for it.

Maverick then went on to brag about how Teddy Roosevelt,

a New Yorker, organized his Rough Riders, and Blackjack Pershing strutted up and down Peacock Alley, of the St. Anthony Hotel, before going to the trenches of France after first thanking the French people for their contribution to the American Revolution. As a matter of fact, if you look hard enough here in San Antonio you might even see some of Pershing's old Chinese cooks who soldiered with him in his chase after Pancho Villa in Mexico. From our widening world, San Antonio has in retirement, a soldier's solder, Walter Krueger, immigrant. Go to our Irish flats while you are here in San Antonio and you will know a people who came to San Antonio suffering from economic poverty. Go down to what we call, with some humor and much affection, Sauerkraut Bend, and you will learn something about people with names like Herff, Steves, Opprenheimic and Altgelt, who fled a despotic Germany in search of liberty. And while you are weighing the evidence presented at this hearing—go by the Alamo, Texas' greatest shrine, and understand that to a substantial degree the Alamo was defended by foreigners from our widening world.

Maverick felt the Alamo was

important because it belongs to the family of man everywhere. In its time—considering the lack of communications and transportation facilities—the Alamo was sort of pre-United Nations effort of its own. Where did the defenders come from? Let me call the roll: 15 men from England; 10 from Ireland; 4 from Scotland; 2 from Wales; 1 man from Denmark, his name was Zanco; 2 from Prussia; 8 were native born Texans with names like Guerrero and Fuentes and I might also add, like John Alaniz, 32 were from Tennessee and the rest from the other American states, although even some of these defenders also emigrated from Europe.

138   Chapter 8

He then offered his thoughts about Bowie, Fannin, and Crockett:

> Old one-eyed Guerrero, and all the other defenders of the Alamo . . . gave their lives defending the Alamo. You see San Antonio is an aggressive type of provincial city, we and some of us were born, we didn't come from anywhere, we came from everywhere. This is a great melting-pot country that we have here. And a final thought about the defenders of the Alamo. A man named Ramsey Yelvington wrote a play about the Alamo which is produced each summer here. A brave man can see that play and weep. At the end of the play the dead defenders of the Alamo assemble on the stage. Satan walks out and mocks the dead defenders and asks them why they died. This is their reply: "We died there: And from our dust the mammoth thing Freedom, Received a forward thrust, The reverberations we continued, Are something to which man may respond, Or not respond at pleasure." Every man who has ever served in the Texas House of Representatives as I did and as you are now serving, is an old colleague, and so on that friendly basis, I put the question to you as if I were standing at what you and I call the "Snorting Pole." How do you committee members respond? Will you give freedom a forward thrust? Do you believe in academic freedom? Don't you generally agree that the State of Texas already has an adequate screening process for the selection of book? Don't you agree that we cannot adopt the censorship tactics of a Fascist Spain or a Communist Russia? Don't you agree that he who would not intelligently cope with any Totalitarianism must first love Democracy most of all?

He concluded his testimony with a Texas saying that folklorist J. Frank Dobie taught him, which "describes a man who won't run out on you or on an ideal. It goes like this, 'He'll do to ride the river with.' I know you committee members will do to ride the river with. Ride it for liberty, ride it for academic freedom, ride it for good school teachers to keep them from being bullied around, ride the river for the glory of Texas and these United States of America. I Thank You."

When Maverick finished his testimony, Rep. Nelson Cowles asked him if he thought those testifying against the history books were insincere. Maverick answered that he thought they were "completely sincere but don't understand the real meaning of the American dream."[13]

The House textbook hearings had opened a floodgate. Both conservatives and liberals presented their opinions on the selections of state-approved school textbooks in a highly publicized forum. But soon the debate would spread beyond the realm of the classroom to explore a new horizon—the public school library. The question of what books should appear on library shelves would open up a larger conservative versus liberal debate about book censorship amid a who's who of American writers as the great Texas textbook war raged on.

9

Fighting in the Library

The Texas House Hearings and
Literary Censorship

DURING HEARINGS by the Texas State Textbook Committee in September 1961 and those by the Texas House of Representatives Textbook Investigating Committee in January, February, and April 1962, members of Texans for America and Texas Society of the Daughters of the American Revolution questioned the backgrounds and views of various textbook authors. Members of these groups also expressed concerns about textbooks' recommended reading lists and bibliographies, which they felt contained inappropriate, obscene, pro-socialist/communist, and subversive material. In addition, these textbooks often cited unsavory, un-American, and dangerous individuals in their discussions of literature, fine art, and science.

Dr. Donald I. Riddle, of Paris, Texas, chairman of Texans for America, addressed these issues in his September 14, 1961, public testimony before the Texas State Textbook Committee. During this testimony, Dr. Riddle "stressed that he was not allowed adequate time to adequately document item by item the affiliations of those individuals . . . but the records of all of these individuals are matters of public record." He also argued:

> Apparently there has been some confusion in the minds of some
> people and the minds of some of the publishers as to our reason

Fighting in the Library

for objecting to the conclusion in the recommended reading list, the bibliography, and in some cases the text material of these individuals of questionable loyalty. In some cases the individuals are mentioned in the textbook material and not protested by our group, depending entirely on how this individual is treated. If, however, he is exalted or built up, or in any way given status or authority in the mind of the child, this we object to; and our attitude toward these individuals is this: if this individual is included in a recommended reading list or treated in a manner which would tend to give him status in the textbook material, this we object to.

He concluded:

it is entirely possible that the recommended book in the recommended reading list may be completely innocuous, but where our protest comes, if this individual is included in the recommended reading list, we are giving this individual status an authority in the mind of the child, then subsequent statements by that same individual will be accepted by the child as being authoritative. Secondly, we object to using the tax moneys of the State of Texas to promote and enrich these individuals which, in essence, we are doing if his books are recommended through a Texas purchased book. Do I make myself clear on that?[1]

Another textbook critic, Lewis C. Gilbert, summed up Dr. Riddle's concern with the following assertion: "As I pursue my study and investigation of these textbooks, I will look into the records of the authors, the selected library references and reference readings, to see why references which would promote National Patriotism and Private Enterprise have been replaced by references in support of socialistic one worldism."[2]

Texans for America's list of suspect authors, artists, scientists, and more included Ernest Hemingway, J. Frank Dobie, Sherwood Anderson, Stephen Vincent Benet, Aldous Huxley, Thomas Wolfe, George Orwell, McKinley Kantor, John Steinbeck, Herman Wouk, Lincoln Steffens, Ida M. Tarbell, Aaron Copeland, Stephen V. Benet, Maxwell Anderson, Ralph Bunche, Theodore Dreiser, Bernard De Voto, Albert Einstein, William Faulkner, Sinclair Lewis, Upton Sinclair, Eugene O'Neill, Willa Cather, Jack London, and Carl Sandburg.[3]

142   Chapter 9

As a result of Texans for America's concerns about these authors, some books were temporarily pulled from public circulation in the libraries of all high schools in Amarillo, Texas, as well as the library at Amarillo College. The list of banned books included Pulitzer Prize winner *Andersonville* by McKinley Kantor; Pulitzer Prize winner *The Grapes of Wrath* by John Steinbeck; *The Viking Portable Library*, which contained writings by Steinbeck; Pulitzer Prize winner *Laughing Boy* by Oliver LaFarge; Pulitzer Prize winner *The Way West* by A. B. Guthrie, along with his *The Big Sky*; Pulitzer Prize winner *Marjorie Morningstar* by Herman Wouk, also the author of *The Caine Mutiny; Of Time and the River* by Thomas Wolfe, also the author of *Look Homeward Angel; Brave New World* by Aldous Huxley; and *Nineteen Eighty-Four* by George Orwell.[4]

Amarillo superintendent Robert Ashworth and Amarillo College president Dr. A. B. Martin claimed they had pulled the books on their own initiative and that removal of the books from their respective libraries was a "routine matter." Dr. Martin said his action served to set a policy governing "additions in our library in the field of fiction . . . and other related areas of general reading." Ashworth said he wanted to review the books "to see what is in the books and also see if the excerpts that were questioned are in the books."[5] Prior to their respective decisions, Texans for America had sent out a pamphlet claiming that forty-two books at the Midland ISD high school library were "totally unfit for consumption at any age level." This list included all titles removed from library circulation in Amarillo.[6]

Dr. W. D. Kelly, a dentist from Midland, Texas, was a board member of the Midland ISD and was also in the process completing his doctorate in the science of education at the time of the controversy. Kelly was the only member of the Midland ISD school board who voted to remove the protested books from general circulation in the Midland High School library. The following is the public testimony he presented before the House Textbook Investigating Committee on January 31, 1962. During his testimony, Kelly emphasized that he represented only himself and was not speaking for the Midland ISD school board. His concern focused on the need for more involvement by local school boards in the selection of textbooks and library books.[7] Part of his testimony covered the various rules regulating the adoption of books for the public schools of Texas. Among other things, he complained that the current frameworks allowing private citizens to submit their concerns regarding state-approved textbooks allocated little time for citizens to adequately evaluate the submitted programs.

> I feel sure that each member of this committee can say along with Thomas Jefferson that, "If a nation expects to be ignorant and free in a state of civilization it expects what never was or ever will be."
>
> I would not have you ignorant—it is with this end in view that I say: "Today our American way of life is challenged from within and directed from abroad. This threat comes not from a great military force, but rather in the books of our children."
>
> The converts of this atheistic, communistic, totalitarianism are devious, subtle and prolific writers. The thing to be afraid of today in America is that we do not give an effective testimony to our youth of the value of American institutions and what they have cost in the history of our people.
>
> As far back as 1925 it has been known by at least a few that this insidious cancer was recognizable in the books of our children—specifically in textbooks. Unless we expose this communist-socialist propaganda for what it is our wonderland of the world will go by default, through a series of persistent half-truths and outright lies.
>
> From time to time we hear of those who contend loudly for academic freedom, for the privilege of the teacher to teach whatever he chooses. They assert that the schools should be open to all ideas and all sides of every question. Let's take a look at this contention and see how it works. When you set food before immature school age children, do you also set poison before them and let them choose? What brings quicker and more intense condemnation on school or home than allowing poison receptacles to be in reach of youngsters? Is it censorship to snatch poison off the food table of children?
>
> When you get out the toys for children to play with, do you also include matches? Is it censorship to snatch away the matches from a child's hands? Do we give our growing youths knives and icepicks to play with or do we give them baseballs and footballs, tennis balls and running tracks? Is that censorship?

In the five thousand years of recorded history adults have learned at least one thing—they must be responsible for the training and guidance of youth during their impressionable and formative years.

A student in our schools has a moral right to trust that his textbooks are the truth and dependable and that even library books are not false and misleading. Even habits and vices tolerated in adults are so much more harmful to growing bodies that we prohibit the sale of alcohol and tobacco to school age students. Are not young and growing minds in as great a need for food and protection?

Children can be made mental cripples and moral misfits for life by communist ideology in the classroom. To face life with perverted ideas on economics and political institutions cripples a youth more destructively than automobile collisions or polio diseases. Certainly the state must not employ teachers who cripple minds and morals. Books by communist authors have this same destructive power. Books are written by people. Books have personality. A book is the extension of ideas and personality of its author. A book is no better than its author.

At our present state of development a communist leader will sharply condemn an author if he puts as much as 5% subversion in a textbook. This same communist leader will praise an author for 2% subversion. Why? It is obvious that at the 2% level our children never know they have been poisoned-they just lay down and die. If you do not believe this junk ask any physician who was in Korea. Hundreds of our American boys 18–21 years of age, without a scratch, just laid down and died. We didn't even have a medical term for it—the troops called it give-up-and-die.

Others will appear before you today and prove to you beyond the shadow of a doubt that there is communist infiltration and subversion of state adopted textbooks here in Texas today. I shall not infringe upon their time—My concern has long been WHO IS RESPONSIBLE FOR THIS CONDITION. [All capitalized words appear in the source transcript of Dr. Kelly's public testimony.]

In Texas, like other states, the Legislature has wisely placed the control of our schools, the management thereof, largely in the hands of the home folks; the parents and tax-payers of each community. Of course the Legislature has set up uniform state standards for the guidance and direction of the local boards, but each

Fighting in the Library

board is empowered to make the decisions of management and selection to fit the needs of each separate community. This local control is typically American and an effective defense against subversion.

Few facts about the world communist conspiracy are so well established as that education is their first objective even ahead of military power. Lenin has stated the world communist policy over and over again to be to first infiltrate the public schools and kindergartens with their ideology. So our school board members are sentries on duty in the front line of the ideological contest in America and they are facing enemy action. Our school board members can guard our impressionable children. If they fall like a sleeping sentry in our military forces, countless innocent young Americans may be hurt and the battle may be lost by the board members' failure in their definite duty.

The Educationist will shout long and loud about the merits of his having the exclusive right to select our children's books. However, to set the educationist up as the sole authority over what is taught would be to deny freedom of choice to the citizens of that district, to deny them the freedom to direct their own government of which the schools are an important part.

There is an academic freedom that we can all believe in and that is the academic freedom of the student and parent from having foreign ideologies rammed down the throats of the students against their will. Government in America is by the people and for the people. Our people must always have the power and the opportunity to correct unsatisfactory performance by government agencies and employees including teachers.

Is it censorship if, in selecting books for our school children's desks and libraries, that our school board members insist on books that impress on the minds of the pupils the principles of morality? If that be censorship, let's have more of it. Is it censorship for board members to insist on the selection of books that will encourage truth and justice? Is it censorship to insist on the selection of books that teach patriotism? Patriotism, like everything else, has to be taught and to be taught effectively it has to permeate all our books and it has to be lived sincerely by both parent and teacher.

I know that there are authors who laugh at the virginity of young womanhood, but their writings need not be selected for our young people. More than half of our public school students come from Christian homes where God and His Holy Scriptures are respected. Shall their ideals and standards be insulted and derided by our school books? They need not be. There are plenty of good books. The best science supports morality, truth, justice and patriotism. True science of government, correct science includes all, these attributes of loyal citizenship.

As in the case of our own schools, Midland, the question of removal of books [from the public school libraries] is a difficult one. The Administration and School Board has been too trusting. Believing that others acted on the same high ideals as theirs, they have been slow to criticize, reluctant to condemn. Those who would corrupt our youth have presumed on the natural tolerance of Americans. They have hidden their vicious wares under the cloak of an academic freedom designed for mature adults. The results have been that materials derogatory of our American history and achievements and laudatory of totalitarian government have found their way into the schools for our youth. When such books came to our attention, the reaction of the teachers and board members was to place the books where they could do no harm—not remove them. That is, they set up departmental libraries for the select few—the gifted children are to read them and become corrupted. But how did they get there in the first place? Who chose them? There is no record in ninety-nine cases out of a hundred.

In the case of the Midland Schools I made the motion that the board set up a record [or listing] of who recommended the selection of the book or material. The Administration put up a howl that sounded throughout our community. Therefore the motion died for lack of a second. . . . BUT THERE SHOULD BE A RECORD. NO OTHER MEANS WILL INSURE ADEQUATE THOROUGHNESS, in the selection of these books which are vital tools in shaping the ideals of our youth in their formative years. . . .

Would you hesitate to throw a rotten apple out of a box of sound apples prepared for distribution to your young people? Is that censorship? Would you give the rotten apple to your child? It takes only one false book to raise doubts in the minds of inquiring youth with their natural and proper curiosity about this big world around them. Not only must our educational methods be patterned on American Freedoms, our Texts vibrant with the recitation of the true facts of American liberties and accomplishments, but we must

Fighting in the Library   147

seek, as authors for all school books for our youth, loyal leaders who are deeply in love with American liberties.

We depend on physicians for our health. We place our earnings in banks. But for the development of the highest ideals of character in our children, for their training and competence in the affairs of this life we depend on school board members to provide good texts in the hands of good teachers. There is no greater earthly trust, no higher responsibility.

IT IS MY RESPONSIBILITY AS A SCHOOL BOARD MEMBER TO TAKE THE GREATEST CARE TO INSURE THAT OUR SCHOOL MATERIAL WILL—through the hands of our excellent teachers—BUILD STRONG WILLED YOUNG PEOPLE CLEAN IN BODY AND MIND. . . .

Let me point out the fallacies of this [current adoption] system [in Texas]. Take for example the process of selecting a 9th grade history book. Let us suppose that 100 books are submitted for adoption. Of the 100 books, let us say that 50 are subversive and 50 are not. Now take 15 persons [on the State Textbook Committee], all of whom represent only a very, very narrow segment of our population. All of whom, so they say, have been brainwashed by the same basic ideologies—that is, the view of the educationist. This has been drilled into them through the years in college—through the years as teachers. I say that they by education are not true representatives of the people. I believe that most of them would not know a subversive book if its cover were red and it had the hammer and sickle on every page.

Let us say that they choose 5 books of which 4 are subversive and 1 is not. Let us now follow the chain of command, and the Commissioner of Education removes the one non-subversive book for some technical reason. Now the four go to the State Board of Education. Here the State Board of Education rubber stamps them, or may even throw out the worst of the four. This will leave three books - all subversive on the multiple lists. . . . The local school board must select one of the three subversive textbooks. . . .

Let us go to Midland now and take a new situation: Say that of the three bocks up for adoption one is subversive and two are not. . . .

The local Board of Trustees may only ratify or reject the recommendations of the textbook committee. The [local] board

148   Chapter 9

> does not have the right to recommend a textbook [as was true
> in 1962]. . . . THE LOCAL BOARD IS NOT ONLY DILUTED
> BY THE STATE BUT ALSO BY LOCAL ADMINISTRATIVE
> CONTROL. . . .
>
> I say to you with all the power I possess the people of Tex-
> as have no control whatsoever over the selection of textbooks.
> THEY DO NOT EVEN HAVE A REPRESENTATIVE CONTROL.
> TEXTBOOK SELECTION IN TEXAS AS OF THIS DAY IS NOTH-
> ING MORE THAN A CAREFULLY CAMOUFLAGED PRIEST-
> HOOD OF A VERY FEW PROFESSIONAL EDUCATIONISTS
> WHO HAVE ABSOLUTE CONTROL OF THE MINDS OF OUR
> CHILDREN.[8]

As noted previously, in 1962 State Representative Bob Bass proposed a bill
to the Texas legislature to make changes to the organization and powers
of the State Textbook Committee, Office of the Commissioner of Education, and State Board of Education, as recommended by A. A. Forester
of the Texas Society of the Daughters of the American Revolution. The
purpose of the bill was to alleviate some of the complaints about textbook
selection noted by W. D. Kelly. However, Bass's fellow legislators did not
act on any of those proposals.

While Riddle, Gilbert, and Kelly had their suspicions about some of
the further reading and references recommended by textbook authors,
Dr. Douglas Morgan and Rev. Lee Freeman did not.

Douglas Morgan, a University of Texas philosophy professor, in his
public testimony said that if parents properly raised their children, they
would be good even if "they read some naughty words in books. We
have to have ideas presented openly. God allowed Christ to be tempted.
Christ resisted because he was stronger inside." Morgan went on to argue that parents should educate children rather "than to indoctrinate
them. If we indoctrinate our children with only one idea, whether it be
right or wrong, we will be following the same path as the Russians." In
regard to the so-called controversial books questioned in the Midland
public school library, Morgan said, "I can find examples of sex, decay,
and sin in another book that I think should be in every library and in
every home." That book was the Bible. Morgan added: "Perhaps a word
ought to be uttered in defense of our own kids. I do not think that the

Fighting in the Library

mere mention of a man who was once called a Communist by a Senate investigating committee is going to make a Communist out of your kid or out of mine. If we confuse indoctrination with education, we are doing the same things the Communists. In Russia the only educated man is a Party member."[9]

Rev. Lee Freeman was Associate Pastor of the University Baptist Church, Austin, Texas. The following excerpt is from the public testimony he gave before the House Textbook Investigating Committee on January 24, 1962. Here, Freeman discusses what he felt was an inherent problem with the writing of history books, stressing, "To grind a particular political ax in the twentieth century would be very poor history writing, and we certainly would not want that sort of thing."

> In various points of history, groups of people have attempted to get history written, so that it will favor their particular point of view. In Nazi Germany, when Hitler took over, one of the things that he was interested in was writing the history of the German nation to prove his theories of racial superiority and etc. Now the bug-a-boo there was the Communist and the Jew. Hitler, of course, saved the Germans from the Communists and blamed many things on the Jews. And so history was written so as to point out that all ancient evils started with the Jews, all modern evils started with the Communists. This was just flat not true, but I mean that this was the way that history was written. The Communists write history in this way today. They claim they invented everything and so on, etc. . . .
>
> [It is] not the purpose of the study of the American history simply to be propaganda. It is not the purpose of the study of the American history to inspire patriotism. We love our country. We are proud of the things in our heritage, but we are interested in knowing the truth about things, primarily. This is the first thing, to understand what was going on in our history. There are things in our history of which we will be ashamed. There are many things of which we will be proud of, but we want to know the truth because we are a nation of free people who do not subscribe to the theory that the truth has to be distorted in order to protect us. We are not interested in building up a methodical history that simply will thrill our hearts, but not be in accord with the facts. We don't

need this. As a Democratic society, a society that depends on the intelligence of the people, to understand issues, they need to understand how things have come to be. And this is the reason that we need an objective kind of writing history. And this is the reason and concern for my being here. You would, in your investigation, take very seriously the nature of history and I would think, consult with competent historians, who are recognized in their field, as to whether these books are historically accurate, in terms of the cannons of scientific study of history in our time and not be swayed by political extremes, one or the other or anyone but rather try to maintain an objective presentation of the truth. Because we have nothing to fear from the truth. . . . Let's always be true to the facts, as they were understood and received and more important, in the content in their own time. This is the kind of history that we are interested in.

Reverend Freeman then concluded:

One other thing that I would like to mention and this touches my own concerns maybe a little more directly. There are passages in the Bible that I would not read in the pulpit. Portions of the Song of Solomon are somewhat embarrassing and would be considered decidedly risqué in some circles. Several ministers have appeared before you and spoken about various books that contain obscene words, etc. I am not a man who particularly enjoys bad language any more than the rest of the folks, but a book ought to be judged on its total content in what it is trying to say and not on passages taken out of context and words of this sort. I heard someone earlier mention that a man like Ernest Hemingway was an author of pornography. This is a very loose definition of pornography, and in the first place, pornography is defined I think, by the courts and you can't send it through the mail and this sort of thing. This is not pornography. He uses some language that I certainly would not use in polite conversation or from the pulpit, but he is writing a novel, he's not preaching a sermon. He's reflecting an aspect of life as he sees it. This is his right. I think we need to have a balanced unemotional sort of approach to these things.[10]

Fighting in the Library

Through their various testimonies, Riddle, Gilbert, Kelly, Morgan, and Freeman addressed the issue of whether censorship is justified for library books, state-approved history textbooks, or textbook recommended reading lists. Censorship was also a major concern for many others who appeared before the House Textbook Investigating Committee when individuals from the Texas Institute of Letters confronted members from Texans for America. The resulting conflict pit liberal against conservative and led to further public disagreements as the war of words raged on.

10

Liberal and Conservatives

The Texas Institute of Letters versus Texans for America

PROTESTS BY TEXANS for America and the Texas Society of the Daughters of the American Revolution regarding school library books and state-adopted social studies textbooks quickly prompted a response from liberal members of the Censorship Committee of the Texas Institute of Letters. Speakers representing the Texas Institute of Letters included Lon Tinkle, Frank Wardlaw, Rev. Joseph M. Dawson, Frank E. Vandiver, and J. Frank Dobie. Counterpoints from the conservative Texans for America soon followed, with arguments presented by James Donovan and J. Evetts Haley.

Members of the Texas Institute of Letters Voice Their Concerns

Members from the Texas Institute of Letters were particularly concerned with J. Evetts Haley's prior endorsement of a statement he presented to the Texas House of Representatives Textbook Investigating Committee. In his January 17, 1962, presentation, Evetts cited that "stressing of both sides of a controversy only confuses the young and encourages them to make snap judgments based on insufficient evidence. Until they are old enough to understand both sides of a question, they should be taught only the American side. . . . If this struggle meant anything, it is the perpetuation of the Christian ethnic. There is not freedom except under the Christian ethnic as enshrined in the Constitution and the Bill of Rights."[1]

Texas Institute of Letters president Lon Tinkle was an award-winning historian, a biographer, a book critic for the *Dallas Morning News*, and a professor at Southern Methodist University. He was the author of *Thirteen Days to Glory: The Siege of the Alamo* (1958) and went on to write several other books, including *The Story of Oklahoma* (1962), *The Valiant Few: Crisis at the Alamo* (1964), *J. Frank Dobie: The Making of an Ample Mind* (1968), and *An American Original: The Life of J. Frank Dobie* (1978). Tinkle also went on to be the coeditor of *Treson Nobel: An Anthology of French Nobel Prize-Winners* (1963) and *The Cowboy Reader* (1969). He was a member of Ordre des Palmes Academiques in France, received an honorary doctorate from St. Mary's University of San Antonio, and served as president of the Texas Institute of Letters from 1942 to 1952.[2]

In his January 31, 1962, public testimony before the House Textbook Investigating Committee, Tinkle began by telling the legislators:

> The Texas Institute of Letters is a non-profit organization established by the Historical Centennial Commission of the State of Texas in 1936. As a part of this celebration of the independence of the republic days of statehood of Texas, The Historical Commission invited some leading scholars and writers and thinkers to establish the Texas Institute of Letters for two purposes. First, to commemorate the intellectual heritage of the state and second, to foster the writing and reading of good books in the State of Texas. . . . By training, by profession the members of The Texas Institute of Letters have a profound concern for the fate of books in our society and ever profound concern for the scrupulous definition of key words in our existence and in our lives . . . The Texas Institute of Letters believes with Stephen F. Austin that "all restrictions, on the introduction, sale, or reading of books are calculated to prevent the diffusion of intellectual life and knowledge—to retard the improvement of the nation by perpetuating ignorance, superstition is contrary to the genius of free institutions and shall never be imposed under any pretext whatever."

154 Chapter 10

He added:

> Sharing Austin's faith in intellectual freedom and his suspicion of those who think it is ever possible to defend freedom by destroying it, the Texas Institute of Letters stands opposed to all encroachments and restrictions on the right of people to write as they think and to read what they choose. . . . [The Texas Institute of Letters goes] on record as being in total opposition to all forms of extralegal hindrance on all expressions of a creative or analytical mind at work in any field, whether that field be literature, art, science or economics or any other phase of human behavior.

He concluded:

> Whether the hindrance be motivated by moral, political or other grounds and when it be in the form of arbitrary police censorship, blacklisting, boycott, esthetic vigilantism or any other action that by-passes the orderly processes of the duly constituted State and Federal Courts.[3]

Frank Wardlaw was a former president of the Texas Institute of Letters; he established the University of South Carolina Press before becoming director of the University of Texas Press. In the following public testimony before the Texas House of Representatives Textbook Investigating Committee, Wardlaw offered his observations about the need for literary freedom and also defended the textbook authors and publishers whose works were used in the state's public schools.

> We are Americans, and this fact demands our complete and unswerving loyalty. In our own time being an American also implies a particular and rather frightening obligation. Never in all our history had there been so compelling a necessity for us to keep the beacon light of freedom shining in the world. We must never fall into the trap of thinking that we can make this light shine brighter abroad by dimming it here at home.
>
> There are in America today many well-meaning, patriotic people who feel that it is their duty to protect their fellow-citizens from error by removing from bookstores and libraries books which they think are harmful or dangerous. But this, it seems to me, is contrary to the genius of America.

Liberals versus Conservatives

I know that there are many bad words and some vicious books published in this imperfect world, and I know that many sincere people believe we have gone too far in opening up the whole range of human experience to inquiry by novelists and other writers. But, in the final analysis, there are no men wise enough to be censors, and we always lose more than we gain by censorship. Proper home training and the nurturing of sound literary tastes are the best defense against bad books.

In recent months we have witnessed prolonged and concerted attacks against the textbooks used in our schools. We are told in effect that there exists an all-pervading conspiracy among the writers and publishers of textbooks to seduce our boys and girls away from loyalty to America. Children shouldn't be taught both sides of controversial questions, only the *American* side, these textbook censors declare. Our Founding Fathers and other American heroes must not be portrayed as fallible human beings who sometimes made mistakes, but as supermen whose acts and motives were unvaryingly pure. Above all, children must *not* be taught that this is One World. They must not learn too early about life in other countries until they are rooted and grounded in a special brand of Americanism, or they will be sure to put other loyalties above that which they owe to their country!

These agents of the communist conspiracy who write our textbooks are terribly subtle, we are told—witness the fact that they sometimes refer to the United States as a democracy rather than a republic (Hamilton and Jefferson both did the same thing, but that is beside the point). They even omit the old painting of George Washington praying at Valley Forge which was in all the textbooks fifty years ago. And these and similar methods are successful, we are informed; our young people are no longer loyal to America!

I simply don't believe in the existence of this conspiracy among the people who make our textbooks. The textbooks which our children use are sometimes dull, occasionally inaccurate, and frequently innocuous, which is probably traceable to the desire of the publishers to please everybody, but they aren't subversive. If I am wrong, and this conspiracy exists, it is too subtle for me to grasp— and it is completely ineffectual. I regard as a baseless slander the charge that our young people no longer love this country. They are just as patriotic as they were in any youth—and vastly better informed.

We are the heirs of Western civilization, and our national character, culture, and achievements are a blend of elements derived from many lands. Furthermore, like it or not, our destiny is inextricably tied up with that of other peoples of the world, and it is desperately important that we understand them; this is simply enlightened self-interest. We should never lose sight of our own glorious heritage, but it will be fatal if we forget that we are "involved in mankind."

America's great strength lies in the fact that it has provided an effective system for people of widely divergent points of view to participate in the formation of national policy and the corollary fact that no one point of view has ever permanently gained complete ascendancy. The history of our nation bristles with controversial issues in which Americans of equal patriotism, courage, and intelligence have taken diametrically opposite positions.

What is the *American* side of the Civil War, for instance? And what about the two sides of the American Revolution? The textbook censors regard themselves as conservatives, but they would object strenuously if the textbooks presented much of a case for the conservatives of 1776—the Tories who cast their lot with the status quo and against the wild-eyed radicals who led the nation into rebellion. Most Tories believed deeply in the righteousness of their cause; they were even willing to die for it. Those loyal Britons were wrong, we know now, but they were not knaves or fools. Much of the philosophy and many of the institutions of our freedom are a legacy from Great Britain; the authors of our liberty include Cromwell and Locke and Pitt as well as Franklin and Washington and Jefferson and Paine.

The America that I love has been enriched and glorified by the blood, sweat, and tears of Rebels and Tories, Yankees and Confederates, of Republicans and Democrats, of Liberals and Conservatives, English and Scots, Irish and Germans, Italians and French, Swedes and Mexicans, Negroes and Chinese, Protestants and Catholics, Jews and Deists, Baptists and Methodists, Episcopalians and Presbyterians, Christian Scientists and Holy Rollers—even Freethinkers and Atheists. A single *American* point of view on any controversial issue? This is dangerous nonsense. . . .

I do not impugn the motives of those who think differently; I question neither their sincerity nor their patriotism. I simply believe that they are wrong and that they have misapprehended the nature of America and the sources of its strength.

International communism is a frightful menace in the world, and we must face up to this danger with all the stamina and resolution we can muster. But the irresponsible sowing of suspicion can only serve to weaken us in this fight. We need more faith— faith in our young people, faith in the vitality of America, faith in the validity of freedom, and the eternal power of freedom's God.[4]

Dr. Frank E. Vandiver was also a former president of the Texas Institute of Letters, a history professor at Rice University, and later a president of Texas A&M University. A leading authority on the American Civil War, Vandiver is the author of several books, including *Rebel Brass: The Confederate Command System* (1956), *Jubal's Raid: General Early's Famous Attack on Washington in 1864* (1960), *Mighty Stonewall* (1957), *Tattered Flags: The Epic of the Confederacy* (1970), and *Blood Brothers: A History of the Civil War* (1992). He gave the following public testimony before the House Textbook Investigating Committee on January 24, 1962, expressing his disapproval of the censorship of history books:

State education authorities must have the right to select textbooks and must exercise careful professional discretion in selections from among the books offered. At the same time, the right of selection must not be warped into the power of oppression. Some have objected to mention of certain persons in textbooks because they have been cited by congressional committees, have condemned some economic views because they do not agree with the views of the protesters, and have opposed some authors because they advanced locally unpopular views. The people who object have a right to do so. But the history of the United States stands as a monument to freedom—freedom of protest, freedom to advocate, freedom of choice, and freedom of thought. . . .

Stephen F. Austin, like Thomas Jefferson before him, stood bluntly against any sort of restriction on books. Whatever restrictions were imposed, he saw them as hazards to the Republic. And what was true in the crisis-ridden days of the Texas Republic is even more true in the world crisis of today. If America is to remain the beacon light of freedom in a world threatened by slavery, it

158   Chapter 10

must remain free and unfettered at home. Those faint-hearted who fear that American youth are not capable of judging for themselves what is right and wrong condemn the very system they profess to support. If we suppress from consideration anything involved in today's complex world struggle, we will only advance the cause of hostile ideology by rejecting our own. Liberty is not defended by surrendering it. . . .

Free minds are not built easily; quickly, or by any prefabricated shortcuts. Freedom is its own best advocate: let those who grow in it use it as their answer to totalitarianism everywhere. At the center and heart of the American dream is freedom of thought. It is our greatest triumph and our greatest weapon. Blunt that weapon here, and freedom suffers everywhere.[5]

Dr. Joseph M. Dawson, from Austin, Texas, was an eighty-three-year-old ordained Baptist minister who for thirty-one years was pastor of the First Baptist Church in Waco, a well-known Baptist leader on both the state and national levels, and a president of the Texas Institute of Letters. The following is public testimony he gave before the House Textbook Investigating Committee on January 31, 1962.

In his testimony, Dawson noted Rev. J. Frank Norris, who became one of the best-known preachers of his day and was one of the first radio preachers setting the stage for such later televangelists as Pat Robertson and Jerry Falwell. Norris attended Baylor University, where he helped lead the effort to fire the more liberal school's president, O. H. Cooper. After graduation from Southern Baptist Seminary of Louisville, Norris, an adamant anti-Communist, gained control of the *Baptist Standard*, and as pastor of the First Baptist Church of Fort Worth, he led one of the largest congregations in America. He targeted those who accepted the theory of evolution and did not adhere to literal interpretations of the Bible. He once had apes and monkeys placed near his pulpit to show his church members the "kinfolk" of those who supported Charles Darwin's *Origin of Species*. It was also Norris who persuaded John Birch to become a Christian missionary to China, where Communists murdered him. Norris likewise helped create the mid-twentieth century movement to criticize textbooks, first led by such groups as the John Birch Society, Texans for America, and the Minute Women, followed in

1962 by Mel and Norma Gabler's Educational Research Analysts Textbook Corporation. Norris died in 1952 at the height of the McCarthy era.[6]

Reflecting on the censorship legacy of Norris and many others, Dawson gave the following public testimony before the House Textbook Investigating Committee:

> Censorship has always been objectionable to strugglers after freedom. It harassed men of independence in ancient Greece and Rome. In not a few European countries it has produced tragic effects upon liberties. Everywhere censorship has been a major weapon of aristocratic governments and authoritarian sects. Censors have been hated because of their ruthless disregard of human rights, their violent partisanship, their vicious stifling of the creative mind. In the opinion of objectors to it any honest review of man's historic experience with censorship leads to the conclusion that it has blighted individuals, grossly mistreated minorities, encouraged monstrous dictators, and impeded progress for the masses. This adverse pre-judgment therefore must not be charged to irritation or prejudice but regarded as a challenge to fullest investigation.
>
> Perhaps the loudest protest in our mother country against censorship in respect to printing was made in 1644 by the greatest English poet John Milton. Milton addressed his *Areopagitica* to the English Parliament against a decree of the Star Chamber that all printing should be entrusted to the Bishop of London and the Chancellors of Oxford and Cambridge. The practical effect was to give Archbishop Laud absolute control over every press in England. He used his authority after the manner of the Inquisition.
>
> Milton's masterpiece is strong meat, too strong for pressure groups today. In it he declared that the attempt to keep out evil doctrine by censorship is "like the exploit of that gallant man who thought to round up the crows by shutting the park gates." He reminds his readers that ideas are spread as effectively by word of mouth as by the use of printing. He argues that censorship, if attempted over printed matter, to become effective must be extended to garb, pastimes, eating, in fact to almost everything. Moses, Daniel, and Paul and the Church Fathers, he claimed, by pre-

160   Chapter 10

cept and example, enjoyed freedom in the pursuit of knowledge. Milton ended with a paean to England, which through freedom of the press had come to be recognized as "a nation not slow and dull, but of a quick, ingenious and piercing spirit." In a final burst he prayed, " Give me liberty to know, to utter, and to argue freely, according to conscience, above all liberties."

This freedom to read and write became an American tradition. The founders of our Republic, steeped in Milton's contentions, wrote into the first article of the Bill of Rights a guarantee for it. We are not shocked when we read that Thomas Jefferson, on being informed that a book had been suppressed, exclaimed, "I am really mortified to be told that in the United States of America . . . a question about the sale of a book can be carried before the Civil Magistrates. . . . Are we to have a censor? Those imprimatur shall say what books may be sold and what we may buy? . . . It is an insult to our citizens to question whether they are rational beings or not. . . . For God's sake let us hear both sides, if we choose."

Sadly do we recognize the current rash of attempts at the hated practice of censorship. Self-appointed guardians of what they proclaim as the only correct views are seeking to impose upon others coercively their warped concepts.

Look intently at this. What the would-be censors are doing, be it said, is not in behalf of free discussion, which is fundamental to the democratic process in an open society—the unquestioned right of dissent, whether from ultraliberal or ultraconservative. The censors cannot tolerate hearing sides of an issue; seemingly they are hell-bent on silencing all expression outside their own. Of course it is obvious that they are trying to seize media which belong to all the people for the purpose of forcibly propagating the peculiar views of a part of the people.

The shame of such endeavors is seen in the fact that they turn out to be thinly disguised political stratagems or poorly concealed sanctimonious fanaticisms. Pity is that so many good people are unwittingly misled by them.

For whatever it may be worth I wish to cite an illuminating episode out of the past. In the early 1920's while I was serving as a member of the Board of Trustees of Baylor University, the Reverend J. Frank Norris, equipped with a large church, a powerful radio station and a widely circulated newspaper, attacked certain textbooks and teachers [for teaching such things as evolution in science courses at] Baylor. His noisy, prolonged attacks incited a nasty disturbance. Finally, amidst the rising tumult, the Baptist General Convention responded to Norris' demand that as owner of the institution the Convention appoint an investigating committee. He said he knew what was the only true faith, and as a representative of "people from the forks of the creek," he called for authoritative correction of dangerous areas. Fortunately the Convention named a competent committee. Following a diligent examination, the committee came up with the report that it was inadvisable for a mass meeting such as the Convention to handle matters like this, that selection of textbooks and teachers properly belonged to the trustees in consultation with the faculty and faculty. The report was approved, quiet reigned, and that policy has been pursued to the satisfaction of Baylor's constituency.

Self-appointed censors usually concentrate on alleged evils in publications around three areas: politics, obscenity, and religion.

Charges or alleged political bias often are made by those who resist change, those who are determined to maintain the status quo. More often than not they wish to obscure knowledge of what has happened in their own nation and fear to let others know the facts about new political systems elsewhere. One such person offered the law school of my university a million dollars provided it would agree not to teach any decisions of the United States Supreme Court rendered after the advent of Franklin Delano Roosevelt! How different is the appeal of the American Bar Association to our schools to teach the full truth about communism and our system.

Others of the suppression ilk employ persecuting tactics. They label advocates of political theories and platforms which they reject as socialistic or communistic. Listening to critics of textbooks before the legislature's investigating committee, one gained the impression that each presumed every author of an offending text either was a card-carrying Communist or had been one. . . .

Next let us face up to obscenity. I take it none of us would condone the infamous furtive dealers in pornographic materials who slip their wares into the hands of school children. I am supposing too, that few would disagree with the historic June 24, 1957, decision of the United States Supreme Court: " . . . it is apparent that the unconditional phrasing of the First Amendment ('Congress shall make no law . . . abridging the freedom of speech, or of the press') was not intended to protect every utterance. . . . The protection given speech and press was fashioned to assure unfettered exchange of ideas for the bringing about of political and social changes desired by the people. . . . All ideas having even the slightest redeeming social importance—unorthodox ideas, controversial ideas, even ideas hateful to the prevailing climate of opinion—have full protection of the guarantees. . . . But implicit in the history of the First Amendment is the rejection of obscenity as utterly without redeeming social importance." . . .

Some time ago, I wrote for [*Christianity Today*] an article in which I said: "If citizens grow excited over pornography, they should do something besides wail. They should, before resorting to court action, certainly before organizing a censorship committee, endeavor to take other positive steps. An influential Christian magazine editor advises that our real reliance must be upon spiritual disciplines which produce 'a sensitized conscience.' A home counselor asks if those whose children are susceptible to corruption from salacious literature have provided an abundance of attractive wholesome literature for their homes. A pastor advocates church libraries with a promotion of offerings that will win readers. The churches should induce high standards and produce good taste. Their task is to teach youth to approve that which is excellent. It is of the utmost importance that Christians try to see life whole, and not fatuously imagine that youth is lost through a single evil."

Finally there is the question of religion in the public schools, about which many confused citizens are censorious.

When I went to Washington, DC, to give direction to the Joint Committee on Public Affairs for six national bodies of my denomination, I was asked by the head of the Christian Amendment Association to go over to Capitol Hill and lobby for the passage of a bill he had persuaded an unthinking congressman to introduce. I promptly refused. He looked at me aghast. "What, don't you believe in Christianity?" he asked. I replied that I most assuredly did, but not by legislative enactment and tax support. "Why should any citizen beg Congress to do what is expressly forbidden to do by the Federal Constitution? The first of the Bill of Rights reads, 'Congress shall make no law respecting the establishment of religion, or prohibiting the free exercise thereof.'"

Quite to my brother's chagrin, I pulled down the history books and showed him plainly that from the birth of the nation devoted Christians had been trying in vain to get Congress to do what

Liberals versus Conservatives 163

its better informed members knew it must never do. The House Judiciary Committee in 1874 explained congressional refusal in these words: "The Christian fathers of the Republic decided, after grave deliberation, with great unanimity, that it was inexpedient to put anything into the Constitution or frame of government which might be construed to be a reference to any religious creed or doctrine."

That is why the name of God is not in the Federal Constitution and the name of Jesus Christ is not in the constitution of any state of the Union. The founders wanted every citizen—Christian, Jew, Moslem, and men of no belief—to enjoy absolute freedom of conscience. This does not mean that the government is atheistic or hostile to religion. It is secular in the sense that it is not under the control of any church or set of churches but protects every citizen in his right to believe or not believe. Ours is not officially or in fact a Christian nation.

For this nature of our government, I, for one, am unspeakably grateful. For more than sixty years I have tried as best I could to preach the gospel of Jesus Christ, but I am sincere in saying I would not use a feather's weight to compel anybody to be a Christian. I hold with Thomas Jefferson that to compel a man to support any faith he does not accept is both a sin and a tyranny.

What then of the outcry of the censorious about the neglect of religion in our public schools, particularly in respect of rituals and formal teaching? I answer: Except for the teacher's use of the literatures of religions and insistence on spiritual values, instruction in the faith of any sect is positively unconstitutional. The United States Supreme Court in its interpretation of the Constitution has consistently and expressly said so, as in the Everson case: "The 'establishment of religion' clause of the First Amendment means at least this: Neither a state nor the Federal Government can set up a church. Neither can pass laws which aid one religion, aid all religions, or prefer one religion over another. Neither can force nor influence a person to go to or remain away from church against his will or force him to profess a belief or disbelief in any religion. . . . No tax in any amount, large or small, can be levied to support any religious activities .or institutions, whatever they may be called, or whatever form they may adopt to teach or practice religion."

In conclusion I affirm that American nonsectarian public schools, the pride of our land the envy of all lands, whatever their

164   Chapter 10

real defects, by actual test produce as fine a type of citizen as any system of schools on earth. They are the greatest single source of national unity and the hope of real democracy on this continent.[7]

During his public testimony, Rev. Dawson elicited gasps from some in the audience when he said the United States is not a Christian nation, and while he had spent most of his life trying to persuade people to be Christians, he would not raise a featherweight to compel anyone to be Christian. Rep. Bill Dungan asked Reverend Dawson, "If this is not a Christian nation, what is it?" Reverend Dawson replied, "This is a nation of free men with religious liberty. My experience has taught me that self-appointed censors are nuisances and that small minority pressure groups can cause a great deal of harm." He added that the question of what should be taught in public schools should be the responsibility of teachers and the boards of education.[8]

J. Frank Dobie, a world-renowned folklorist, received his BA degree from Southwestern University at Georgetown and, for a time, worked as a reporter for the *San Antonio Express* before becoming a high school teacher and principal in Alpine, Texas. He received his MA in English in 1914 from Columbia University and was a reporter for the Galveston *Tribune* before going to Austin to teach at the University of Texas. He became a full professor of English there in 1943. With few interruptions, such as while he served as a first lieutenant during World War I, Dobie worked on his uncle's ranch, taught for a year at what is now Oklahoma State University, and lectured in American history at Cambridge University in England, but most of his career during 1914–47 was at the University of Texas, where he became good friends with historian Walter Prescott Webb and naturalist Roy Bedichek.[9]

Dobie's career as a professional writer began when he helped reorganize the Texas Folklore Society in 1922, went on to serve as its editor and secretary, and became a leading authority on the multicultural aspects of folklore as part of the life and literature of the Southwest. With Texans such as J. Mason Brewer, John Lomax, Soledad Perez, Jovita Gonzales, Mody Boatright, Americo Paredes, and Francis Abernathy, he helped make the study of southwestern folklore a respected academic discipline. His books about the Southwest encompassed a variety of topics, including unusual characters, ghost stories, songs, weather conditions, multi-

Liberals versus Conservatives

ple occupations, wildlife, buried treasure, and lost gold and silver mines. Many of Dobie's numerous books received national and international recognition, including *A Vaquero of the Brush Country* (1929), *Coronado's Children* (1931), *The Mustangs* (1934), *The Flavor of Texas* (1936), *The Longhorns* (1941), and *The Voice of the Coyote* (1949). He wrote 21 books and produced more than 800 magazine articles, as well as some 1,300 newspaper columns.

Along with his enthusiasm for the academic study of folklore and his opposition to racial segregation, Dobie also spoke out for academic freedom and condemned textbook censorship when he gave his public testimony before the Texas House of Representatives Textbook Investigating Committee. He told its members that any censor "is a bigot and an enemy of the free world" and that "the more textbooks are censored, the weaker they will become.[10] He continued:

> Censorship . . . is never to let people know but always to keep them in ignorance. Never to enlighten but always to darken. It is, and for thousands of years, has been a main force used by dictators and all manner of tyrannical governments from Nero to Nikita Khrushchev. As Thomas Jefferson said, "Error of opinion may be tolerated where reason is left to combat it," and that's all we are asking for. Leave reason free to combat error, and don't any of us think we know what all the errors are, or wisdom will die with us. After the press had attacked him violently, Jefferson still held that he had rather live in a country of free newspapers and any sort of government, than under a well-meaning dictator without newspapers. . . . Censoring military secrets in time of war is something else—it's necessary in mortal combat with an enemy. A censor is always a tool—or as Winston Churchill called Benito Mussolini during the late war a "utensil." Not one censor in history is respected by history or by enlightened men of any nation. An individual can be a patriot and still have a different idea of Americanism. . . . Any person who imagines he has a corner on the definition or the conception of Americanism and wants to suppress all conceptions to the contrary is a bigot and an enemy to the free world.
>
> A government, in accordance with the principles of such an individual who fancies he knows it all, would be no better than any other tyrant. . . .

It is easier to appeal to prejudice than to reason, to ignorance than to enlightenment. That is the way of the demagogue. . . . No use kidding ourselves—school children aren't fools. They don't live in vacuums. They're not going to be much influenced by some dull piece of propaganda, tale-twisting and flag-raising put into a textbook. They're just not. It goes over them just like water goes over a duck's back.

When Edmund Burke, one of the great friends of America, before the American Revolution, was running for Parliament—he had an opponent who said he would vote any way his constituents wanted him to vote. Burke wrote a letter . . . in which he said "I will not vote the way you suggest I vote. I will study the subject and then will vote according to an enlightened conscience." Now, there is a vast difference between having an ignorant conscience, an enlightened conscience, and merely being conscientious is not enough. The road to hell is paved with people who mean well, but who don't know. . . .

I'm reminded of a fable out of Aesop—of an oldish man and a youngish boy and a donkey. They were going to take this donkey to sell and started out leading him. They met somebody and he said, "Here you have a strong little donkey and both men are walking. Why don't you ride?" So the father put the boy up on the donkey. They went a little farther, and they met somebody else, a censor, and he said, "Look's here, this young, agile, vigorous, lively little boy riding the donkey and his father, who is already so down and tired, walking." That's not Americanism. And so the boy got off, and the father got on. So they met somebody else and he said, "The idea of a grown man riding when his little son has to walk." So the father pulled up the little boy, and both were riding the donkey, and before long they met another "censor" and he said, "That's not the way to 'write it' or ride it, rather," he said, "Two cruel, human beings on a poor little donkey." So they both got off, and they threw the donkey down, and they trussed him up and tied the four legs together and then ran a stick between the tied legs and put one end on the shoulder of the man and the other on the shoulder of the boy and started carrying the donkey to market. By that time they were about to have the "blind staggers" and got to the bluff of the creek and dropped him off into the water. Well, that's what happens to your textbooks when every Tom, Dick, and Harry

—everybody who has a corner on patriotism and who considers somebody else who doesn't agree with him is not now a patriot. . . . I know most of [the texts] are very dull. One reason that they are so dull is that the publishers are so anxious to present something that nobody will object to.

And I have here the resolution formulating this Committee. Chairman, I don't want to arouse a prejudice against me from the members of the committee, but let me read one of these "Whereases" by which this committee comes into existence. "Resolved that the House of Representatives of the 57th Legislature expresses its desire that the American History courses in the public schools emphasize in the textbooks our glowing throbbing history of hearts and souls inspired by wonderful American principles and traditions." If you get so much throbbing and inspiration in textbooks, you're not going to get knowledge. Blake, the poet, says "To generalize is to be an idiot for knowledge consists of particulars." This goes back to the old textbooks—they were readable. I remember yet selections that I memorized out of the 5th grade reader from a one-teacher school on a ranch in Live Oak County. And one of those selections I feel has made me a better person. It made me love history. I don't know, it makes me love freedom more. "At midnight in this guarded tent, The Turk lay dreaming of the hour, When Greece, her knee in suppliance bent, or nee in suppliants bent, Should tremble at his power."

I was for the Greeks then, and I was again for the fighters for freedom ever since—but not for the Daughters of the American Revolution's, the Minute Women, the John Birchers and other fanatics [meaning Texans for America] who fear vitality and intelligence and seek to perpetuate petrifaction.[11]

Texans for America Respond to the
Texas Institute of Letters

James P. Donovan was an attorney from Highland Park, Texas, and worked as legal consultant to Texans for America. What follows is the public testimony he gave before the House Textbook Investigating Committee on January 17, 1962. While J. Evetts Haley preferred that parents select the books their children would use in schools, attorney

168 Chapter 10

Donovan had a different suggestion for more local control of school textbooks. In Donovan's testimony, he noted the process for adopting textbooks in Texas and then proceeded to dwell on the problems he felt were inherent to this process.

> It was my privilege to work in both espionage and counter-espionage, during World War II, both domestically and foreign, in and against the Communist. I might say that in this time of confusion and excitement, in name calling and classification of people by men of the press any of the political lights who are sometimes dazzled perhaps by the brilliance of their own intelligence, who tend to lose face across the world, and we tend to put ourselves in jeopardy by our own attitude. It is not a time for name calling; it is not a time for characterization of philosophies. We have one enemy which Liberal, Conservative, Progressive, Democratic or Republican must face, and that's the Communists. . . .
> [T]he election of the Board of Education at a local level and on the state level, is relevantly unimportant because under the statutes as they now stand, the [State] Commissioner of Education is the only man who can make nominations for the [State] Textbook Committee. Now, when he makes those nominations, they go to the [State] Board of Education for approval. Now, should the Board of Education decide that some of those nominations are not good, that Board has the right to reject the nomination offered . . . then the Commissioner of Education will then submit additional names, so that the actual control and nomination of the members of Textbook Committee in the State of Texas, is in one man. He is the man to pick the persons who can be appointed. No other person has any authority. . . . The local Board of Education has nothing to say, not one word. The only power that the local Board of Education has under our present law, is to make a selection between the minimum three, or maximum five books, that were chosen by the Textbook Committee and approved by the Board of Education. So that it may be in some instances a choice of evil. They have to have the Textbook and whether it's good or bad they have to pick one. They have no alternative.

Liberals versus Conservatives

169

In regard to private citizens obtaining copies of the textbook up for adoption, Donovan elaborated the following:

> [The Textbook Committee] has to be appointed by law on the first of May, and then the Board of Education has to move to approve or reject the list or parts of the list in November, and the books are not put into use until the following September. Now in the period and with the way the system functions (this is not said with criticism of any individual), there is no time or opportunity to get a book and study it and find out what it is; whether it's good; whether it's along the lines that we believe in as a nation. As individuals, we have differences and that's what has made us great, but the system doesn't allow the time for serious and careful study and consideration. Now you will say, these are teachers, specialists in their field; that's true, but there are ninety books and there are fifteen people. You don't get the books; the supply is limited. Even those people don't have the time to cover the problem, and be sure that we are getting the right material. . . . [Instead] of entrusting our future to one man's judgment or fifteen people's judgment, why can it not be sent to the people at the local level? Let these [local school] Boards take the responsibility of examining these books. Make it a matter of law, these are only suggestions, make it a matter of law that they examine them and express their opinions to the State Board and then when they have the consensus of opinion over the State under our form of government, the majority will control and then let's adopt the texts that are right. Now that's one possible solution.

He noted the following about other speakers before the House committee:

> [T]had a great deal of discussion about what is socialism and what is communism. I don't think that anybody can define it from day to day. communism is the most difficult threat in the world. It's very much like a rising snake, getting ready to strike. It will grab and get into the position which is most advantageous, at the moment. The question was asked, "Are there Communists in our unions?" I

would say, "Yes." "Are there Communists in our schools?" I would say, "Yes." "Are there Communists in our Armies?" I would say, "Yes." "Are there Communists in our Federal Departments?" I would say, "Yes," and don't forget that this Communist conspiracy has been in operation since the early 20s, has spread worldwide, and has only one goal. Now you can talk about Communists and Socialists at the theoretical level, but when it gets down to everyday business, be assured that they hope to take you by the philosophy which was long ago established, divide and conquer and bore from within. They are actively participating in this policy now. They will change overnight. They will adopt any patriotic movement and follow it and utilize the people in it. By the same token, they will make fun of and smear and call names anything that is prejudicial to their cause.

Donovan concluded:

[These] are things that I believe are important in our consideration of this matter. I think that this is the only country in the world where men from all walks of life can come here; we've had railroad men, teachers, engineers; doctors, and lawyers here tonight, all interested in the same thing, not in the sense of condemnation, but in the sense of protection. You ask the question, "Are there good books?" Sure, there are good books, but nobody is perfect. This group, Texans for America, has examined books, they have been short on time and, strangely enough under the Texas law . . . the Texans [for America] cannot come in and say, "We recommend this textbook for adoption." That's against the law. You can criticize any text, but you can't say that's a good text taken. Now that's the situation that we are in today.[12]

Apparently never intimidated by anyone, J. Evetts Haley seemed to relish in taking on members of the Texas Institute of Letters. Haley was a former member of the organization and recipient of one of its writing awards. He had been longtime friends with many of its members, including Tinkle, Wardlaw, and Dobie, but they parted ways with him over the censorship issue, as well as Haley's opposition to racial integration and his conservative views on other political, economic, and social issues. With his voice showing great emotion, Haley's presented

Liberals versus Conservatives

his public testimony before both the committee and his former friends regarding the issue of book content:

> I regret the absence of some of the gentlemen [from the Texas Institute of Letters] who testified this afternoon, former associates of mine and erstwhile friends, particularly J. Frank Dobie whom I've known for many years. . . . Texas historian J. Frank Dobie of Austin will head a 21 member group here and for this committee today. . . . Personally, I am a historian, and I've admired J. Frank Dobie in the field of folklore, mythology, in particularly, and he is noted for the fact that he stood up for years for the literary lives of Texans. My only objection is in regard to Dobie is when they start leaving off the authentic. Now, in further respect, personally, may I say gentlemen, that I am a historian. I happened to be with the University of Texas for eight years at least, as a member of the history department at that institution. I happen and I say it without particular pride that it's a matter of industry that I have written some 12 books on Texas history, the valid facts and conclusions of which have never been successfully challenged in the public forum or in court. I am sad to say as a historian, and I would be remiss if I did not say it to you that I think we witnessed today in this room one of the saddest and most significant features in Texas modern education. We saw here a group apparently recruited very largely from the institution on the hill [the University of Texas at Austin], my former alma mater which I am a graduate and I was a member of the history staff, and a group that cheered enthusiastically, a flippant reference that the fact of this is a Christian nation. That is a sad and a significant fact. If this struggle means anything, it means the perpetuation, gentlemen, of the Christian ethic. [Dr. Joseph M. Dawson] who alleged to be a minister referred flippantly to "In God We Trust." Not only that, the Christian ethic is enshrined, as you gentlemen so well know, in governmental form in the Constitution and the Bill of Rights. There is no freedom except under the Christian ethic in this world as enshrined in the Constitution and the Bill of Rights, and that is why we are here today protesting. These books [adopted by the State of Texas] that these youngsters all ordered [have] this false philosophy that holds the man can be free and still not be a Christian. I should like to say further gentleman, this committee, that after seven years on the

faculty of the University [of Texas] I was fired, and I was fired for speaking my honest convictions in the press and in the forum as to what was going on in this country with its Fascist tendencies, and there's not a one of this bunch of bleeding hearts [in the audience] who testified here today who stood up and claimed that I should be protected in my legal rights to speak my mind. Not a one of them. Where were these bleeding hearts? Where were the Dobies and the rest of them when I was being fired from the University of Texas for speaking my honest convictions [in opposition to President Franklin Roosevelt's New Deal]? Where were the youngsters marching in support. They were getting ready to be marched into Germany and into Russia because their rights, your rights, were being defiled and I was being tried for what? For telling the truth. That's the reason, gentlemen, that this is such a tragedy and important issue. It means little to me. I am in essence an old man, but these youngsters have a right to know that in Texas and America with all its great ideals, and you and you alone are being betrayed and you are the ones who should be concerned; not a bunch of old broken down cow punchers. You can just sit here and smile superciliously, but you're being shipped all over the world under military compulsion for what? Ostensibly to fight communism. Now, where is the battlefield? We're drawing it right here in Austin, tonight. Now, there was some illusion to the Texas Institute of Letters. I happened to be a member of the Texas Institute of Letters before the super-sophisticate [Lon Tinkle] here who introduced this matter today was even a member of the thing. I refer to the book editor, of course, of the *Dallas Morning News*. My erstwhile friend of that institution. Where was he? He now is preaching that by some curious and distorted means of reasoning, by some distortion of moral character that every man should and must as they do, have a right to write and to publish. Who better to defend that than Evetts Haley? And yet what do they say? They imply that their right to write and read what they wish presupposes a violation of our right to buy and present to our children what they must read and ponder. This freedom is not a one way street, but what they assume and arrogate to themselves is complete authoritanism— their right, and, of course, they have a right to read and publish what they want. By what distortion gentlemen, of what purvity, do they contend that that right presupposes that they can override

Liberals versus Conservatives

173

my right and your right to force you to buy a book that you don't think your child should read. It happens, too, I'm sure it was just an inadvertent oversight on the part of Lon Tinkle that when I was a member of this group, this Texas Institute of Letters years ago, that I won a thousand dollar reward for a book submitted to history [on Charles Goodnight]. He just inadvertently overlooked that. That book hasn't been challenged yet. It is still on the history shelves, for the delectation and instruction of the children of this state who have pride in their ancestors and pride in themselves. That oversight was of little moment except that I want to point out that I am no longer a member of the Institute of Letters. And when Lon Tinkle got up here and laid down the predicate that anything should be written even when it trespasses moral grounds, they lost Evetts Haley from the Institute of Letters. And I've not been back, and I'm not going back. That is the sort of flux that's here today. These long haired super-intellectuals who are trying to preach to us that they have a right—of course they've got right— to write all the filth they want, but by what right do they have, what right can they have to force the people of Texas to buy and feed it to their children? There never was a more authoritarian dirty-doctrine preaching than this bunch that paraded here today, and I have known them for 30 long years. Where were they turning their shirts when I was being kicked out of the University of Texas for speaking what I honestly believed?

Gentlemen, there are some other things but I want to draw just one very formal illustration as to what this arrogance on the part of Lon Tinkle and Frank Dobie and Frank Wardlaw and the rest of them presupposes. You saw Lon Tinkle stand right here today and say that they have the right, anyone must have the right, to write and preach and say anything he wants. Let me draw a homily of somewhat crude illustration. What if Lon Tinkle is a firm be-liever in homosexuality and the alleged pleasure thereof? Does Lon Tinkle have a right then to write into his book or into any article the alleged pleasure in the process of homosexuality and pass that on to our children? Under his sweeping dictum, he does, but there happens to be a law on the State of Texas books that makes ho-mosexuality and sodomy a crime. Now where does freedom, your so-called academic freedom which your bunch out here on the hill [the University of Texas]—your left-wingers out there so love to

174   Chapter 10

preach. I'm talking to you folks, you young folks [students at the University of Texas who were in the audience], where does freedom stop and morality start in? Where does license start in and the destruction of Christian morality end? That's the issue here. That should be enough to express the most supercilious who sat there and grin at this thing that this is serious business and when not any of you don't think it isn't, and if it's practiced on anybody in my family, you're gonna find out it's serious business, and the district attorney can put it on the docket now.

But there are other serious matters. Who is trying to censor what? Who is trying to censor what? It's perfectly all right according to the distorted and the crooked and the devious in the dishonest reasoning that's been paraded here tonight for anybody to write anything he wants to, but if you don't want to buy it, and I'm talking about the people of Texas, if we don't want to buy it for our children, that is censorship. That is bad. Freedom can't be a one-way street. All we want is not censorship. We want the right of free choice. And the right of free choice should extend to what we read or what we're willing to pay for. We should certainly grant that. Even the fat-heads at the University of Texas should wake up to that.[13]

Haley criticized Dobie for defending the Civil Rights Congress (CRC), which opposed racial segregation. The CRC also had its lawyers defend African Americans and American communists the organization deemed unjustly persecuted by any segment of the American government. Haley then basically repeated many of the same criticisms he made about the Boller-Tilford book before the State Textbook Committee on September 14, 1961, and the State Board of Education on November 13, 1961.

When Haley finished, Rep. John Alaniz asked him, "You object to the mentioning of social classes in these [history] books?" Haley said, "Yes," because a lack of social class was "why your people and mine came to this country." Alaniz waited about fifteen seconds and then in a monotone said, "Part of my people were here already." Even Haley's supporters laughed at that.[14]

Haley also would later refer to Dobie as "the doddering old daddy of the do-gooders."[15] Rep. Bob Bass went further and claimed that Dobie brought with him to the hearings a group of "beatnik" University of Texas students, with his only interest being to destroy the House textbook investigation.[16]

The Controversy Continues

The debate over the censorship of library books continued. In a report from Rep. Bob Bass regarding the findings of the 1962 Texas House of Representatives Textbook Investigating Committee, he noted, "It is obvious that the trend is toward socialism in many of the books used in the Texas public schools. We now have to take the poison out of the textbooks, and they're full of it. This country is heading toward socialism just as fast as we can, and they are trying to teach it through the books of our youth. There is too much socialism in the school textbooks." Bass was also especially concerned, for example, with McKinley Kantor's Pulitzer-winning *Andersonville*, which he felt should not be in public school libraries, declaring, "To be specific, I don't want any sex teaching in the schools."[17]

Bass went on to urge authors and publishers to devote considerable time and effort to improving the materials contained in their textbooks—particularly those used for the study of economics.[18] He also proposed a bill (which his fellow legislators in the legislature failed to act upon), providing "that no public school librarian or similar official shall permit literature containing obscene language to be deposited in the library by which he or she is employed" and that those "failing to remove such literature on orders from the school board should be subject to a fine between $50–200."[19]

The controversy between the Texas Institute of Letters and Texans for America also elicited a quick response from some other groups. One was the American Studies Association, which repudiated and condemned "such organizations as the Minute Women, the John Birch Society, the Communist Party, Texans for America, and any organization which attempts to subvert American values or destroy American institutions." The ASA added, "We invite all citizens to join with us in pledging allegiance to the faith of our Founding Fathers and to our American heritage of freedom, independence, and justice guaranteed by the due process of law." It also defended its "confidence in the personal

176   Chapter 10

integrity and professional competence of Dr. Paul Boller, Professor of American History at Southern Methodist University, and in Dr. J. Frank Dobie of Austin, one of Texas' most distinguished men of letters" and recommended to the Texas Education Agency and state officials that "in the future textbooks be adopted by competent members of the teaching profession unhampered by efforts of unqualified laymen to impose their professional prejudices upon our professions."[20]

The Texas Library Association also responded to Representative Bass and other members of the House Textbook Investigating Committee, issuing its own protest of the charges raised against textbook authors and their publishers, while also decrying the removal and censorship of library books. It stated it was "unalterably opposed to extra-legal, irresponsible attempts by self-appointed censors to discredit a book or other printed publications or its author through unfair quotations out of context; misrepresentation; substitution of personal bias for qualified opinion from competent authorities; guilt by association; character assassination; and other odious devices foreign to the spirit of American democracy and fair play."[21]

That was not all. A parting criticism of Texans for America came from John Howard Griffin, writing in the summer of 1962 issue of the *Southwest Review*. He argued:

> [E]xamination of the objections of Texans for America demonstrated that the group rarely questions the truth of the historians' findings. No, they object to points of emphasis, inclusion, and exclusion. One can pick almost any work to pieces in this manner. They demand that textbooks be slanted toward purely "nationalistic history." They require the historian to alter or "edit" historical facts to conform to their group prejudices. If he does not, he will suffer character defamation and possible financial reprisals. This could become a punitive form of censorship if it caused the product of years of work to be nullified.

He added:

> [W]hat about the young? Are high-school students really subverted by so-called "four-letter obscenities" that they have heard all their lives? Are they really so fragile they cannot take nourishment

from truths that make other men strong? Will they not later resent and completely distrust their education when they discover it was designed as a therapy? Will they not feel cheated that truths were deliberately kept from them? Will this not turn that cheaply-sponsored patriotism into no patriotism at all?[22]

Finally, an editorial in the *Corpus Christi Caller Times* was even more blunt when it charged:

[The House Textbook Investigating Committee] has turned into a sounding board for extremists based against the United Nations, foreign aid, respect for civil rights in combatting communism, public welfare programs, and the course of federal policy generally over the past generation. . . . It has treated professional educators and experts in the fields covered by history and social science textbooks as hostile, not to say suspect witnesses. There is no wonder that moderates, respectable civic leaders, and others likely to represent a community consensus on the matter have strayed away from its hearings in droves. If there is any one indisputable essential to sound textbook selection it is that the system should be strictly nonpolitical.[23]

That the 1962 debate over social studies content for the Texas public schools was far from over. New voices, new testimonies, and new objections were raised. Then some heavy hitters added to the melee: Norma and Mel Gabler joined with Texans for America and the Texas Society of the Daughters of the American Revolution, offering their public testimony before the House Textbook Investigating Committee. The Gablers eventually became two of America's most prominent conservative textbook critics of the mid- to late twentieth century.

11

Conservative Uprising

Mel and Norma Gabler
Join the Fray

WHEN MEL and Norma Gabler first testified before the Texas House of Representatives Textbook Investigating Committee on January 24 and 31, 1962, little did they or anyone else realize the couple would become the most well-known American textbook critics of the twentieth century. Norma, a housewife, had a high school education, and Mel, who served in the US Army in the Azores during World War II and worked for Exxon Mobil, had one year of college. As a result, few felt they were properly qualified to evaluate textbooks for schools. Nevertheless, they raised their concerns as citizens in a pluralistic society, on a conservative platform of family values and moral decency.

The Gablers Voice Their Concerns

The Gablers became involved in textbook issues when their oldest son complained to them that he felt something was wrong in his 1956 American history book, *Our Nation's Story* (Laidlaw Brothers). Upon close examination, Mel and Norma disagreed with certain elements of the book. For example, they felt the text (and textbooks in general) should include more information about the Pilgrims and American heroes such as George Washington, Nathan Hale, and Patrick Henry. Like many conservative critics, they were fans of Barnes's 1885 *A Brief History of*

Conservative Uprising 179

the United States and favored earlier works such as Rev. Parson Weems's book about George Washington and the cherry tree episode, along with the McGuffey Readers. These older publications depicted a heroic age that the Gablers felt would inspire patriotism in students. Additionally, the Gablers felt *Our Nation's Story* devoted too much space to coverage of the twentieth century.[1]

With their increasing interest in education reform, for their public testimony before the Texas House of Representatives Textbook Investigating Committee in 1962, the Gablers acquired copies of textbook reviews from such conservative groups as Texans for America and the Texas Society of the Daughters of the American Revolution—reviews both groups had used when protesting the social studies books considered for Texas adoption during the fall of 1961. Armed with this material, the Gablers submitted a twenty-six-page report containing 273 specific objections about history textbook content before the Texas House of Representatives Textbook Investigating Committee. Their report concerned nine of the textbooks already approved by public school personnel of the Texas State Textbook Committee and adopted by the Texas State Board of Education in 1961. Those textbooks were *American History* (Ginn), *This Is Our Nation* (Webster), *Rise of the American Nation* (Harcourt), *The American People* (Row Peterson), *History of a Free People* (Macmillan), *The History of Our World* (Houghton Mifflin), *Men and Nations* (Harcourt), *This Is America's Story* (Houghton Mifflin), *Story of Nations* (Holt), and *The Record of Mankind* (Heath), in addition to *Our Nation's Story* (1956), which was not up for adoption in 1961 but also had been protested by Texans for America and Texas Society of the Daughters of the American Revolution. In essence, the main concerns of the Gablers about those textbooks were the same as those that had been raised by Texans for America and the Texas Society of the Daughters of the American Revolution before the State Textbook Committee on September 14, 1961.[2]

On January 31, 1962, Mel Gabler offered a summary of what he and his wife firmly believed when he told the House Textbook Investigating Committee:

> To the vast majority of Americans, the terms "values" and "morals" mean one thing, and one thing only, and that is the Christian-Judeo

morals, values and standards as given to us by God through His Word written in the Ten Commandments and the Bible. . . . After all, according to history these ethics have prescribed the only code by which civilizations can effectively remain in existence. . . . The fact that our nation was founded on Christian principles is badly slighted [in the history textbooks]. The great Christian heritage of our nation seems of no concern of the [textbook] authors.[3]

Determined to have a lasting impact on education reform, the Gablers continued their search, reviewing virtually every new textbook produced in 1962. Mel posited: "Kids become what they're taught and textbooks mold nations because they largely determine how a nation votes. If you don't tell students what's right and wrong, you have anarchy. Why shouldn't we fight? It's our children, our tax money, and our government. And it's our rights that are being violated." He continued:

The public school system of this country has . . . [become] a propaganda agency to support the projects, campaigns, crusades, ideas, and personal philosophies of a self-appointed group of educators that now asserts the right to dominate and control that system. There is no place in that system for individuals desiring to use their position or authority to promote any New Deal, Square Deal, Fair Deal, Re-Deal, or any other kind of Deal. It is a violation of our constitutional rights to make the public school system an instrument for the dissemination in the community. The parents of the children of America have a right to a public school system where the instruction is based upon the truth. They have the right to oppose any and all school programs and activities where propaganda is substituted for the truth. . . . We want the schools to return to the basic academic skills rather than to go about changing values. There are better ways to spend classroom time than by examining student's emotions and thoughts, and other trivial matters . . . Every publisher will sell good, bad, or questionable books. They're out to sell-they don't care what's in 'em. Those who bring textbook content to the public's attention are often referred to as "textbook censors." However, this is not true. Traditional American values are now being censored from textbooks even before they reach the reviewer.

The Gablers felt that "until textbooks are changed, there is not possibility that crime, violence, VD, and abortion rates will do anything but continue to climb. Textbooks mold nations because textbooks largely determine how a nation votes, what it becomes and where it goes." They wanted textbooks to stress the importance of the free enterprise economic system, emphasizing the disadvantages of socialism, communism, and big government. They also opposed alternative or critical interpretations of history, which they felt had a negative connotation. At the time, new principles and ideas were being raised in mathematics, and the Gablers feared the "New Math" spillover, arguing that when a student "reads in a math book that there are no absolutes, suddenly every value he's been taught is destroyed—And the next thing you know the student turns to crime and drugs."

They opposed materials that sanctioned permissive child-rearing, one-worldism, the occult, role playing and sensitivity training, or the benefits of insulin for diabetics, since such material "is instilling in student minds that the term 'drug' refers to a beneficial product." In addition, they felt textbooks placed too much emphasis on the Elastic Clause of the US Constitution. Mel wondered "why the story of *Uncle Tom's Cabin* should take up space in a history book that makes no mention at all of the story of Francis Scott Key and 'The Star Spangled Banner,' or the story of Nathan Hale."

In addition, the Gablers also raised the following concerns:

1. They wanted the less emphasis on the rights of federal authority over the rights of states with more emphasis on the importance of the Ninth and Tenth Amendments to the US Constitution.

2. They opposed the federalism of Pres. Franklin Roosevelt's New Deal programs during the Great Depression, as well as Pres. Harry Truman's Fair Deal and Pres. John F. Kennedy's domestic programs—regarding all of them as Fabian socialism or creeping socialism. They also felt that "socialism is preferred in most of the economic books."

3. They felt that US membership in the United Nations caused America to give up its national sovereignty to a world organization.

182 Chapter 11

4. They wanted phonics taught along with other reading techniques in language arts classes.

5. They felt depicting the problems of American society, such as treatment of such issues as American Indians, child labor, or that of massive unemployment during the Great Depression of 1929–41 left a negative image for students, which would "only succeed in raising doubts about our [economic, social and political] system." As for American slavery, they felt too much information about it was included in the history books, since slavery "has long been eliminated."

6. They opposed the adoption of any history book if it "devotes too much space to the Vietnam War, Watergate and farmworker Cesar Chavez, while leaving out temperance leader Carry Nation."

7. They asserted that "with no absolute values considered, a seed of doubt about the firmness and validity of traditional values is planted each time a choice of alternatives is made. Value clarification programs are based on the anti-Judeo-Christian ethic of humanistic relativism. It places students adrift with no fixed moral values or guidelines."

8. They argued that Christianity should be stressed in social studies texts and claimed, "Our nation was founded on Christian principles and has a rich Christian heritage" and "the Ten Commandments . . . are the basis for most law."

9. They wanted texts to depict a "traditional" American family with father, mother, and children, the father having the dominate role in the family, and opposed any mention of gay marriage.

10. They opposed women's liberation or the equal rights movement, which Mel said had "totally distorted male and female roles, making the women masculine and the men effeminate" and felt pay equity between men and women could occur only if women "abandoned their highest professions as mothers molding young lives."

11. In a number of interviews, such as on the television program *Textbooks on Trial*, the Gablers disapproved of stressing contributions of minorities, such as Rosa Parks, who Mel

Conservative Uprising

called "a lesser known person" over what he claimed were more worthy contributions by "the great men" who truly made significant contributions to America.

12. They wanted curriculum to stress patriotism, respect, courtesy from all students, a dress code, and strict discipline.

13. In the tradition of Rev. J. Frank Norris, a prominent mid-twentieth century antievolutionist and anti-Communist, the Gablers wanted creation science—a fundamentalist Christian belief of a literal interpretation of the creation story in the first chapter of Genesis, with the universe being only about six thousand years old—taught in science courses along with scientific explanations of evolution. They felt the theory of evolution had too much evidence against it and feared the teaching of evolution would lead students to become secular humanists.

14. They felt that "[a]llowing a student to come to his own conclusions about abstracts and concepts creates frustration. Ideas, situation ethics, values, anti-God humanism—that's what the schools are teaching. And concepts. Well, a concept will never do anyone as much good as a fact."

15. They suspected at least some textbook authors active in the civil rights movement might be possibly associated with subversive organizations or have ties to Communist front groups.

16. The Gablers preferred home schooling to public schooling or students attending fundamentalist Christian schools but had some reservations about schools involved in a state-funded voucher system.

17. They opposed any kind of progressive education, such as that promoted by philosopher John Dewey.

18. They opposed any sex education programs except those that stressed only abstinence.

A more detailed philosophy of the Gablers appears in their *What Are They Teaching Our Children? What You Can Do about Humanism and Textbooks in Today's Public Schools* (Victor Books, 1985), and James

C. Hefley's *Textbooks on Trial* (Victor Books, 1976) and *Are Textbooks Harming Our Children: Norma and Mel Gabler Take Action and Show You How!* (Mott Media, 1979).[4]

After presenting their testimony before the Texas House of Representatives Textbook Investigating Committee in 1962, the Gablers established the nonprofit Educational Research Analysts Corporation in Longview, Texas. Mel retired early from his job at Exxon Mobil, and the Gablers took no salary for their work with their corporation, instead accepting a $300 honorarium plus expenses for their speaking services. After 1962, and before their health began to fail by the late 1990s, they appeared before the Texas State Textbook Committee and the Texas State Board of Education every year to protest textbook programs on subjects in the K–12 curriculum.[5]

When the Gablers became more experienced with their textbook evaluations, one journalist noted they "brought their supporters to public comment portions of the [Texas] State Board of education meetings unrolling their 'scroll of shame,' which listed objections they had to the content of the current reading material." One scroll was fifty-four feet in length.[6]

As social studies programs became more extensive by the 1980s, new ones began to be written by committees composed of various writers, in-house publishing staff members, editors, and outside consultants helping produce the programs. Different groups were enlisted to write the teacher guides, testing programs, and any auxiliary materials, editing what professional historians, political scientists, economists, and so forth had written in the original drafts for each textbook program. Thus textbook programs were produced via curriculum composition endeavors by various committees. The result was that some parts of the programs contained obvious errors, with one even positing that Pres. Harry Truman had dropped the atomic bomb during the Korean War— an error no professional historian would have made. Errors such as these provided the Gablers and their reviewers with more ammunition.[7]

Once the Gablers became more widely known as textbook critics, they also regularly made their concerns known to members of the Texas State Board of Education, regardless of the political composition of the board. One scholar of the textbook adoption process in Texas noted that over the years the Gablers became "quite influential through their

Conservative Uprising 185

personal relationships with a number of Board members. One SBOE member acknowledged the Gablers worked toward this end. 'We received letters, primarily from the protestors who came [to the hearing] on a regular basis. Some of them, particularly the Gablers, would call around and talk to everybody trying to influence their vote.'"[8]

The Gablers also became effective in urging others to carefully read the "questioned" parts of textbooks they planned to protest. To assist interested protestors, the Gablers told "their followers they do not have to read entire books—only the 'questioned' parts. And to find the 'questioned' parts, the would-be censors have only to refer to the Gabler-distributed reviews." Thus concerned citizens used the Gabler reviews to underscore the "questioned" parts from textbooks, "making it appear as if [they had] read the books [in entirety] before protesting them."[9]

By the end of the twentieth-century, the Gablers had made presentations coast to coast and in Canada, Australia, and New Zealand. American, Canadian, Australian, New Zealand, French, British, and Japanese broadcasting companies filmed them, and they appeared on CBS's *60 Minutes*, ABC's *20/20* and *World News Tonight*, various PBS programs, NBC's *Today Show*, *The Phil Donahue Show*, William F. Buckley's *Firing Line*, Jerry Falwell's *Old Time Gospel Hour*, Pat Robinson's CNN show *Crossfire*, and other television and radio talk shows. Additionally, the Gablers were featured in *Time*, *Newsweek*, *Reader's Digest*, *People*, *Parade*, *Christianity Today*, *US News and World Report*, *Texas Monthly*, the *Wall Street Journal*, the *New York Times*, the *Chicago Tribune*, the *Atlanta Journal*, the *Baltimore Sun*, and many other print media sources.[10]

For their efforts, the Gablers received the Texas Good Citizenship Medal from the Sons of the American Revolution, Texas Senate Awards of Appreciation in 1975 and 1999, various high-profile awards from conservative groups like the Texas Freedom Forum, and a Congress of Freedom Award (ten times). Endorsement for the Gablers came from conservative individuals and groups such as Jerry Falwell and the Moral Majority, Phyllis Schlafly's Eagle Forum, the Committee for the Survival of a Free Congress, the Texas Pro-Family Forum, and Texas governor Rick Perry. Another honor came on May 7, 1999, from the conservative Republican–dominated Texas State Board of Education, in the form of a resolution to "honor and commend Mel and Norma Gabler . . . for thirty-eight years of sacrificial service both in textbook review and in

186 Chapter 11

the textbook adoption process in textbook decisions made in Texas and elsewhere," which thanked the Gablers for "critiquing textbooks and . . . alerting parents . . . concerning textbook errors, omissions, contradictions, and detours."

After falling at his home and suffering a brain hemorrhage, Mel Gabler, age ninety, died on December 17, 2004. Norma Gabler, age eighty-four, died on July 22, 2007. Neal Frey, the Gablers' senior textbook analyst, became the head of their Education Research Analysts organization and continued their work.[11]

Mel Gabler's testimony before the Texas House of Representatives Textbook Investigating Committee on January 31, 1962, was very lengthy, but in essence it argued the following:

> I'm here in opposition to the censorship of our textbooks. Censorship eliminates one or more viewpoints leaving only the viewpoint desired by the censor. Continued study of the textbooks which have been restricted to the censor's viewpoint will result in the gradual indoctrination of the students. Over a period of years, an entire nation can be indoctrinated in this manner. There are of course exceptions, and in certain subjects there is only one viewpoint worthy of discussion; that is to the decent and honorable people. Morals, for example. A book for grammar school children should be limited to morality of equality for which our nation should aspire. And I believe that you all agree with me that only an anti-American would want the morals of our school children defaced. Before I continue with my testimony, I would like to explain the reasons for my concerns. As little as just a number of months ago, I was like most parents—kids brought the books home from school—we never opened the cover. Didn't look at 'em.[12]

Then Gabler recounted an incident when his thirteen-year-old son came home from school and told him, "There's something wrong with this book." He continued:

> I just shrugged it off because I had so much confidence in our educational system, I didn't believe there could be anything wrong with the book. Then, of course, I began reading and hearing just

Conservative Uprising

a little bit about the books. Then, last summer I read about the hearings here. Then, this fall when my older boy got to the 11th grade, the first thing you know, he comes home and says "Daddy, there's something wrong with this book." By that time, we were concerned enough to finally open the book, like we should have done to begin with—actually, we should have been looking at those books all these years. Because after all, they are our children. It is our tax money that's educating the children, and I think we as parents should be concerned about that.

Gabler then made a point of stressing he was not an authority on history, but added:

I am very much concerned about the trend that any person that would look about him can see what is happening in our nation. Now there's a lot of people who could be here and do a better job than I am, but since I'm here, I'm going to do the best that I can. Now I mentioned I'm not an authority on textbooks and textbooks are written by authorities so the first thing is why can you see something wrong with a textbook when an authority can't?

He then posited:

If an ordinary person like me can see that something is wrong with a book, then it's mighty obvious that somebody that writes that book and knows better is doing that on purpose. He's bound to, and you've heard enough testimony here today to see that the books are slanted. Now I thought, as I said, I was so naïve that I thought history was history but I found out that it can be written to transmit the viewpoint of the author regardless of the subject material. Getting back to my opposition of censorship in textbooks, those of us who want decent books are sometimes saying we want the books censored. No. What we want is the stoppage of the censorship because most of the books . . .

One, censored of much that is patriotic.

Two, many of them have been censored of practically all of the Christian precepts upon which our nation was founded.

188   Chapter 11

Third, they have been censored of much about the fact that the early settlers came to our land to find freedom, particularly religious freedom.

Four, censored to the fact that our nation prospered so greatly because of our free enterprise system because we didn't have the shackles of collectivism which has held other nations down and what proponents of our slanted textbooks seem to want forced on our nation.

Fifth, censored of the character building and features of old textbooks. For instance, you heard a whole lot about the McGuffey Readers in recent years. Right? Our books have been censored of much of the character building features we used to have.

Sixth, many of them have been censored of the fact that many of the government programs of recent years are so generously described in these books are actually nothing but Fabian Socialism. [that is to promote the principles of socialism by gradual and reformist means instead of by revolution.] That is socialism in disguise. You don't dare call it socialism, but it amounts to the same thing. More and more government control. More and more government functions to get more and more government control. And to put big government, big brother government, in a good light.

Seven. Censored to the fact that many of the persons given under outside references are individuals with many anti-American affiliations.

Eight. Censored to the true facts regarding Pearl Harbor, the fall of China, the fact that we stopped for two weeks on the banks of the Elbe so that Russia could occupy East Germany and so forth.

Nine. Censored to the fact that we must give up patriotism for our country in direct proportion to the allegiance we give to internationalism.

Ten. Censored to the fact that the location of the U. N. in our country is a communist criminal conspiracy almost unlimited opportunity for spying with diplomatic immunity.

Eleven. Censored to the fact that during the years since the formation of the U. N., there has been more aggression than during any other period of history. For example, there were one-fourth of a billion persons under the iron control of communism when the U. N. was born. Today there are approximately one billion.

Gabler concluded:

> [I want] to remind that books which give only a one sided view cannot help but influence our children and in this case, influence them away from the very precepts on which our nation was founded. Now we'll agree that there are people who like these books. That'll include those with liberal socialist leanings, those who favor internationalism over nationalism, those who favor powerful centralized government over the rights of individuals and states, and those who favor a one-world government in preference to our own nation. Now this type of person will be favorable to these newly adopted history books.[13]

When Mel Gabler finished his public testimony, he proceeded to engage in the following dialogue with Rep. John Alaniz:

> Representative Alaniz: "Gabler, are you against the government owning anything. You said in your opinion that communism was state owned of everything?"
>
> Gabler: "[The state owning a business is] included in communism . . . No, not anything. Just to abide by our Constitution and own what the Constitution says the federal government can; not go out and own things and do things that the Constitution doesn't give us the leeway to do, because it can't. The 10th Amendment very clearly limits federal functions named in the Constitution. We'll just use the 10th Amendment, and I'm afraid that most of these textbook writers have just more or less ignored it because some of them don't hardly mention the Bill of Rights, and those that do usually give about five of the Bill of Rights, but I haven't found any of the new ones that even list the 10th Amendment."
>
> Representative Alaniz: "And it's important. [Alaniz then proceeded to tell Gabler that the federal government runs the US Postal Service and asked if that was communism and a violation of the Constitution.]"

Gabler: "Well not the federal Constitution although it's a possibility that private enterprise could run the post office better."

Representative Alaniz: "Among other things in San Antonio the city owns the water board, the transit company, the electric system and some districts own schools. What was wrong with that?"

Gabler: "Well, I don't know where you put the complete distinction. There's a certain amount of ownership that's necessary to transact the business of the nation. It's a matter of when continually we try to educate children to want more and more federal control; more and more federal function because the encroachment on private enterprise or individual freedom increases as government functions increase."

Representative Alaniz: "[Do you favor] keeping Christian principles in the public schools?"

Gabler: "I think that they should be mentioned because I did not read in the interest of time part of a speech by J. Edgar Hoover in which he says the nations that emphasize God do not have the moral problems that nations do that skip the glorification of God."

Representative Alaniz: "What denomination of Christianity should be taught in the public schools?"

Gabler: "I don't think we should teach any particular denomination, but we could at least in our history books refer to the fact that the nation was founded on Christian principles where the introduction of some of these books don't even mention that they came here for religious freedom. In other words, it's just a strictly materialistic view point that's given in most of these books. What I'm saying is we should acknowledge the fact that we do have a Christian heritage. I don't mean we ought to teach religion in school, but we should acknowledge that we as a nation were founded on basic Christian principles."[14]

A Response to the Gablers

A response to the Gablers came from Dr. William Martin, the Harry and Hazel Chavanne Emeritus Professor of Religion and Public Policy in the

Conservative Uprising
191

department of sociology at Rice University and a Senior Fellow for Religion and Public Policy at the James A. Baker III Institute for Public Policy at Rice University. He received BA and MA degrees in Biblical Studies from Abilene Christian University, a Bachelor of Divinity degree from the Harvard Divinity School, and a PhD in Religion and Society from Harvard University. One of his areas of specialization is religious fundamentalism and its impact on politics. He is the author of numerous scholarly articles on religious fundamentalism for such publications as *The Atlantic Monthly*, *Harper's*, *Esquire*, *Texas Monthly*, and *Foreign Policy*, in addition to numerous books, such as *A Prophet with Honor: The Billy Graham Story* (William Morrow, 1991), *With God on Our Side: The Rise of the Religious Right in America* (Broadway Books, 1996, 2005), as a coauthor, *With God on Their Side: Religion and American Foreign Policy in Twentieth Century America* (Woodrow Wilson Center / Johns Hopkins University Press, 2003).[15]

For the November 1982 issue of *Texas Monthly*, Dr. Martin wrote an article entitled "The Guardians Who Slumberth Not," the result of his in-depth interviews with Mel and Norma Gabler. Known for his writings and research about the Religious Right, Dr. Martin concluded the following about the Gablers and their desire to improve education as they saw fit:

> If we assume, as seems justified, that Mel and Norma Gabler do indeed wield sizeable influence over American education, what are we to make of them and that circumstance? I found them to be courteous, pleasant, good-natured people who are earnestly, honestly, and unselfishly committed to helping the young obtain what they regard as the best possible education. I found myself applauding their concern, admiring their dedication, and agreeing with a number of their objections to specific texts. Yet I believe their crusade, if successful, will have a devastatingly negative effect on American education and culture.
>
> To begin with, their attack on humanism as an evil spell that has been cast over Western civilization—an attack in which they are joined by most of their New Right colleagues—is dangerously misleading. There are a few people who fit the New Right image of a humanist, who are indeed antireligious atheists and who blaspheme on the side. But for most people whom the New Right

lumps into the secular humanist category, humanism is not a religion but an approach to the world. It is not, I think, an inherently reprehensible approach. It conceives of humans as having capacities of reason, mind, and will that far exceed those of other creatures and endow them with a singular dignity. It values diversity of opinion and rejects imposed or authoritarian approaches to knowledge, such as appeals to tradition of Scripture or other ostensibly revealed truth, in favor of free and critical inquiry, scientific methods, and individual and collective reflection. It maintains that to deserve our allegiance, beliefs about the world, society, and humanity should be based on—and not contradict—available evidence. It is skeptical of all claims to ultimate truth, because it has learned that not all the evidence is in.

In education, this humanistic approach does not seek to ply children with pot, pills, pornography, and polymorphous perversity. Rather, it strives to instill in them habits of mind and qualities of spirit that will include a love for knowledge, a depth and breadth of understanding, an ability to think well and critically for themselves, a belief in their essential worthiness and in that of others, and a desire and ability to work for the common good. It is not only part of the heritage of Western civilization, it is one of its best parts, and those who lump humanities into the same category as robbers, murderers, perverts, and "other treacherous individuals" as prominent New Right leaders have done, are guilty at best of serious ignorance and at worst of slander and immorality of a contemptible sort in which Jews and Christians and other men and women of goodwill and integrity should have no part. . . .

The shortcomings of the Gablers' view of education—as a process by which young people are indoctrinated with facts certified to be danger-free, while being protected from exposure to information that might challenge orthodox interpretations—can be seen by looking at three areas: history, science, and the social sciences. One may or may not agree with the particular objections the Gablers make to various history books, but it is clear that they are oblivious to the idea that the writing of history has never been, nor can it ever be, factual in any pure sense. Those who provided eyewitness accounts and other records with which historians work were engaged in interpretation, not only in adjusting the light under which they chose to display the materials they dissembled but even in their selection of events, dates, and people from the infinite possibilities open to them. And to imagine that they or anyone else engaging in the historical enterprise does so free of the influence of his or her values, perceptions, and ideological biases is to believe something no reputable historian has believed for generations.

The Gablers seem incapable of considering the possibility that a textbook might meet their criteria of fairness, objectivity, and patriotism and still be critical of any aspect of American life. To bend a metaphor, it is as if they hoped that by refusing to acknowledge the existence of new materials, techniques, social conditions, and fashions, they might somehow persuade the emperor to keep wearing his comfortable, if somewhat threadbare, old clothes. To be sure, new versions of history may be inferior to earlier ones. But with free inquiry each new construction can be examined for accuracy, adequacy, method, logic, and insight. When orthodoxy is the only criterion, there can be no search for the broader, deeper, more lasting truths that make men and women and children free.

Efforts by the Gablers and other fundamentalist Christians to negate the teaching of evolution are probably even more detrimental to the educational process and the long-term welfare of the country. Fundamentalists typically belittle evolution as mentalists typically belittle evolution as "just a theory, not a fact," as if theories are mere speculations or guesses dreamed up by scientists in idle moments. As scientists use the term, however, a theory is a description of natural phenomena, based on long observation and, if possible, experimentation. To obtain the status of theory— as in cell theory, quantum theory, and the theories of gravitation and relativity—these descriptions must be supported by an abundance of evidence that has been critically examined, argued over, and organized into what is regarded as the best explanation for the phenomena in question, or one of a very small number of competitors. Evolution is such a theory. Creationism is not.

Millions of fundamentalist Christians believe in sudden creation and a young earth because that appears to be required by a literal reading of Genesis. Other millions of Christians regard the Genesis account of creation not as a scientific description of the origins of the earth and humankind but as a religious story —a myth, if you insist—whose purpose is to affirm the belief that behind the universe is God. Other cultures have comparable stories. This one is ours. It is a fine story, perhaps "true" in some ultimate sense, but it should not be asked to bear the weight of a scientific theory, because it cannot. Creationists can mount a case that sounds impressive to a layperson and can sometimes score points against scientists unaccustomed to defending their views in-public-debates or on radio and television talk shows. But when they tackle true scientists who are on to their game, as in the Arkansas creationist trial[s] [*Susan Epperson v. Arkansas; McLean v. Arkansas* or Scopes II; and *Edwards v. Aguillard*, which ruled that states cannot approve laws which forbid the teaching of evolution in public schools or allow scientific creationism as a religious belief to be part of a public school's science curriculum], they lose, and they lose because creationism is neither demonstrable fact nor theory but a religious belief that .runs counter to available evidence. The case for creationism is not made by people who have had any noticeable impact as scientists. As the Arkansas trial revealed, no reputable scientific journal has published an article espousing scientific creationism. Moreover, several leading spokesmen of creationism claim doctoral degrees from institutions that, if they exist at all, are unaccredited. . . .

The Gablers' attack on moral and cultural relativism is aimed primarily at the social sciences. Without question, the loss of certainty engendered by opening windows on a wider world can be distressing. It is probably true, as many social commentators have observed, that civilizations work better when there is consensus on basic values, and that some of our most pressing social problems—crime, for example—are closely related to a breakdown of such consensus. We have, since at least the sixties, experienced a crisis of values that has led to a crisis of legitimation in which we have withdrawn from basic institutions—family, schools, business, government, and religion—the confidence and trust we once granted them, replacing those attitudes with skepticism, cynicism, and hostility. This is not a benign development, and the upsurge of evangelical religion, the Moral Majority, the Coalition for Better Television, Educational Research Analysts, and other manifestations of conservative ideology is a reaction to it.

One of the great challenges facing our society—and there is no guarantee that we will meet it successfully—is to reestablish a bal-

Conservative Uprising

ance between adherence to a set of basic values and acceptance of individual and cultural variation. I appreciate the Gablers' desire to participate in that effort. I do not, however, think we will be well served by believing that either Longview or Houston is the center of the universe, that all flags should be red, white, and blue, or that "Jesus Saves" should be adopted as the international anthem. We live in a multicultural world—something children learn very early, mainly from television but also from newspapers, from movies, and, particularly in large cities, from their neighbors and schoolmates. If we cannot learn to accept that fact and its profound implications, which social scientists are committed to explore and explain, we may not be able to keep our world.

A final quarrel I have with the Gablers is their contribution to a growing climate of censorship. In the two years since the New Right's impressive show of muscle in November 1980, complaints to the American Library Association about attempts to remove or restrict access to materials in classrooms and libraries have risen by more than 300 percent. As one consequence, some teachers admit that they avoid introducing anything controversial into their classes, or they tape class discussions that might conceivably be misconstrued, or they teach material that is no longer relevant or in which they do not believe, simply to keep from losing their jobs or being hassled by unhappy parents.

As noted earlier, the Gablers claim they are not censors because they do not try to say what can be published. They also object to being judged by a double standard. "When we try to get changes made," Norma said, "it's called censorship. When minorities and feminists do the same thing, nobody complains." But whether regarding them as censors or as honest competitors in the marketplace of ideas, their critics have become increasingly vocal. . . .

I have three children. Two are now grown men; my daughter entered the eleventh grade this fall. My wife and I have attempted for over two decades to expose them to a kind of education and cultural experience that is radically different from that endorsed by the Gablers. And yet they have mastered basic skills, they have good values, they work hard, they know a great deal, they think exceptionally well, and they have made solid contributions to the varied groups in which they have participated. They are not perfect, but they please me enormously. What is more, I have taught thousands of young people who have experienced a similar kind of education and who seem to me to be, well, almost as promising as my own offspring.

It may not be possible to prove that an open mind is better than a closed one, or that the proper antidote to a bad idea is not censorship but a good idea, or that a society in which some questions are never answered may be preferable to one in which some answers are never questioned, but I believe these things to be true. I not only believe them; I have bet my life on them.[16]

As the Gablers and Martin alike continued their respective work, the debate over what content should be included in Texas social studies programs would continue, with contrasting philosophies put forth by both conservative and liberal legislators of the Texas House of Representatives Textbook Investigating Committee. Since the committee could not collectively agree on a joint report, each member (after he had listened to 124 witnesses offer public testimony) made his views known in a series of final reports regarding the public hearings. These individual reports emphasize the clash of conservative versus liberal values so inherent to the great social studies textbook war. The battle was heading up as a civil conflict loomed, pitting legislator against legislator.

12

Disorder in the Court

The Contrasting Texas Legislative Reports

DURING THEIR meetings, representatives on the House Textbook Investigating Committee often disagreed with one another. Given their varying viewpoints, rather than issue a joint report, they decided that each would write a separate report. They agreed that their reports would not include any criticism of other representatives, and they limited their respective reports to include the testimony of no more than five witnesses each. All but Rep. Bill Dungan voted to halt any further public hearings after the one in Dallas on May 31, 1962. Proceedings from that hearing were excluded from any report, because of the five-member committee, only Dungan was present to hear the public testimonies; thus the committee did not have a quorum.

A speaker at the Dallas hearing, Gen. Erwin A. Walker, managed to dominate much of the newspaper coverage because of what he had to say. Walker was an outspoken anti-Communist, opponent of racial desegregation, and soon to be a losing candidate for Texas governor in 1962. That led Rep. Bob Bass to call the Dallas hearing a "political frame-up" intended to help the more conservative political candidate, state senator Preston Smith, gain a lead over the more liberal Speaker of the House of Representatives James A. Turman in their contest for lieutenant governor (which Smith did go on to win).[1]

The final reports of John Alaniz and Ronald Roberts regarding their investigation of the teaching of American history were in stark contrast

198 Chapter 12

to the comments by Bill Dungan, Nelson Cowles, and Bob Bass. Alaniz and Roberts advocated a much more liberal Democratic trend in the legislature. Dungan, Cowles, and Bass leaned more in the older conservative mode. Arguments made by these legislators provide a classic point-counterpoint exchange regarding the issues of (1) academic freedom, (2) censorship of books, and (3) what public school students should be encouraged to consider in their study of an academic discipline. Indeed, their differing viewpoints are as relevant in the twenty-first century as they were in 1961–62.

In his final report, Dungan agreed with Cowles that economic textbooks used in the public schools of Texas needed to do a better job of getting students to "appreciate the superiority of our capitalist system over all others." (On this topic, Cowles's report on economic books appears in chapter 5.) Bass and Cowles also urged major changes in the textbook adoption process, such as allowing more time for citizens to evaluate proposed programs, making copies of those programs more available to the public, and limiting the power of the Commissioner of Education to appoint members of the State Textbook Committee—in essence, what A. A. Forester of the Texas Society of the Daughters of the American Revolution had proposed during her public testimony before the Textbook Investigating Committee (described in chapters 4 and 10). None of these suggestions were enacted into law by their colleagues in the Fifty-Eighth Legislature. Thus only selections from the final reports of Alaniz, Cowles, Dungan, and Roberts will be presented as follows.

The representatives based their final reports on the results of listening to eight long days of testimony from 124 witnesses, and each report provided either rebuttals or support for what those witnesses said to the committee. For the purposes of this review, only selected excerpts in representatives' own words will be used to illustrate a summary of their opinions, especially since their full report to the Speaker of the House of Representatives totaled more than three hundred pages. The summary excerpts from each legislator appear under three categories that have been added for the purposes of clarification: "Overview," "Witnesses," and "Recommendations and Conclusion." As agreed on by the members, the reports appear in the following order: Alaniz, Cowles, Dungan, and Roberts.[2]

Disorder in the Court 199

Textbook Report by John C. Alaniz

Overview

After three or four hearings, the testimony became repetitious. I reached the conclusion that most of the witnesses were getting their material from the same sources. The testimony of 90% of all witnesses could be inserted in the following categories:

1. United Nations—The testimony of the witnesses indicated that any book that mentioned this organization or any of its works was taboo or communistic or socialistic.

2. The Roosevelt Era—The witnesses protested any books that mentioned Social Security or any of the other programs started during the Roosevelt Era as socialistic or communistic or both.

3. Patriotism—If every textbook that witnesses would read failed to mention or glorify our early American heroes, this was a communistic plot to undermine the minds of our youth in our public schools. Many of the books that were protested were world history books and even one world geography book came under attack for its failure to mention our early American heroes. Somehow the committee was never able to impress these witnesses that our early American heroes were adequately covered in American history books dealing with early American history.

4. Obscene Material and Sex—Some of the classics came under attack here. It was difficult to follow the thinking of many of the witnesses on this subject. Even some of the witnesses who appeared protesting this subject matter could not agree. The present laws on obscenity are adequate. The Supreme Court of the United States has legally defined obscenity. . . . In this manner a different jury each time will determine under the facts of each case whether or not a certain writing comes within this definition set out by the Courts and statutes. This is due process without the dangers of a censorship board of bureau as many communities have established in the United States.

Witnesses

This writer, from the very beginning, tried to confine those appearing before the committee to only those persons who had actually read textbooks that are being used, or are up for adoption in our public schools. I was not successful. Everyone was allowed to testify. Well over half of the witnesses appearing never had read any textbooks being used in any public schools. They just pondered generally on the evils of our time and somehow thought our public school system of education was to blame for them all. . . .

Seventy-five percent of the witnesses appearing before the committee, in my opinion, received their source material from one of the following: "Lifeline," the "Dan Smoot Report" [Dan Smoot was a former FBI agent, television commentator, author of many anti-Communist pamphlets about alleged Communist infiltrations in the US government, and a writer for the John Birch Society's anti-Communist *American Opinion* magazine], and or the John Birch publications. Most were sincere but misguided individuals. Anyone who differed with their position or even questioned their ideals, was, they thought, against them and by inference, Communistic. In trying to protect and preserve the American way of life, the ultra-right is undermining the very foundation of our democratic system, the free and open expression of ideals, with room for disagreement without the danger of being called anti-American or disloyal because one disagrees with their position.

Two notable exceptions were the appearance of a band of college professors from SMU, Rice, and Texas University, and a group of brave citizens from San Antonio, who testified as to the dangers of censorship in a free and open society. Their appearance was like a breath of fresh air in a London smog. They are a brave and courageous lot. The people of Texas are indebted to their testimony and their appearance.

Recommendations and Conclusions

Two of the members of the committee [Representatives Alaniz and Roberts] were abused and harassed by the audiences and witnesses appearing before it. It is not important that it was personal and aimed at two members of the committee; what is important is that the dignity of the House of Representatives and the State of Texas was irreparably damaged. I recommend that the 58th Legislature adopt rules of procedure for study committees with the aim of eliminating such spectacles and assuring that the dignity of the House be maintained and upheld at all times. I feel that the people of Texas deserve no less.

The greatest disappointment to this writer was the absence of public school teachers or administrators as witnesses in defense of the public school system of this State and the textbooks used therein. I can well understand their absence in view of the delicate positions they hold, where school boards hold a club over their head, whereby they can be fired without rhyme or reason, by just refusing to renew their contract at the end of each school year. I can well imagine the future of any school teacher in this State if a band of John Birchers set out to have his scalp.

As to the methods of selection of textbooks in this State, and to the contents found therein—we have in Texas the soundest and most economical system of all the States. Each local school district passes on the books to be used by it, the books are recommended by a State Textbook Committee that is appointed by the members of the elective State Board of Education. There are no basic improvements that could enhance this method of selection of textbooks in our State.

I will never say that every textbook adopted in Texas is perfect or that it will satisfy every viewpoint. This is never possible; not even the Bible has satisfied every viewpoint, but I will say that it is impossible for any foreign ideology, Communistic or otherwise, to creep into our textbooks and our system of public education in Texas.

Most of the witnesses appearing before the committee were sincere but badly informed or poorly prepared or both. They could well learn from this poem: "A little learning is a dangerous thing; Drink deep or touch not The Elysian Spring."[3]

Textbook Report by Nelson Cowles

Overview

There is evidence that in recent years, a definite trend has developed in American History textbooks which portray and instill in the minds of our youth the flaws and failures in our society and our American way of life. A history book which fails to create a feeling of pride in our nation and a love of country, should not be adopted for use in our public schools. There have been such books adopted and in use. In such books we find important men in history completely left out or in many instances slandered or criticized. Many important events are not given proper consideration.

News coverage of [our] hearings followed the same general line that they had previously followed regarding textbooks. That it presented news of the hearings as the opinions of individuals from either of two opposing views, with those who objected to the textbooks generally pictured as extremists or censors, etc.

Witnesses

In the first group were those who were objecting to the textbooks. Some of this group, including those who had fought the longest, felt that the books should bring out only that which is commendable about our country. For this reason they were often called "censors."

The other portion of the first group, and a goodly majority, felt that it is all right to present the pro and con of Americanism, provided that all of the good about our system were presented positively and that a thorough treatment be given the evils of the communist criminal conspiracy-socialism.

The second group, which generally received by far the greatest amount of favorable newspaper coverage, consisted, for the greater part, of university professors, American Civil Liberties Union members, or college student "beatniks." Some students were most discourteous, particularly when mention was made of morality, virtue, Christian heritage, etc.

It should be noted that the first group came prepared, with books, and other documentation, and gave page, paragraph, and line number references in much of their testimony. The second group, instead of bringing facts, page number, etc., spent most of their time attacking the members of the first group, and several times implied that the first group was attacking teachers.

Recommendations and Conclusion

Testimony has revealed that many adopted American History textbooks list as required or recommended reading, such books as *Andersonville, The Way West, Marjorie Morningstar, Laughing Boy, Grapes of Wrath, Big Sky* and many others, I contend that such reading material should not be made available for young people or Junior High or Senior High School age. We have anti-obscenity laws which apply to motion pictures and pornography. Those who speak for such literature contend that to prohibit such is censorship.

Actually, there are many teachers who are seriously concerned about the content of textbooks. They express their concern but do so only on the condition that it remain confidential because they fear loss of their teaching position if they speak out against things they know to be wrong.

It is apparent that due to lack of time and the number of books involved, most selections are made strictly as spur of the moment decisions based on general impressions. Book reviews of the books under consideration are, of course much quicker to read than the book itself, but the fallacy here is that, almost without exception, all well-known book reviews are definitely left-wing, in that they commend highly those books which are "slanted," and find fault with the type of books that should be taught our children. It seems that nearly all books offered by textbook publishers are slanted to varying degrees.[4]

Textbook Report by W. T. Dungan, Chairman

Overview

The books and school material criticized could be classed in four groups. First, pornographic or obscene, which included a large number of library books and reference material. We were given plenty of examples taken directly from school libraries, and I must say that some of them were very shocking. Individuals from Midland, Texas, were the first to appear in criticism of lewd library books, some of which were reference material for history courses being taught in the high school. Among the books criticized were *Andersonville* by McKinlay Kantor, *1984* by George Orwell, *The Grapes of Wrath* by John Steinbeck, *Laughing Boy* by Oliver La Farge, *Marjorie Morningstar* by Herman Wouk, *The Big Sky* by A. B. Guthrie Jr., and quite a few others. We received reports of many protests of this type of books by citizens to their local school boards in several Texas cities, particularly Midland, Corpus Christi, and Amarillo. Two ladies came to see me from Beaumont and brought a copy of *The Tropic of Cancer* which they said was being read by students there and circulated quite freely. They did not appear before the committee but said they would if we held a hearing in that area as they were very concerned about such literature being read by students, and felt that it should not be allowed.

The second group of textbooks criticized was history books, particularly US History. Several books were singled out that are now being used in the public schools. The main objections being omission of facts the critics considered pertinent and necessary for students to acquire patriotism and pride in the development of the United States. Another criticism was outright falsification of facts or a different presentation from earlier authors' writings. Some of the witnesses criticized what is termed "slanting" or changing the meaning and interpretation of certain facts of history. Others said there is a definite trend by certain authors to belittle some of the great men of American History as well as leaving out references to God or the part religion played in the founding of this nation.

Witnesses

[At our] public hearings . . . we heard citizens from all walks of life. The people appearing before the committee may be classed into two groups. The first group was composed of people who feel that something is basically wrong with our textbooks in particular and parts of our educational system in general. They feel that something should be done to correct the situation. This group was composed of individuals such as business men, former teachers, professional people, students, and even some educators. Organizations that had representatives to appear were Texans for America, Daughters of the American Revolution, the American Legion and its Auxiliary.

The second group was composed of people who appeared to defend our present system of education as being the best and found nothing wrong with textbooks. They felt that authors and educators should have a free rein in the field of education and their works be exempted from censorship or criticism and no obstacles placed in restraint of their academic freedom. This group was composed of individuals from the field of higher education principally. Also two organizations had representatives appear. They were The American Civil Liberties Union and The Texas Institute of Letters. The membership of these organizations seemed to be made up principally of college professors, writers, and ministers.

Representative Dungan then noted that some of those testifying had criticisms of Progressive educators John Dewey, Harold Rugg, and George Counts whose material they deemed "socialist propaganda." (Summaries of their careers appear in chapter 3.) Dungan included selections from the writings of those educators in his report as follows. John Dewey in *My Pedagogic Creed:* "Education, therefore, is a process of living and not a preparation for future living. We violate the child's nature and render difficult the best ethical results by introducing the child too abruptly to a number of special studies, of reading, writing, geography, etc., out of relation to this social life. The true center of correlation on the school subjects is not science, nor literature, nor history, nor geography, but the child's own social activities." Dr. Rugg in *The Great Technology*: He said that teachers had the important job of conditioning "a new public mind" for the "new social order." Dr. Rugg gave teachers specific suggestions: "The teachers must disabuse their pupils' minds of any archaic ideas they might have about our history. They must be told that the American Revolution was not a revolt of men who wanted to be free against an all-powerful, tyrannical and tax-eating government. It was just a brawl between American landlords and the British nobility, and the men who led the Revolution were merely interested in their own property. The students must be taught that our free enterprise system is a failure- it breeds poverty and inequality and the only fair system is a planned one, run by the government." Dr. George S. Counts expressed the purpose of "Dewey's progressive education as follows: "In the collectivist society now emerging the school should be regarded, not as an agency for lifting gifted individuals out of the class into which they were born and of elevating them into favored positions where they may exploit their less favored fellows, but rather as an agency for the abolition of all artificial social distinctions and of organizing the energies of the nation for the promotion of the general welfare. Throughout the school program the development of the social rather than the egotistic impulses should be stressed; and the motive of personal aggrandizement should be subordinated to social ends."

The witnesses [during the public hearings also] supplied information that a plan is being worked upon to give control of all education to Federal agencies and through them eventually to UNESCO, a branch of the United Nations. The National Education Association came in for criticism of its part in the plan to "standardize, socialize, and federalize" our educational system. There is definite proof that such plans do exist. A bulletin entitled *A Federal Education Agency for the Future* distributed by the US Dept. of Health, Education, and Welfare, Dept. of Education, gives a fairly comprehensive program for federal participation in education in the United States. It also advocates closer relationships with foreign ministries of education, international bureau of education and UNESCO. After reading about some of the plans and programs of UNESCO which is largely controlled by Communists, I do not feel that the people of this country wish cooperation with that organization and certainly not control of our educational system by it.

Recommendations and Conclusion

First, I think that our pornographic and anti-obscenity laws should be strengthened to eliminate the filth and trash, called literature by some people, from our *public school* libraries. I recognize this is a delicate subject and needs to be treated as such. I am convinced though that immature minds can be adversely affected by this type of trivia and cause, in some cases, irreparable damage.

Second, I feel that many of our History textbooks are of an inferior quality and should be improved or replaced. I feel that books by authors whose loyalty to this country, whose dedication to the principles upon which this nation was founded are doubtful, should be carefully studied before a decision on their adoption is made.

I think many, many good loyal Americans in positions of influence in this country who would like to see a full socialist government here are aiding and abetting the communist movement without even realizing they are doing so. I think it is the duty of all loyal citizens to help awaken people to a realization of these facts, and I think the best place to begin is in our schools.

[It] is my considered opinion that in some instances our educational systems, and particularly some textbooks, are being used to indoctrinate students with beliefs and ideologies foreign to those their parents believe in and in direct opposition to the moral and spiritual values upon which this nation was founded and only upon which it can continue to exist as a free and independent Republic.

I feel that much information can be obtained by listening *to the people*, so to speak. I do not subscribe to the belief held by some theorists that the "masses are asses" but rather to the theory that the people as a whole are the best judges of what is best for them if they still have the power to choose. Loss of the power to act locally, or what is known as "local self-government," is in my opinion one of the great dangers facing this nation today. Many of the rights given the people under the Constitution are gradually being usurped by the State in some cases and in many cases by the Federal Government.

It is an established fact that many people who are placed in positions of power and influence lose contact with the needs and desires of the public and begin to see themselves as a superior being who knows what is best for the "masses." I have seen many politicians acquire this idea and many unceremoniously relieved of it at the polls.

Unfortunately, many of our educators who likewise have this feeling of *superiority* are placed in their secure positions for life and cannot be reached by public opinion. This has led to abuse of this security in some instances. . . . They seem to forget that the public does pay the bills and furnishes the "clientele" to keep our educational institutions in operation, and are more interested in the quality of the product turned out than the educators themselves.

These criticisms are aimed at some of the professional educators in our higher institutions of learning who influence education in lower echelons through textbooks and policy-making, rather than at teachers in our public schools. I have the utmost respect for the classroom teachers in our public schools, the vast majority of whom are sincere, patriotic and dedicated persons who are doing great work in their chosen fields, in some instances under severe handicaps . . . and one dedicated teacher told me that, "if the administrators would turn the job of educating the kids back to the classroom teachers without some of the newer and more modern frills, then the public would see better results."[5]

Textbook Report by Ronald E. Roberts

Overview

Apparently the reason there's so much controversy over textbooks, academic freedom and the quality of our schools results from the tensions caused by the "Soviet Menace."

We as a free society have two choices in the field of education to make in deciding how to cope with the Communist drive for mastery of the world.

We can adopt similar patterns of "thought control" over education and our people as the Communist have done, which of course will result in the loss of academic freedom and all other freedoms. We can meet the Communist challenge by a complete rededication to our own democratic values as a means of preserving our free society.

This second choice will require our people to believe in the potential accomplishments of education as they never have before as a means of maintaining a democratic society. It will, of course, mean permitting academic freedom in our schools and universities. It will mean that our schools will educate for "responsible citizenship," not just train scientists, mathematicians, technologists; this will not preserve the future of a free society.

A nation of free men is a nation of citizens who "all" share our commitment to freedom on all levels and segments of our society, political, social, economic, and educational. Education will be a powerful instrument for the preservation of the achievements of mankind, particularly freedom, if our teachers have the courage to assume their academic responsibilities, particularly in teaching "about" the more controversial subjects. Controversial subjects, particularly political, economic, and social issues should not be "watered down" or skimmed over if we are to prepare young citizens for responsible citizenship.

Teachers and educators have both a right and a responsibility to open up the search for TRUTH to as many individuals as possible. The future of our nation will depend to a great extent on the equipping of our citizens to seek answers to controversial issues facing our nation and the free world.

In summary I want to mention one of the real thorns academic freedom is plagued with. Will our educational program consist of true "intellectual freedom," or will the teacher be pressured into a program of "narrow indoctrination" by outside pressure groups? For example some groups are pacified as long as the teacher is "dishing out" what "they" consider good Americanism. However, if a teacher allows a study of some controversial political or socioeconomic issue, be is immediately a suspect of being subversive. This is the reason some teachers leave out important public and political issues, and as a result the student enters society as an adult unprepared to cope with many of the socio-economic problems he will be faced with for life.

Unfortunately these organizations that "censor" our textbooks, libraries, and other teaching materials are using the same tactics of the Communists, and all other forms of totalitarianism. Instead of challenging the intellectual development of the student they advocate a program which merely amounts to a form of "indoctrination" used by the Communists.

Resorting to short sighted narrow political indoctrination will not lead to victory over communism. These types of methods will lead to the gradual destruction of our precious freedoms, particularly academic freedom.

Witnesses

Probably more than ninety per cent of the testimony was "repetitious" and beyond the authority of the Resolution. A number of "points of order" were raised to keep the Committee operating within the scope of the [House] Resolution [to examine American history textbooks], but each time the point of order was over ruled by the Committee Chairman [Rep. Bill Dungan].

Many hours were devoted to attacking library books in public school libraries. Most all of these attacks were in a "piecemeal" fashion, through the listing of certain offensive words or passages out of context. Nearly all reasonable people realize that a book should be judged on its total content and on the basis of what it is trying to say. By taking words and phrases out of context some people can even make the Holy Bible look undesirable for reading! Obviously the most important point about library books is that the State of Texas has absolutely nothing to do with their selection or purchase. The selection of library books is strictly a "local" matter and should be maintained as a responsibility of the elected boards of the various school districts.

Most of the testimony was highly repetitious and definitely undocumented within the scope of acceptable academic standards. A great deal of the testimony consisted of political and religious bias and personal opinion instead of changes made on the basis of high level academic research and careful study of historical facts.

To a large degree the attacks came from people who objected to certain events in the political and economic development of our nation, particularly from the Administration of Woodrow Wilson through the Kennedy Administration. It appears that many of these individuals do not want historical facts presented which they disapprove of but want a form of watered down political propaganda of their own liking. Most of the attacks came from "right wing" extremist organizations, the John Birch Society and Texans for America.

These groups that appeared before the Committee adopted a very narrow form of Americanism. They adopted the attitude that they had a monopoly on the meaning of "Americanism." Most of the witnesses who admitted they were members of these reactionary organizations seem to have forgotten that our nation has progressed forward because of "Freedom to teach and learn the truth, the freedom to dissent, and to challenge thoughts and ideas." John Milton said: "Give me the liberty to know, to utter, and to argue freely according to my conscience, above all liberties."

Unfortunately, these extremist organizations appearing before this Committee are inclined to suspect you of being subversive if you disagree with them. They are inclined to regard independence of the mind as the forerunner of subversion. It should be pointed out that Thomas Jefferson and Alexander Hamilton were certainly not conformists and certainly were not "un-American."

One of the leaders of the organized attacks of our public schools and textbooks testified that he did not approve of the present system of public schools. From this testimony it is reasonable to assume that these severe critics of our textbooks actually seek the abolition of our public schools.

I cannot think of a more destructive manner of weakening the United States of America than abolition of the public schools which have been the very bulwark of freedom.

Time after time the leaders of these reactionary organizations repeatedly used the same destructive tactics before the Committee. They demand that all teaching be solely along the line of the particular view point or doctrine they themselves adhere. They demand conformity and denounce differences. They do not reason with those who differ with them; they condemn and attempt to destroy them!

Their specific proposals are always of a repressive character. They endeavor to remove what they dislike, whether it be textbooks of which they disapprove or teachers they disagree. To secure these ends they appeal not to educators but to the public whom they misinform and to authorities on whom they can bring pressure. In these operations they indulge in much misrepresentation of facts and issues.

Nearly all of these people have fine motives and are sincere in their concern for our public schools and our American ideals, but they must realize it is not good Americanism to spread fear, hate, and suspicion throughout our state and nation. Unfortunately these reactionary organizations that seek to censor our textbooks, teaching materials, and films are destroying the freedoms they seek to preserve and protect through the tactics they use to achieve their desired results. These destructive tactics bring about a forum of political indoctrination instead of challenging the intellectual development of the student. We need citizens who can learn to THINK and COMPETE in the market place of ideas. Censorship on a narrow basis will develop weak citizens, not strong citizens. This certainly is not the way to meet the Communist challenge. These methods will bring about the gradual destruction of our precious freedoms.

Naturally these types of attacks have the effect of a repudiation of freedom and to repudiate a belief in freedom is to destroy western civilization.

Recommendations and Conclusion

We have stressed in America this belief that our type of democratic society can stay strong only if the fires of individual freedom are emphasized in our public schools. We have always thought of the schools and universities as the back bone of our republic. It has been through the influence of the schools that we have developed the United States into a position of world leadership.

It has always been the pattern of dictatorships to curb the search for "truth and knowledge" in the classroom except in the fields of scientific technology which can be used to enslave the body and mind. In other words, it is essential to permit academic freedom if our western way of life is to remain vigorous and strong.

Justice [Louis D.] Brandeis said: "The greatest dangers to liberty lurk in insidious encroachment by means of zeal, well-meaning but without understanding." Justice Brandeis' statement properly answers 95 per cent of the recent critics of our Texas textbook program.[6]

The final reports submitted by Representatives Alaniz, Bass, Cowles, Dungan, and Roberts should have brought closure to the controversy, but that was not the case. After submitting his final report, Representative Roberts still had two other issues to resolve: First, a private citizen had called Roberts a Communist during the proceedings, and he took high offence to that accusation. Roberts then proceeded to raise a suit against his accuser for slander in a Texas district court. In addition, a conflict between Representatives Roberts and Dungan was on the verge of boiling over—both men accused one another of legislative wrongdoing during the House Textbook Investigating Committee hearings. These two episodes only served to prolong the textbook controversy, as the battle raged on with Roberts on the front line.

13

Unfinished Business

A Civil Lawsuit for Slander and Accusations of Legislative Wrongdoing

THE HOUSE textbook committee hearings in Amarillo on February 26, 1962, proved to be among the most contentious in the state's legislative history to that time. They began with Billie Frances Boots objecting to *Stories of Young Texans*, a state adopted supplemental text, claiming that it advocated Roman Catholicism and was full of Catholic propaganda. She then asked committee member Rep. John Alaniz what schools he had attended in San Antonio and what schools his children were enrolled in. Alaniz told Boots he went to public elementary school in Bonham, Texas, and was a graduate of Brackenridge High School in San Antonio. His children attended a parochial school. Boots replied, "That's what I thought. I'm not a heretic. I'm a Baptist."[1]

At the same hearing, Rep. Ronald Roberts asked witnesses if they were members of the John Birch Society, knew the differences between socialism and communism, and how a "democracy" compared to a "republic." He also stated that most of the book "attacks came from right wing extremists organizations, the John Birch Society and Texans for America." When he was out of the hearing room, Boots said, "I'm sorry the man from Hillsboro [meaning Roberts] isn't here. I had a question for him, too. I wanted to ask him how long he has been a card-carrying Communist."[2]

The Boots-Roberts conflict caused Alaniz to tell Rep. William Dungan, "I want to see one real live Communist. In 100 hours of testimony one hasn't turned up yet." Dungan replied, "Some people think we have one on the committee. I did not say I agreed. I simply said that someone said that. One might turn up yet. You might learn a little something."[3]

Shortly thereafter, Larry Williams, who had spoken earlier at the hearing, took the floor to say: "Please accept my apology for the radical and unfair testimony given by Boots. A feeling of shame was certainly prevalent among all of us [the audience]. I suppose in a hearing like this unreasonable attitudes will be expressed." When he finished, the audience gave him a standing ovation.[4]

Upon learning what Boots said about him, Roberts told a reporter: "I consider the remark very unfortunate. When communism is introduced, it is a menace regardless of one's political views. In my opinion, when people resort to name calling, it plays into the hands of Communists. Anybody who creates suspicion in our country is emphasizing the menace. I strongly believe in our constitutional form of government which provides for freedom of speech, press and religion." He concluded that as "a legislator and teacher, I am dedicating my life to conserving our constitutional republic. I have never been a Communist, card-carrying or otherwise."[5]

Boots said she felt Representative Roberts "tried to make everyone who expressed the belief that the textbooks were expressing subversive attitudes look like a stupid idiot and make light of such testimony. He was the most rude person I have ever seen." She also added that Representative Alaniz should not have been on the legislative Textbook Investigating Committee because he was a Roman Catholic.[6]

Even the politically conservative Governor Price Daniel became involved by sending Roberts a letter calling Boots's comments about him a "slanderous allegation" and stating he was "shocked to learn . . . of the personal attack made against you."[7]

Willie Morris, editor of *The Texas Observer*, went even further regarding the remarks made by Boots by sarcastically writing: "It is a typical trick of communism, of course, to place some of their own card-carrying comrades in places of great trust, but to have imagined one on the textbook committee itself! This discovery, which could only have been made in the [Texas] Panhandle, is fraught with implications. Suppose, in the committee's future peregrinations, we are to learn that a *majority* of the committee are card-carriers—a frightening prospect and a dangerous omen for our very textbooks themselves." Morris added: "Where will the awful truth strike next? Dungan, a special agent for Mao Tse-tung? Bass, a secret director of collective farms in the Ukraine? Cowles, a soul mate of Alger Hiss at Harvard? Already we have been warned in the Amarillo hearings that Alaniz is a Roman Catholic. It has been almost two months, and the orders may have been sent out from the Pope long ago." Morris finished his satire: "These are disturbing thoughts, but we may at least take solace in the knowledge that the textbook investigations have finally flowered. Where will it all end? We demand, for the safety of our commonwealth and its citizens, that the textbook committee cease investigating textbooks and start forthwith investigating itself."[8]

Within weeks after the Amarillo hearings, Representative Roberts sued Boots for slander for $85,000. He filed his suit in the Hill County, Texas, judicial district court. That $85,000 is about $700,000 in today's money.

Boots's lengthy answer to the suit filed against her by Representative Roberts could be considered a summary of some Texas conservative concerns at the time, especially as a more liberal political agenda was starting to emerge in Texas and as reflected in the public testimony of many of those who opposed the 1961 Texas adoption of the history programs. A condensed account of Boots's response to Roberts and his reply to her are included as follows.[9] In her defense, Boots cited numerous cases where her comments about Roberts were not subject to a civil suit, since according to a state law of 1901 her comments were a "fair, true and impartial account of all executive and legislative proceedings" and her statements during the textbook committee hearings were "absolutely privileged and therefore not actionable." She went on to make seven major responses to Roberts:

1. She claimed Roberts "adopted communist techniques and espoused communist causes" when he voted for a Texas House resolution praising the US House Un-American Activities Committee, which she felt was "an action being consistent

with established Communist policy of public profession of patriotism while secretly striving to undermine and destroy capitalism through aiding and abetting the communist conspiracy."

2. Although none of the history textbook authors ever had their names appear on any such lists, she argued that Roberts initially opposed the creation of the House Textbook Investigating Committee to review state-adopted books because she felt those books were "authored by admitted communists or fellow travelers listed by the House Un-American Activities Committee or the Texas Department of Public Safety."

3. Boots claimed that Roberts, once on the Textbook Investigating Committee, used free speech guarantees as a Communist device she felt were "designed to ridicule, embarrass, harass and smear those citizens of Texas" who only "protested the insidious implantation of the communist philosophy in the minds of the children attending our Texas Schools and official contribution to moral delinquency through reference books, carried in Texas School libraries." This, she argued, "ridiculed the Supreme Being recognized by the Christian world, emphasized and glamorized immorality, and sexual license in such lewd, lascivious, foul and vulgar language."

4. She felt Roberts, in his effort to intimidate witnesses at the committee's public hearings, "inquired as to witnesses' membership in the John Birch Society, whether they knew the difference between socialism and communism, the technical difference between a democracy and a republic, and by implication as to whether or not the protesting citizens subscribed to 'book burning' as exemplified by Hitler's fascism."

5. She maintained Representatives Roberts and Alaniz "insulted housewives and mothers by inquiring as to whether or not they didn't number among their associates, people who used language such as was contained in the extracts [from school library books], deemed by the Committee chairman [Dungan] too filthy, rotten and obscene to be read in public." For Boots, the action of Roberts also gave "official sanction

to licentiousness and amorality, known factors contributing to the rise and acceptance of communism, and the decay of representative democracy founded in a Christian belief in freedom under law."

6. She claimed that when Roberts failed to intimidate witnesses, he "pursued the well-known communist tactic of smearing those who did not agree with his profligate philosophy of life." This she said he did by having a letter published on January 25, 1962, in the *Beaumont Enterprise*. In that letter, he wrote the following about some of those protesting the history books: "In my opinion these extremist groups that have been appearing before this special committee are more dangerous than the Communists. These fanatical groups would actually destroy democracy because of the methods they seek to impose on our society."

7. Finally, she argued, her comments were "provoked by the conduct of Roberts" and "made in good faith, without malice, and in the public interest."

In his reply, Roberts noted that Boots's statements about him were not absolutely privileged unless the charge made by her was grounds for his removal from office. He then asked: "Did the words used by Billie Boots impair my fitness for the office of the legislature? Clearly a statement that a man is a Communist, un-loyal to the United States of America and the State of Texas, are words so obviously hurtful to the person that they require no proof of their injurious character [since when she made her accusation] I was and am the representative of Hill County, Texas, to the State Legislature." Roberts then included the following transcript from the Amarillo hearing:

MR. DUNGAN, CHAIRMAN: Boots, actually, the witnesses are not supposed to ask questions at all. . . .

BOOTS: Then I will apologize, Chairman.

MR. DUNGAN, CHAIRMAN: If Alaniz wants to go ahead with it, it's all right, otherwise. . . .

MR. ALANIZ: I don't mind, Chairman, I don't mind.

MR. DUNGAN, CHAIRMAN: All right, sir, you may proceed if he doesn't object to the questions.

BOOTS: Well, what happened to the gentleman from Hillsboro? I had a question for him. I wanted to ask him how long he had been a card-carrying Communist. If he has left, then I will omit the question.

MR. DUNGAN, CHAIRMAN: I think that is being a little out of order, Boots. Are there any questions you would like to ask the witness, any member of the committee?

BOOTS: By the way, I am not a heretic. I'm a Baptist.

To Roberts, the comments Boots made about him and reported statewide when he was seeking reelection to the Texas House were slanderous and constituted an accusation that "I was disloyal to this country and tantamount to accusing me of being an agent of the enemies of the United States of America, at a time when this country is engaged in a Cold War with communism. Said accusation was, and is false, unfounded in fact, and slanderous . . . and was a cruel and malicious falsehood, outrageous, and in utter disregard of my feelings and my reputation."

The case was closed on February 16, 1966, when Roberts dropped his suit after the unexpected death of his attorney, Donald Eastland. In legal terms, the suit was "dismissed for want of prosecution." Apparently, the comments Boots made about Roberts did not do any damage his political career. A majority of voters in his district reelected him twice more to the Texas House of Representatives, where he continued to serve until January 11, 1967.[10]

However, Roberts and Rep. William Dungan were not quite through sparing with one other. Their next encounter would soon involve the Texas House of Representatives and the Texas Attorney General. This time, the dispute between the two men began when the House Textbook Investigating Committee scheduled hearings in Dallas for March 30–31, 1962. As noted previously, since Representative Dungan was the only member of the committee present with no quorum, the Dallas hearings never became part of the official record submitted by the committee. The other four members of the committee boycotted the hearing. Rep. Bob Bass called Representative Dungan's Dallas hearing nothing more than a "political frame-up intended to help one political candidate [over] another in one of the state races. The quickest way to destroy [our] committee and its work is to turn it into a political vehicle. . . . I am 100 percent against that."[11]

Reps. John Alaniz and Ronald Roberts agreed with Rep. Bob Bass, who was referring to the more liberal Speaker of the House of Representatives James A. Turman, in his losing contest with the more conservative State Senator Preston Smith for lieutenant governor. Turman was supported by some liberal groups who criticized the hearings. Dungan held the Dallas hearing three days before the Turman-Smith run-off race and said he would "gavel down" anyone who even remotely named either candidate. Representative Alaniz said, "I'm sorry I missed the Dallas hearing. I would have had a chance to cross-examine General Walker, and for an attorney like myself, that is a paradise lost."[12]

Alaniz was speaking of Maj. Gen. Erwin A. Walker, who was a racial segregationist, a member of the John Birch Society, an anti-Communist, and one who demanded the impeachment of US Supreme Court Chief Justice Earl Warren for the court's 1954 unanimous decision in the *Brown v. Topeka* case to desegregate public schools. He also had called Harry Truman, Eleanor Roosevelt, and former secretary of state Dean Acheson "definitely pink." He feared racial integration would result in the miscegenation of blacks and whites. He also supported a racially segregated Rhodesia and, while in the US Army, urged his troops to vote for extreme conservatives. After Pres. John F. Kennedy forced General Walker to retire from the US Army in September of 1961, Walker organized protests against the desegregation of the University of Mississippi. When those protests turned violent, US Attorney General Robert Kennedy arrested Walker for five days on charges of "seditious conspiracy, insurrection, and rebellion." As another form of protest, Walker flew the American flag upside down in his front yard. Walker was also an unsuccessful candidate for Texas governor in 1962, ending up sixth and last in the Democratic Party primary election.

At the Dallas hearing, General Walker did not talk about any of the textbooks in question but nevertheless managed to dominate media coverage of the proceedings by asserting, for instance, that the faculty at Southern Methodist University and the University of Texas at Austin were following the lead of Harvard and MIT by replacing basic Christian education with that advocated by "elite sophisticates." General Walker also claimed this "is liberal opportunism taking advantage of our weaknesses . . . to depreciate our strength, our accomplishments and our future as a Christian free country." Walker concluded his testimony by insisting that Texas state educators were waging an "effective attack on Christianity, morals and the American tradition." Later, when Representative Alaniz asked Representative Dungan if General Walker had read any of the American history textbooks used in the Texas public schools, Dungan replied that "[t]he General is widely read, and I'm sure he did."[13]

By then, the emotional intensity of the legislative hearings had increased to the point that State Rep. Bob Hughes, one of four state legislators to observe the Dallas hearings, told the audience: "It is a painful duty for me to say this, but I only learned this morning that members of this [House Textbook Investigating Committee] have been subject to threats and pressure—threats with financial, legal and personal reprisals." Even Helen Blackman of Austin, secretary of the committee, said she received a telephone call threatening loss of her job if she attended the Dallas meeting. She nevertheless showed up for work anyway.[14]

In spite of the controversy, Representative Dungan had eight hundred copies of the transcript of the Dallas hearings printed at state expense and sold some of them for two dollars a copy, at a financial loss to him. When Rep. Ronald Roberts learned of this, he claimed such a practice was a possible misuse of House printing facilities. The result was a House investigation of Dungan regarding the "propriety" of his actions. Dungan responded by claiming that Roberts received reimbursement and vouchers for not being in full attendance when the House Textbook Investigating Committee held hearings in San Antonio and Amarillo.[15]

To resolve the charges made by both men, Speaker of the House Byron Tunnell, on March 12, 1963, appointed a House committee of five members to investigate the charges made by the two men.[16] On May 24, 1963, a House investigating committee cleared the charge against Representative Roberts by stating he was in San Antonio and Amarillo on the days for which he made "application for reimbursement, and vouchers authorizing such reimbursement were approved by Dungan," and that

220   Chapter 13

Roberts attended all the meetings and followed the rules of the textbook committee.[17]

In regard to the charge against Dungan, the House investigating committee, along with an opinion by State Attorney General Waggoner Carr, then reported that a "member of the Legislature is not authorized to prepare, at state expense, printed matter he intends to sell to the public, for the reason that printed material prepared at state expense must be used for governmental or public purposes and not for private purposes."[18] But the committee noted there is no statute or rule prohibiting such sale, and that Dungan's family business financially suffered from neglect due to the time he had to serve on the House Textbook Investigating Committee. It then added that even though his sale of copies of the Dallas hearing was "contrary to public policy," there should be specific rules to prohibit it. The House of Representatives followed by approving such a resolution.

In justifying his actions before the House of Representatives, Dungan probably got the last word. He ended defense by concluding: "Now, Speaker, if this House decides to have another Textbook Committee, I'm not asking for the job, as I got enough experience to last for a while; but if I'm needed, so help me God, I'll give it another round. But please don't put me on one with some of the same members."[19] As was the case for Roberts, when Dungan ran for reelection, his constituents reelected him to office for two more terms.

By then, most members of the legislature had become very weary over the issue of textbook adoptions. Their fatigue over the issue was quite evident, as shown by what occurred at the final meeting of its House Textbook Investigating Committee, when it ended its public hearings on the subject.

14

A Last Meeting but Far from a Conclusion

AT THEIR LAST meeting in December of 1962, members of the Texas House of Representatives Textbook Investigating Committee undoubtedly were expecting a rather routine and calmer closure to their endeavors, especially after holding seven highly contentious and very lengthy public hearings while listening to public testimony from 124 witnesses. That was not to be the case. The trouble began when Rev. W. S. Arms, pastor of the University Temple Baptist Church of Austin, handed Chairman Dungan a petition. Dungan did not accept the petition from Reverend Arms on behalf of the committee but said he would give it to the Speaker of the House, who would decide if it merited consideration by the full House.

Included among the concerns of Reverend Arms, which reflected those expressed by many of the frustrated conservative Texas textbook protestors during 1961–62, was a petition calling for laws regulating what he called pornography in textbooks and library books used in the state's public schools; he also asked the Texas House of Representatives to look into the "question of perjury" before the House Textbook Investigating Committee by any witnesses who might have testified in a "facetious manner." He went further in his petition by asking the committee to eliminate the testimony of anyone who defended or was a member of any subversive or Marxist group, as well as any witness "who defended or sponsored any book or books whose authors have Communist citations."[1]

That was not all. Reverend Arms urged that any books written by Communists or groups or individuals who were Communist sympathizers "be removed at once from the shelves and use in state supported schools as detrimental to the welfare and security of the state." He also asked that groups such as labor unions not be allowed to influence the State of Texas' textbook selection process.[2]

Finally, Reverend Arms wanted any witness who defended textbook passages containing "amoral content" to appear before the legislature and read aloud what they defended; any Texan regarded as "dangerous, subversive, or of Marxist persuasion," who sought "by any means to change, subvert, overthrow by force, violence or any other methods our constitutional form of government," should be indicted by the committee of the House.[3]

When the House textbook committee did not accept Reverend Arms's petition, he still tried to make his point, at least to the media, by continuing to interrupt the committee members. Seemingly frustrated, Reverend Arms finally declared, "I don't think anyone should be frightened by this, unless they have cause to." He said he could "get 20,000 signatures [for his petition] before January 8. I'm going to the Baptist Convention in Fort Worth."[4]

Finally, Representative Bass told Representative Dungan, "If this man [Arms] can't be silenced, let's clear this room." Bass and Representative Alaniz then suggested calling the sergeant-at-arms to "keep him [Arms] quiet." With that, Reverend Arms remained silent.[5]

Rep. Bob Bass did include in his final report one petition, that being from W. H. Kellogg of Huntsville, Texas. Kellogg's petition, signed by forty-seven persons, requested "that in view of facts brought to light by this investigation that this work be broadened and continued by the next House of Representatives."[6]

In January 1963, after all the publicity from hearings conducted by the Texas State Textbook Committee, the Texas State Board of Education, and the Texas House of Representatives Textbook Investigating Committee, the Texas Legislature had three options: (1) continuing with the legislative textbook investigations; (2) considering petitions like the ones suggested by Kellogg and Reverend Arms; or (3) giving attention to proposals like those from J. Evetts Haley and A. A. Forester, or those from Representatives Bass, Cowles, Dungan, and Roberts, re-

A Last Meeting but Far from a Conclusion

garding changes to role of public school librarians and changes to the format of the textbook adoption process. Indeed, even after the many public hearings, all the requests for changes in the textbook adoption process and those regarding school libraries and school librarians went for naught in the Fifty-Eighth State Legislature, and the Texas textbook adoption process would remain basically the same until early in the twenty-first century. Indeed, by 1962, a majority of state senators and representatives, as part of a changing political climate in Texas, seemed very weary of the whole textbook business and did not act on a single one of those options or suggestions. Rep. Rayford Price of Frankston probably summed up the feelings of many of his colleagues when he said, "I'm not convinced that there is a need for any change in textbook selection." Rep. Chet Brooks of Harris County facetiously added: "Although I don't see this as a major issue, but we may be faced with fighting off attempts of John Birchers and other extremists to institute book-burning programs."[7]

Their sentiments in 1962 seemed to be echoed by an editorial from the *Corpus Christi Caller Times*. It supported the then current format for adopting textbooks in Texas and for free speech allowing public criticism of textbooks, but objected to what it claimed was "nit-picking and statements being taken out of context by textbook critics." The editorial went on to add: "Somehow overlooked is the obligation of every critic to judge a book or other work on its merits as a whole. The task of a historian writing a text for public school children is a monumental one. It becomes more difficult each year. The historian is faced continually with these questions: How much space should I devote to this or that period in American history? . . . Can I, in fact, write a history text that will please everybody?"[8]

The textbook war had originated on September 14, 1961, with very limited press coverage of two conservative Texas groups protesting the content (or lack thereof) in some social studies textbooks being considered for state adoption. It went on to become one of the most extensive of its kind in the nation's history. At the time, it is quite possible that few people realized that these textbook protests were only a prelude of what was to come—protests in Texas that escalated with such intensity and scope as to acquire an increasingly confrontational momentum all its own, causing repercussions that have endured to the present day.

This would soon lead to numerous other groups, regardless of which Texas political group was in power at the time (conservative or liberal), becoming even more involved in such cultural wars, regarding what should and should not be emphasized in social studies programs, often with very contentious disagreements. The conflict continues in the present day.

Epilogue

AMERICAN PROTESTS of social studies textbooks dating back to just after the Civil War have generally involved two main schools of thought. One is embodied by the position taken by early seventeenth century Puritan minister and lawyer Nathaniel Ward of Ipswich, Massachusetts. He felt society should not tolerate ideas deemed intolerable because to do so would only cause people to doubt their own beliefs. A variation of Ward's advice came from Winston Churchill, who maintained, "History will be kind to me for I intend to write it." And, if protesters could not write history, they could at least follow George Orwell's dictum in *Nineteen Eighty-Four* that "he who controls the present controls the future, and he who controls the past controls the future."

These men could easily have been describing the differences of opinion of historian J. Evetts Haley and folklorist J. Frank Dobie, who as early as 1962 disagreed about what students should be allowed to study in a democratic society, particularly in regard to American history. Haley felt that "stressing of both sides of a controversy only confuses the young and encourages them to make snap judgments based on insufficient evidence. Until they are old enough to understand both sides of a question, they should be taught only the American side. . . . If this struggle meant anything, it is the perpetuation of the Christian ethnic. There is no freedom except under the Christian ethnic as enshrined in the Constitution and the Bill of Rights." For Dobie, "Censorship . . . is never to let people know but always to keep them in ignorance. Never to enlighten but always to darken. It is easier to appeal to prejudice than to reason, to ignorance than to enlightenment. That is the way of the demagogue. . . . No use kidding ourselves—school children aren't fools.

226 Epilogue

They don't live in vacuums. They're not going to be much influenced by some dull piece of propaganda, tale-twisting, and flag waving put into a textbook. . . . It goes over them just like water goes over a duck's back."

At the time, it is highly unlikely when Haley and Dobie testified before the Texas House of Representatives Textbook Investigating Committee in 1962 that they realized they were contributing to the beginning of a renewed post–World War II national debate over the evolution of American historiography, especially in regard to social studies programs and particularly to the writing and teaching of American history. They would become a vital part of one of the most extensive social studies protests in the nation's history. While doing so, Haley and Dobie managed to summarize much of the 1961–62 Texas social studies debate, during a time of negative reactions to Pres. Franklin D. Roosevelt's New Deal, Pres. Harry S. Truman's Fair Deal, an emerging civil rights movement, and the election of liberal Democrats John F. Kennedy as president of the United States and Lyndon B. Johnson as his vice president, carrying Texas in the process of that election, along with their political agendas and an emerging civil rights revolution. The debate over the social studies programs also embodied some American fears associated with McCarthyism and a Cold War with the Soviet Union. Texan concerns about those issues resulted in some conservatives calling for social studies textbooks to place greater emphasis on the free enterprise capitalism, states' rights, American exceptionalism, limited national government, Protestantism, and opposition to a civil rights revolution, progressive education, communism, and US membership in the United Nations.

By then, so many changes had occurred during the first half of the twentieth century that some of the population of the United States was left in a state of intellectual and moral whiplash. There had been two world wars, a Great Depression, and the Korean conflict. The New Deal under Franklin Roosevelt and the Fair Deal from Harry Truman again demonstrated how a growing federal government could continue to invoke more power than individual states. The Soviets, formerly World War II allies, proved themselves to be dangerous and untrustworthy, and there were some American spies working for them. Atomic weapons were replaced by even more powerful hydrogen ones, and many US citizens could hardly comprehend much less feel like they could control what was going on around them.

Epilogue

During the post–World War II, well into the 1950s, there were differences primarily among academics over the proper place or role of history in the social studies curriculum and some local conservative complaints about certain political science textbooks being too pro–New Deal, but overall there existed a temporary lull in serious, extensive, or major American social studies wars during 1945–60. That was about to end by the late 1950s into the 1960s, with more ethnic minority groups and women demanding rights that they had never had before, including, for example, more inclusion in social studies programs. By then, publishers and authors were also beginning to formulate guidelines to make their social studies programs more inclusive. In addition, publishers no longer produced two distinct American histories—one version for select southern states and the other for rest of the nation. In addition, there was the advent of the federally funded Project Social Studies projects, with their New Social Studies programs involving more inclusiveness and emphasizing inquiry-oriented, problem-solving, and point-counterpoint approaches. All this would only ignite other social studies wars, beginning in many other places in addition to Texas, such as in Michigan, New York, California, North Carolina, and Georgia, and spreading elsewhere, as shown in the annotated bibliographies of appendices D and E, thus shattering the temporary lull in debate during the immediate post–World War II era.

Convinced they might be losing the political-cultural war, some Texas conservatives during the late 1950s to 1961 had to look elsewhere to maintain the perpetuation of their philosophy. One area they could try to control was the content of school textbooks that their children were reading. Thus the scope and content of textbook adoptions on a state level again became a center of controversy. Texas conservatives had the most unique opportunity in the world staring them right in the face, with their state being one of the nation's leading adopters of textbooks for the elementary and secondary levels. This became evident with the adoption of social studies textbooks in Texas by the late 1950s and early 1960s, with Texas being one of the largest buyers of textbooks that were also used in many other states. Indeed, the timing and historical setting could not have been more opportunistic for Texas to have its own major conservative-liberal confrontation involving the content of social studies textbooks, mainly history ones.

228   Epilogue

Thus the scope and content of social studies textbook adoptions again became a center of controversy. This became evident with the adoption of social studies textbooks in Texas by the late 1950s and early 1960s. To be more specific, some Texas conservatives, frustrated with continuing to lose battles with the federal government, a rising civil rights movement, and the beginning decline of their political influence at the state level, adopted tactics long used by various others by turning to an area where they hoped to have their point of view exposed to a wider audience—students in the public schools.

If successful in getting their conservative philosophy into those social studies programs, it would also appear in many other states, which found it more convenient to purchase the same textbooks, with less expenses for publishers not having to print different versions of their products. And while there had also been earlier disagreements in Texas about public school social studies textbook content during the late 1950s, previous protests in the Lone Star State were minor compared with the way the 1961–62 hearings about proposed social studies programs developed into a series of highly significant controversies between conservatives and liberals. The result was the great Texas social studies war of 1961–62, which not only shattered the somewhat temporary lull in the nation's social studies conflicts after World War II but also, as already noted, was only the first of a renewed group of major social studies textbook wars to spread nationally well into the twenty-first century.

The Texas protests of 1961–62 involved a star-studded cast of both conservative and liberal spokespersons. The conservatives included historian J. Evetts Haley representing Texans for America; A. A. Forester, as textbook chairperson for the Texas Society of the Daughters of the American Revolution; Mel and Norma Gabler, who became nationally prominent textbook critics; and retired general Edwin Walker. They were pitted against liberals such as folklorist J. Frank Dobie; historians Lon Tinkle and Frank Vandiver; University of Texas Press director Frank Wardlaw; ACLU civil rights attorney, former World War II US combat marine, and state representative Maury Maverick Jr.; as well as Texas Baptist leaders Rev. Joseph Dawson and Rev. Lee Freeman, all with support from such groups as the Texas Institute of Letters, the Texas Library Association, and the American Studies Association. Confrontations between the two groups ignited a monumental debate with extensive media coverage.

Some textbook critics, mainly from Haley's Texans for America, claimed that American history textbook authors or individuals mentioned in their books or included in some of their recommended reading lists were anti-American, subversive, or had pro-Communist leanings. Those suspect persons included many Pulitzer Prize recipients and other well-known Americans, such as J. Frank Dobie, John Steinbeck, Thomas Wolfe, George Orwell, Pearl S. Buck, McKinley Kantor, Ernest Hemingway, Stephen Vincent Benet, Maxwell Anderson, Albert Einstein, Willa Cather, Jack London, Aaron Copeland, William Faulkner, Carl Sandburg, Ida Tarbell, and Lincoln Steffens.

All of the fifteen adopted history textbooks by Texas in 1961 were protested by the Texas Society of the Daughters of the American Revolution, and fourteen of those fifteen were protested by Texans for America. After all the members of the State Textbook Committee recommended the adoption of those history programs and the vast majority of members of the State Board of Education adopted those textbooks, Forester was unhappy because she felt most of her major complaints had been ignored by those two groups. As a result, she, along with support from Texans for America, persuaded the Texas House of Representatives to create a special legislative textbook investigating committee. Its five members, John Alaniz, Robert Bass, L. Nelson Cowles, William Dungan, and Ronald Roberts, held seven official public hearings around the state, with a total of 124 citizens testifying before them, which was all the witnesses the committee could accommodate even though many, many more people wanted to testify. The hearings by that House committee proved to be among the most disruptive and contentious in the state's legislative history.

Multiple confrontations also erupted between a series of award-winning Texas scholars over the issue of censorship of textbooks, including arguments between members of Texans for America in opposition to those from the Texas Institute of Letters.

In an unusual move during the textbook adoption process, the Texas State Commissioner of Education removed four geography textbooks from the list of those very highly recommended for adoption by the Texas State Textbook Committee. The Texas Society of the Daughters of the American Revolution complained that the books were in violation of the standards set by the Texas State Board of Education because they had an interdisciplinary social studies approach advocated by progressive educator John Dewey. The books in question incorporated the study of history, economics, government, and sociology within a study of geography.

Textbook evaluators Mel and Norma Gabler also made their initial statewide public appearance by testifying before the Texas House of Representatives Textbook Investigating Committee in 1962. The Gablers soon became two of the nation's most prominent conservative critics of textbooks during the next four decades.

For the first time in the history of the Texas State Board of Education, it refused a request from the Commissioner of Education to extend, as a money saving action, the readoption of high school economics textbooks. The Texas Society of the Daughters of the American Revolution and a majority of the members of the Texas State Board of Education felt some of the texts did not adequately stress the free enterprise system, although the books in question were preferred by more than 90 percent of the state's economics teachers.

Members with conservative political beliefs, usually from Texans for America, unsuccessfully attempted to permanently ban from Texas public schools and state college and university libraries, as well as public libraries, works by some of the nation's who's who of best-known authors, all for allegedly containing content deemed obscene, subversive, or anti-American.

Southern Methodist University historian Paul F. Boller's *This Is Our Story*, coauthored with Evelyn Jean Tilford, was the target of extensive protests, primarily from historian J. Evetts Haley and other members from Texans for America. Although Boller made only a few minor changes in the book (none of any significance), as requested by the State Textbook Committee and the State Board of Education, criticisms of the book from conservative protestors resulted in the book obtaining very few local adoptions in Texas, but it sold well in other states. Boller went on to write numerous other books, many best sellers, and held the Distinguished Lyndon Baines Johnson Chair of American History at Texas Christian University. Jean Tilford would go on to become president of the National Council for the Social Studies.

Epilogue 231

After the legislative textbook hearings, Rep. Bob Bass proposed a bill to have public school librarians subject to prison time and fines for failing to remove books judged to contain obscene material. The Texas Legislature failed to enact his bill into law.

Private citizens petitioned the Texas Legislature to approve a law that would allow the government to indict for perjury those individuals who testified before the House of Representatives Textbook Investigating Committee if those individuals testifying failed to reveal any associations with suspected Communists or other subversive groups. The legislature also failed to enact their petition into law.

Rep. Ronald Roberts filed a civil law suit for slander against Billie Boots, a private citizen, who, during one of the legislative textbook hearings, accused Roberts of being a Communist. In today's money, the amount in damages Representative Roberts requested was $700,000. He later withdrew the suit.

Serious disagreements occurred among members of the Texas House of Representatives Textbook Investigating Committee about what public school students should be allowed to study in a social studies course. Their disagreements caused committee members to depart from the usual custom of issuing a joint report and instead submit individual reports, with conservative Democrats Bass, Cowles, and Dungan pitted against liberal Democrats Alaniz and Roberts.

Representative Roberts accused Representative Dungan of illegally selling for private gain printed state materials about one of their textbook hearings, and Representative Dungan accused Representative Roberts of illegally accepting state reimbursement for legislative meetings Dungan claimed Roberts did not attend. Their accusations against one another resulted in investigations by the Texas House of Representatives and the Texas Attorney General. The House cleared Roberts of any wrongdoing, and because Dungan took a financial loss for sale of the materials (and because there was no House rule against what he did), the House approved, with advice from the Texas Attorney General, a resolution forbidding such sales in the future. Afterward, both Roberts and Dungan were reelected to office for two more terms.

Nevertheless, that was far from the end of this story. The conservative-liberal clash of values prominent during that ancestral great Texas social studies war of 1961–62 would only increase in intensity in Texas

232 Epilogue

over social studies programs during the following years. Indeed, the Texas social studies war of 1961–62 was part of a transition from earlier national battles on the topic and those that followed into the twentieth-first century.

Regardless of which group at the time dominated the Texas political scene, whether conservative or liberal, on most matters after 1962, liberals prevailed, at least during the next six major secondary level social studies adoptions before the Texas State Board of Education. In 2010, a Republican-led conservative majority on the State Board of Education cited this issue when creating their revised social studies standards.

The Texas textbook protests inspired many groups and individuals to become involved and oppose or defend what materials publishers submitted for the state adoption of social studies textbook programs. For example, well into the twenty-first century, along with the Texas Society of the Daughters of the American Revolution, Norma and Mel Gabler's Education Research Analysts, and the John Birch Society, newer conservative groups to become involved in social studies conflicts in Texas include, for example, those from the Moral Majority, the Texas Eagle Forum, the Texas Public Policy Foundation, the Liberty Institute or Free Market Foundation, various chambers of commerce, the Texas Conservative Coalition, the Wallbuilders, the Texas Tea Party, Truth in Texas Textbooks Coalition, Women on the Wall, Texas Values Action, Americans for Prosperity, and various other religious groups.

In contrast, along with the ACLU, in Texas newer liberal groups to become involved in conflicts into the twentieth-first century over social studies content include members from the National Organization of Women, People for the American Way, Texas Freedom Network, National Council for History Education, Organization of American Historians, Texas State Historical Association, Texas State Teachers Association, the American Federation of Labor Teachers Union, National Japanese-American Memorial Federation, Save Our History, Equality Texas, and Multicultural Alliance for Social Studies Advocacy.

Additionally, also involved in the Texas social studies adoption process are numerous multicultural, ethnic, religious, or secular groups, including the Mexican American Legal Defense Fund, League of United Latin American Citizens, Mexican-American Legislative Caucus, American GI Forum, Antidefamation League of B'nai B'rith, National Association

Epilogue

for the Advancement of Colored People, Hindu American Foundation, Jewish Community Relations Council, Madelyn Murray O'Hare for the American Atheist Society, Responsible Ethnic Studies, Texas Latino Education Coalition, Rio Grande Valley Coalition for Mexican American Culture, Mexican American School Board Members Association, and Sikh Coalition.

As part of the continuing evolution in American historiography, as demonstrated by numerous scholars already noted previously and in appendix E, there likewise has been a continuing repetition of previous issues from those 1961–62 Texas battles in many other places throughout the United States, continuing on into the twenty-first century. Issues in the Texas battles as well as elsewhere focus on the extent to which social studies books should stress patriotism, a free-enterprise capitalistic economic system, limited government, state versus federal authority, Protestantism, separation of church and state, American exceptionalism, and US power and moral leadership among the world's nations, along with opposition to progressive education, communism, Socialism, and even US membership in the United Nations.

Nationally, and even in Texas, by the early 1960s and also continuing into the twenty-first century, other value clashes regarding social studies and history programs in the area of American historiography were already emerging or would soon emerge over the roles and rights of women, minorities and ethnic groups, and LGBTQ individuals and communities; roles played in history by prominent American conservatives as well as by liberals; secular humanism; multiculturalism; religious freedom; public welfare; immigration; creationism; scientific evolution; Common Core Educational Standards; whether the extent the inquiry-oriented New Social Studies should be used by teachers and students; the causes of climate change; environmentalism; the main cause of the American Civil War; Islam; and they role played by the Bible and religion in the origins of the American government.

Moreover, as just another example of some of the many ways the great Texas social studies war of 1961–62 continues to resonate nationally, in 1994 the *National Standards for United States History* were developed, primarily by Gary B. Nash, Professor of History at UCLA; Ross Dunn, Professor of History at San Diego State University; and Charlotte Crabtree, Professor of Curriculum Studies at UCLA, for the National

Center for History in the Schools at UCLA. Conservatives, including Lynne Chaney, former chairperson of the National Endowment for the Humanities, Republican politician Newt Gingrich, and radio commentator Rush Limbaugh, felt the 1994 *Standards* strayed too much from the old themes of American historiography in venturing too far by reclassifying the old theme of US history as signifying a nation of "one people" to a nation of "many peoples," by being too politically correct, by placing too much emphasis on the negative side of American history, and by placing too much emphasis on multiculturalism. Authors of the *Standards* answered that their guidelines stressed a more comprehensive or inclusive coverage of the study of American history, along with emphasis on student decision-making through an inquiry approach to the study of history. Although opposition to the *Standards* caused a rewrite to placate some of the conservative criticisms, various aspects of that type of controversy continued in one way or another in other places and remained very evident during *all* of the Texas adoptions of social studies programs from 1961 to the present. The opposing sides in the issue over the *Standards* were mainly just articulating much of what was said earlier during the great Texas social studies war of 1961–62, including arguments like the ones made by individuals such as J. Evetts Haley in opposition to J. Frank Dobie and Maury Maverick Jr. History may not always repeat itself, but in the area of American historiography, some arguments most certainly do.

Other recent issues are spin-offs and at times direct descendants of that ancestral 1961–62 Texas social studies war, reemerging both nationally as well as in Texas. Some very recent Texas examples include the following, which involve in one way or another involve the education of public school students in Texas.

1. The content and teaching strategies in the Texas Education Service Centers Curriculum Collaborative (CSCOPE), used by most public school districts in Texas, in 2010 was claimed by some Republican conservatives on the Texas State Board of Education to be anti-American.

2. The 2010 the Texas Social Studies Standards, called the Texas Essential Knowledge and Skills (TEKS), received unfavorable national and international publicity. Some liberals claimed the

Epilogue 235

2010 standards contained "highly conservative political historical inaccuracies," including downplaying the role of slavery as a cause of the American Civil War; omitting mention of Black Codes, Jim Crow laws, sharecropping, or the Ku Klux Klan; and placing too much emphasis on the memorization of data at the expense of the development of critical thinking skills, all of which effected social studies programs up for adoption in 2014.

3. Because of the controversies over the conservative-oriented 2010 Social Studies Standards enacted by the Texas State Board of Education, the Texas legislature in 2011 provided state reimbursement to allow public school districts the choice of either adopting textbooks approved by the State Board of Education or purchasing other programs on their own. When Texas chose not to use the national Common Core curriculum standards, a state and *not* federally oriented campaign to increase leaning standards for the nation's school children, the Texas legislature granted its public school districts more choices in adopting printed and digital materials, but only on the condition that any materials purchased and reimbursed by the state meet the 2010 Texas standards (if not, they should be supplemented by lessons taught in the classroom). Meanwhile, publishers continue to develop materials to meet the national Common Core Standards for a national market, but this will not apply to Texas.

4. The critical-thinking framework of the Advanced Placement US History Course Exam (APUSH) caused some conservative Republican members of the Texas State Board of Education in 2011 to feel it was anti-American and radically left/revisionist by emphasizing "negative aspects while omitting or minimizing the positive." The State board wanted the APUSH framework to conform to the 2010 Texas Social Studies Standards, but the College Board refused to comply.

5. A controversy arose in 2016 over content appearing in a textbook program submitted for state adoption, *Mexican American Heritage*, dealing with the study of Mexican American culture. This led critics, including those from academia as well as those representing Responsible Ethnic Studies, Texas Latino Education Coalition, Rio Grande Valley Coalition for

Mexican American Culture, and Mexican American School Board Members Association, to claim the book was offensive to Mexican Americans, contained as many factional errors (up to five to seven per page in a five hundred page book), and classified Mexican Americans as lazy and a threat to Western civilization. The fifteen members of the Texas State Board of Education, including the majority Republican members of the board, unanimously rejected the book for state adoption. The Texas State Board of Education in 2017 also rejected another textbook on Mexican American culture for being too limited in scope. With a majority of public school students in Texas having either a Mexican or Hispanic background, in April of 2018, the Texas State Board of Education voted unanimously to create a high school elective course on Mexican American culture, but, over objections of some Mexican Americans, nine Republican members on the board voted to name the course "Ethnic Studies: An Overview of Americans of Mexican Descent," rather than "Mexican American Studies." The name change led to many discussions between MAS supporters and state board members over just how to properly identify such an ethnic studies program: "Americans of Hispanic Descent" or "Mexicans Americans" (with or without a hyphen). Finally, in June of 2018, the state board finally agreed the elective course would be called "Ethnic Studies: Mexican American Studies." The board also stated it would consider adding African American Studies, Native American Studies, and Asian Pacific Studies in the school curriculum.

6. In February of 2017, the Texas State Board of Education tentatively proposed guidelines regarding evolution in new science textbook programs, an extension of what Mel and Norma Gabler had advocated before the Texas House of Representatives Textbook Committee during its hearings in 1962, and something the Gablers continued to do so well into the 1990s. Critics of the tentatively proposed new science proposals claimed the Republican-dominated Texas State Board of Education (in a preliminary vote of 9–5) in its new proposed science standards implied that scientists were uncertain about the validity of the theory of evolution, possibly leaving room for a version of creationism to become part of the Texas Essen-

Epilogue

237

tial Knowledge and Skills (TEKS), as well as a state-sponsored challenge to evolution. However, the State Board of Education in April of 2017 reversed itself and instead voted that, rather than "evaluate," students would "compare and contrast" evolution and creationism.

7. In October of 2018, the Texas State Board of Education met with its social studies advisory committee to receive numerous suggestions before making any final decisions in November to "streamline" teaching time for social studies standards of the Texas Essential Knowledge and Skills (TEKS) for K–12 grades. In regard to historical figures, the advisory panel considered if certain historical persons caused a significant change, if they were from an underrepresented group, and if those persons would have had an impact to "stand the test of time," as well as consider other significant changes in the social studies curriculum, as seen from the following examples. Among the most controversial suggestions the board received from its curricular advising group was to remove "all the heroic defenders" from the story of the 1836 battle at the Alamo and for teachers not to devote time to discussing William B. Travis's "Victory or Death" letter, which would save teachers about forty minutes of instruction, claiming the "heroic defenders" phrase was too vague. This quickly drew opposition from a number of groups and individuals, including Gov. Greg Abbott, Lt. Gov. Dan Patrick, and Sen. Ted Cruz. The board decided to reject that proposal. The advisory panel also recommended removing a lesson about "holding public officials to their word" from a grade-four program but did not restore it to another grade level. They also recommended removing a lesson on how the government pays for its services from a third-grade lesson to save forty minutes of teaching time. To save teachers additional instruction time, the advisory group likewise evoked more controversy when it recommended eliminating discussions of certain individuals from American history, such as Hillary Rodham Clinton, Eleanor Roosevelt, feminist Betty Fridan, Helen Keller, African American poet Phyllis Wheatley, African American mathematician/surveyor Benjamin Banneker, World War II generals George S. Patton and Omar Bradley, and the World War II Women's Air Force Service Pilots (WASP). The

board, after receiving numerous protests, in November of 2018 decided to maintain discussions of Clinton, Keller, Banneker, and the WASP military personnel. Some other examples of the many controversial changes approved by the board included instructing students about the "factors contributing to the Arab-Israeli conflict, adding the rejection of the existence of the State of Israel by the Arab League and a majority of Arab nations," which led to "ongoing conflicts"; having students "describe how religion and virtue contributed to the growth of representative government in the American colonies"; and asking students to "explain how Jim Crow laws and the Ku Klux Klan created obstacles to civil rights or minorities such as the suppression of voting." In addition, fifth-grade Civil War lessons were changed to include a discussion of how the expansion of slavery, as well as sectionalism and states' rights, contributed to the conflict—even though the general consensus among historians is that slavery was the main cause of that war. The board's advisory committee also recommended eliminating multiple references to "Judeo-Christian" and cutting any mention of Moses, "whose principles influenced America's founding documents," all of which the board rejected. Meanwhile, the Texas Freedom Network, the Texas Council for the Social Studies, and the Texas State Teachers Association paid close attention to what the state board decided, adding their feedback where possible. Note that in the face of these changes, it was emphasized that teachers can still discuss with their students any of the individuals or references omitted from the standards.

And so the social studies debate just goes on and on.

The ongoing battles over social studies curriculum and state adoption of those materials will continue for future scholars to investigate. A rich trove of archival material at the Texas Education Agency, the Texas Capital Legislative Library, and the Lorenzo de Zavala State Library and Archives, as well as numerous newspaper accounts and other writings and recordings, eagerly await those who wish to explore that subject from 1963 to the present. This volume seeks to explain the *birth* of that controversy during 1961–62. Many if not all of the arguments noted throughout this volume have continued to resurface and remain relevant well into the twentieth-first century. Indeed, all sides with their differing philosophies have much to tell us, not only about their respective historical eras but also current social issues related to textbook content, which is complex and not always straightforward.

It is critical to reflect on the issues portrayed herein: What can an in-depth look at a textbook controversy such as the one in Texas during 1961–62 teach us? Just what can be learned from all this? Most importantly, it teaches us to be ever vigilant and seriously consider the following eleven sets of questions regarding the social studies adoption process:

1. What are the current problems facing society? Problems according to whom? Did those problems have a bearing on what social studies programs are up for adoption? What are proposed solutions to those problems? Who made those proposals and why? Who is opposed to those solutions and why?

2. What social studies standards or guidelines dictate what can be adopted? Who approved the standards and for what reasons? How qualified were they to do so? Who selected those who made the final decision regarding the adoption? For what reasons? What qualified them to make that decision? Who helped those who approved the social studies standards? Did anyone else participate in the discussions or the writing of those standards? What qualified them to do so, and why did they participate?

3. Were the hearings regarding the adoption of social studies programs made public? If so, how soon ahead were they advertised and by what means? How much time did concerned citizens have to examine the programs? How available were the materials to the public? How open, balanced, or fair were public hearings about the programs up for adoption?

4. Regarding those who had concerns or support regarding the social studies programs, did they read all of the programs involved? What made them qualified to express their concern or support? Did they rely on reviews of the programs? If so, who wrote the reviews and for what reasons? What made them qualified to do so?

240 Epilogue

5. What did the protestors or those who supported the programs value? Did they possibly have any hidden agendas? During testimony involving reviews of the social studies programs, was anything taken out of context? If so, to what extent and why?

6. Who wrote the social studies programs? What qualified them to do so? How factual is the text, and how balanced are the interpretations therein? To what extent do the social studies programs stress the memorization of data? To what extent do the social studies programs emphasize or stress the development of writing and critical-thinking skills? About which issues? Why were those issues chosen? Were the issues balanced on a pro versus con basis? Could others issues have been added?

7. To what extent did authors of the textbook programs or their publishers' spokespersons respond to bills of particulars and oral arguments made by those in opposition or support of the programs?

8. Were social studies teachers encouraged or allowed to speak or otherwise make known their opinions during public hearings regarding the social studies programs up for adoption? If so, when, how, and to what extent?

9. How accurate and thorough was media coverage of protesters as well as supporters of the social studies programs? Were both viewpoints covered equally?

10. To what extent will the social studies standards and social studies programs help students successfully cope with challenges of the twenty-first century?

11. Whether one is a teacher, librarian, pupil, parent, or other concerned citizen, just what should students in a social studies course be allowed or required to study while in public school?

Finally, with any social studies controversy, consider to what extent all those involved adhered to the advice given by nineteenth-century historian Lord John Emerich Dalberg-Acton. As noted previously at the beginning of this volume, he maintained that no one should have the right to criticize or dispute an opposing view until one can express that view not only as well as but better than its proponents can.

Appendix A

The Texas State Textbook Committee's 1961 List of Recommended Changes

THE FOLLOWING is the full list of changes to history books recommended by the Texas State Textbook Committee in 1961, as presented to the State Commissioner of Education. The failure of the State Textbook Committee to recommend the major changes sought by Texans for America and the Texas Society of the Daughters of the American Revolution led to the creation of the Texas House of Representatives Textbook Investigating Committee.

Laidlaw Brothers

Our United States

Page 191—Col. States: "So far, only twenty-two amendments have been made!" Should read twenty three amendments have been made.

The map on page 28 is referred to several times in the section, "How Geography Affected Settlement," pages 29–34. Some of the places mentioned in the text are shown on the map. It would be helpful to the student if the following places mentioned in the text could also be shown on the map: Mohawk Valley, Puget Sound, Death Valley.

In discussing the voyages of Cabot, reference is made to Newfoundland, Cape Breton Island, or land around the mouth of the St. Lawrence River. By omitting the reference to Cape Breton Island which is small and hard to locate on maps easily available, it would be possible to include on page 68 a page reference to the map on page 70 which does show Newfoundland and the St. Lawrence. Nova Scotia, mentioned on page 69, should be labeled on the map on page 70. (This could be done by striking from the map Acadia, not mentioned in text, and using for Nova Scotia the size type in which Newfoundland is printed.)

Page 128–129—The double page map. "Indians of the United States" cuts into the middle of a sentence and bears no relationship to any of the nearby text. Could this be placed at the end of Unit II?

Pages 135–137—The discussion of routes west, rivers, gaps, settlements needs a more adequate map for illustration. Could the Indian map be replaced, at this point, with one showing more adequately the Ohio Valley and the Appalachian region?

Eliminate from the bibliography Marion Bauer, Ann Sterne. And Dorothy Canfield Fisher for allegedly being subversive.

Ginn and Company

American History

Include twenty-third amendment to the Constitution of the United States.

Page 203—Should read Jackson, not Johnson in caption under cartoon.

Correction required in that the text leaves the impression all colonials are radicals. Clarification of the use of the word conservative—pages 102, 106, 131 and 132. (Suggestion to use the word patriot)

Page 581—Change moral code. Should be rewritten to sustain desirable attitudes.

Bill of Rights should be mentioned in text during Washington's administration.

Page 619—Allied Nations should be substituted for use of the term United Nations.

Page 625—The liberation of White Russians statement is misleading. The White Russians change dictators.

Page 628—"Western Europe and Great Britain were severely crippled and after the war Western Europe was unable to recover its former position of strength and power in the world." This statement should be modified to reflect current conditions in Western Europe.

Page 628—The reasons given for the rapid recovery of Russia should include also some discussion of the power of the dictator to deny its citizens for the purpose of increasing its military might.

Dean, Vera M—Subject is on a list of persons who are extremely well-listed as to their communist and communist front affiliations by various government investigating committee (page 661).

Row, Peterson, and Company

The American People: Their History

Include twenty-third amendment to the Constitution of the United States.

The publishers offer to make changes on pages 617B, 622B, 624A and 618 should be made.

Change of statement to read: "The important New Deal concept that these measures emphasized" etc.

Ask for change in wording of statement dealing with "The Social Security Act set up a system of compulsory savings."

Page 618B—paragraph 3. Ask for change in wording of statement "When the initial program of the Roosevelt Administration was introduced it received almost unanimous support." Change unanimous to overwhelming, Page 622b.

Page 725—Change-Considering the total population of the country, the number proven disloyal was small, but, etc.

Webster Publishing Company

This Is Our Nation

Include twenty-third amendment to the Constitution of the United States.

Page 697—Delete Tales of South Pacific; questioned for high-school reading.

Question on the date of Treaty of Ghent (wrong date).

Houghton Mifflin Company

The History of Our World

Chapter 23 should include a description of capitalism similar to the type discussion which was done on Socialism. Index should include line with reference to Capitalism. Page 767—To show Union of South Africa now out of Common-wealth.

Story of Nations

Page 780 should be extended to include latest facts, such as death of Hammarskjöld, or added to picture on page 488.

Page 619—Gives date of Japanese constitution as 1869, should be 1889.

Page 772—Gives Menderes as leader of Turkey-should be brought up to date.

Page 634—Bring African map up-to-date.

Page 657—Bring section on Congo up-to-date.

Page 307—Date map to show when these facts were true.

Page 306—column 2, drop Cyprus and Singapore from list of crown colonies and Somaliland from protectorate.

Page 377—Delete: "She still retains Belgian Congo."

Page 462—Add sentence to bring up-to-date.

Page 547—Story on Russia needs to be brought up-to-date.

Page 580—Bring story of South East Asia up-to-date.

Chapter 70—Include unit on Cuba.

Page 232—Give fuller explanation of Capitalism; bringing out free enterprise, etc.

Lyons and Carnahan

Freedom's Frontier

The only criticism of Freedom's Frontier was for its reference to seven persons whose loyalty had been questioned. In their reply the publishers say,
"Assuming that the committee is right in its assertions, we are not only willing but anxious to delete any references to such persons in Freedom's Frontier or any other of our publications."

In the absence of documentation of the charges from the Texans for America, Lyons and Carnahan's willingness to delete names they had once considered worthy of inclusion raises a question as to their interest in defending *Freedom's Frontier*.

The names need not be deleted unless the committee finds more adequate evidence to indicate the necessity for such deletion.

Harcourt, Brace and World, Inc.

Story of the American Nation

Page 100—(uncorrected copy) Spain fought on the side of Great Britain against France. In the high school text it reads page 55, Spain, having entered the war as an ally of France had to give up Florida to Great Britain.

Men and Nations: A World History

Page 262e—Pictures are reversed.

Page 615, column 1, paragraph 2—Delete the word "Democratic."

Page 321—The whole last paragraph should be deleted.

Page 357—The date of the Mexican revolt should be 1810, not 1811.

Page 12, second column, second paragraph—In the sentence "Men appeared on the earth," insert "probably."

Page 100—It gives the date 392 A.D. when Christianity was accepted by Rome. It should be 380 A.D.

Page 659—Chart should be extended to 1961.

Page 29—King Tut's tomb was opened in 1922, not 1924.

Page 29—Column1, Alexander conquered Egypt in 332 B.C., not in 375 B.C.

Page 396—Should include a paragraph to show weaknesses of Communism.

Rise of the American Nation

Include twenty-third amendment to the Constitution of the United States.

Page 788—"But after Japan attacked China, the two opposing Chinese factions joined forces against their common enemy." Incorrect statement.

Page 788—The Wedemeyer Report should be recognized as differing from General Marshall's report.

Page 804—"Revolt in Poland." The impression-that Poland-gained freedom of speech, press, and religion should be corrected.

Discussion should be included on the manner in which the Soviet Union acquired the atomic bomb.

Houghton Mifflin Company

This Is America's Story

Page 606—Russia establishes a new society.

"In 1917, while World War I was still going on, the Russians revolted against their government. They overthrew their ruler, called the Czar." "Then they set up a government in which the country was controlled by the members of one party, called the Communist Party."

Could it be rephrased this way?

Before a stable government could be established, the Bolshevists, a Militant Minority, coerced the Russian people and set up a government by which the country was controlled by the members on one party, the Communist.

Page 549, paragraph 2—The sentence: "For better or worse, the United States now had overseas possessions to govern and to defend." The publisher has agreed to substitute the following sentence for the one quoted above: "The United States now had overseas possessions to govern and to defend."

Page 552–553—Referring to the topic, "The Puerto Ricans Are Aided," the publishers have stated that they are introducing new material to provide a more balanced treatment. This is a desirable change. (Answer to protests made by the Texans for America, page 3.)

Page 481–482—Concluding section titled, "How Did the New Inventions Change the Farmer's Way of Life? compare "life in the 1880's with farm life seventy years later." (This would be the 1950s.) This section could be brought up-to-date.

Chapter on immigration might mention post World War II refugees.

The substitution on page 549 of *This Is America's Story* as suggested by the publisher is a desirable change, as is the revision of the material on Puerto Rico on pages 552–53.

The expected revisions have been added to the last chapters, but the book is badly dated at other points.

Starting with chapter 21 through 26, Units 7 and 8, there is a series of chapters in which various aspects of the American scene are examined and, presumably, brought up to date. Time after time, this means brought up to mid-thirties or the immediate post war period.

To ask for changes at all the places where it would be required to bring the book really up-to-date would probably not be practical, but the following examples might be cited.

Page 421—treatment of the America Indian ends with the sentence, "the wartime experiences which large numbers of Indians had outside the reservations may well bring about changes in Indian life." No mention of discovery of oil on the Navaho reservation.

Page 435—chapter on transportation and communication includes this sentence, "In spite of newer forms of travel, the railroads still carry the bulk of the passengers and freight in this country." Freight, maybe, but not passengers.

Page 433—discussion of telephone, telegraph, etc. ends with section titles, "Radio Serves America and the World." This is the concluding section on communication and it ends with these words, "Television makes it possible to see as well as hear a wide variety of programs. Radar is a form of radio which was developed during World War II. Radar warns the pilots of ships and airplanes when they are approaching something that might cause a collision. It also protects our borders against invading aircraft. Indeed, no one yet knows all that radio can do for man." Maybe not, but we know a lot more than this!

Pages 439–440—section on resource and American productivity should have more on plastics, synthetics, and electronics.

Page 444—new methods in industry include the assembly line and mass production, but no mention of automation.

Page 445—describes department stores, chain stores, and the mail order houses as methods of merchandising. The latest thing here is the mail order house. No mention of modern merchandising, advertising, the growth of suburban shopping centers, discount houses.

Page 450—concluding statements on the oil industry are, "During world War II the production and refining of petroleum products in the United States reached unbelievable heights. By 1950 the value of the petroleum produced annually was about 5 billion dollars." Since 1950?

Page 481—discussion of agriculture ends with the following, "Then, during the 1950's farm prices fell off while the government found itself with growing surpluses of unsold foodstuff on its hands." What about figures on increased productivity since World War II, less people engaged in farming, decline of family farm?

Page 528—Modern popular music ends with Paul Whiteman, Duke Ellington, Benny Goodman and George Gershwin. How about South Pacific, My Fair Lady, etc.?

Page 530—"Varied program on the radio—music, plays, quiz programs, news—bring enjoyment to millions in their homes. Television has developed at such a startling rate that it is now found in millions of homes. It promises to have far-reaching effects upon many phases of American life."

The Macmillan Company

History of a Free People

Include twenty-third amendment to the Constitution of the United States.

Page 393—Misspelled "splendid"

More positive stand against communism and socialism. Examples:

Page 435, column 2, paragraph 1—the only objection to socialism in. this country seems to be that "Americans were on the whole too prosperous to want violent change."

Page 686, in "American Foreign Policy and Communism," column 2, paragraph 1, line 9, we find, "The United States can offer no pat substitute for Marxism, since by the nature of a free society, we disagree among ourselves about how to promote the good life." In that one sentence the authors seem to condemn the entire system of free enterprise and the worth of the individual.

Page 42, paragraph 2, "In these circumstances the radicals, the men who led the resistance . . ." (Substitute patriot for radical)

List of Recommended Changes

Page 101—Remove statement "Our Constitution is recommended as a model for world union."

Page 434—Revise statement to give clearer picture of Marxism.

Page 158—"Washington's mind moved slowly"—poor wording and should be changed.

Page 543—Speculation on World War II being averted by League of Nations should be removed.

Had Macmillan eliminate the following: "Had Wilson seen the necessity for compromise, the United States would have joined the League, although with reservations. Had that happened, there was just a chance that World War II might have been averted."

Appendix B

American Groups or Individuals Voicing Concerns about Social Studies Textbooks (Reconstruction to the Present)

Act! For America
Advertising Federation of America
Albert Shanker (Labor) Institute
All American Conference
America's Future
American Association of University Women
American Atheists Society (Madelyn Murray O'Hare)
American Citizenship Foundation
American Civil Liberties Union
American Communist Party
American Family Association
American Federation of Labor
American GI Forum
American Historical Association
American Irish Historical Society
American Jewish Committee
American Legion
American Library Association
American Nazi Party
American Principles Project
American Studies Association
American Turner Bund
American War Mothers
Americans for Prosperity

Americans United for Separation of Church and State
Anti-defamation League
Benevolent Protective Order of Elks
Better American Federation
Better Education Association
Boy Scouts of America
Charles Grant Miller
Christian Coalition
Citizens for Excellence in Education
Citizens for a Sound Economy
Civic League for Immigrants
Colonial Sons and Daughters
Commission on Intellectual Cooperation
Concerned Women for America
Constitution Party
Council on Interracial Books for Children
Council on Racial Equality
Creationists
Dames of the Loyal Legion
Daughters of the American Revolution
Daughters of the Republic of Texas
Daughters of Veterans

Daughters of the War of 1812
Descendants of the Signers of the Declaration of Independence
Eagle Forum (Phyllis Schlafly)
Eastern Star
Education Research Analysts (Mel and Norma Gabler)
Empire State Society
Equality Texas
Federal Trade Commission
Focus on the Family
The Free Market Foundation
General Federation of Women's Clubs
General Society of Mayflower Dames
German American Alliance
Grand Army of the Republic
Group on Advanced Leadership
Guardians of American Education
Harvard Graduate School of Education
Heritage Foundation
Hindu American Foundation
Institute for Curriculum studies
Irish Patriotic League
Jaycees
Jewish Community Relations Council of Greater Dallas Education Liaison
Jewish Welfare Board
John Birch Society
Junior Order of United American Mechanics
Knights of Columbus
Knights of Pythias
Ku Klux Klan
Ladies of the Grand Army of the Republic
League for American Citizenship
League of Nations Nonpartisan Association
League of United Latin American Citizens

The Liberty Institute
Mexican American Legal Defense Fund
Mexican-American Legislative Caucus
Mexican American School Board Members Association
Military Order of the World Wars
Minute Women
Moral Majority
Multicultural Alliance for Social Studies Advocacy
National Association for Constitutional Government
National Association for the Advancement of Colored People
National Association for the Advancement of White People
National Association of Manufactures
National Association of Naval Veterans
National Association of Scholars
National Child Welfare Association
National Civic Federation
National Clay Products Industries Association
National Coalition against Censorship
National Congress of the PTA
National Council of Catholic Women
National Council for American Education
National Council for History Education
National Council for Social Studies
National Education Association
National Grange
National Japanese-American Memorial Foundation
National Organization of Women
National Republican Committee
National Security League

Concerns about Social Studies Textbooks

National Society of Colonial Dames of America
National Society of US Daughters of 1812
National Utility Association
Neo-Confederates
New York Economic Council
Organization of American Historians
Patriotic League for the Preservation of American History
People for the American Way
Pilgrim's Society
Project 912
Republican National Committee
Republican Tea Party
Responsible Ethnic Studies
Rio Grande Valley Coalition for Mexican American Culture
Save Our History
Service Star Legion
Sikh Coalition
Sons of Confederate Veterans
Star-Spangled Association
Texans for America
Texas Conservative Coalition
Texas Freedom Network
Texas Institute of Letters
Texas Latino Education Coalition
Texas Navy Association
Texas Public Policy Foundation
Texas State Historical Association
Texas State Teachers Association
Texas Values Action
Thomas B. Fordham Institute
Truth in Texas Textbooks Coalition
Union Society of the Civil War
United Civil Rights Council
United Confederate Veterans
United Daughters of the Confederacy
Various American Indian Groups
Various Black Militant Groups
Various Chambers of Commerce
Various Protestant Groups
Various Roman Catholic Groups
Various White Citizen Councils
Veterans of Foreign Wars
Wall Street Business Men's League
The Wallbuilders
William Randolph Hearst Newspapers
Women on the Wall
Women's Auxiliary of the American Institute of Mining and Metallurgical Engineers
Women's Christian Temperance Union
Women's Home Mission Society
Women's Relief Corps
Women's Relief Corps of the Grand Army of the Republic
YMCA

Author's Note: Makes one wonder about how one would go about writing a history textbook to satisfy *all* those groups, what the book would look like, and what size it would be.

Appendix C

Point-Counterpoint Dialogue about Content in Social Studies Programs

TO FURTHER explore the nature of appropriate content for social studies programs, and as a review of some major arguments put forth in this book, consider the following imaginary conversation between two concerned parents. It illustrates the major clash of values inherent in the great Texas social studies textbook war of 1961–62, more than fifty years ago, and shows the complexity of the issues surrounding the content of these social studies programs—often without easy answers.

Father: *Censure* only means to assess or judge. Interested citizens have a First Amendment right to offer assessments or judgments of what public school students should be allowed or required to study.

Mother: That is true, but *censure* also means to prohibit something, and censorship can leave students with an inadequate and a distorted picture of something. Moreover, the right to read what one chooses is what Thomas Jefferson and James Madison regarded as a fundamental part of the First Amendment. As attorney Clarence Darrow maintained, "To think is to differ, and if you discourage thought, you violate a student's right to read."

Father: But the right to read *what*? Parents are the ones most responsible for the welfare of their daughters and sons, and thereby have the right to control what they encounter in school curriculum. As William Jennings Bryan argued, "The duty of a parent to protect his children is more sacred than the right of teachers

256   Appendix C

to teach what parents do not want taught, especially when the speaker demands pay for his teaching and insists on being furnished an audience to talk to."

Mother: Yes, but teachers, too, have an obligation to determine what young people learn in school. Teachers are especially educated to do this.

Father: However, students up to a certain age are required by law to attend some sort of school, whether it be public, private, or home. Therefore, materials should be banned if their content conflicts with values stressed at home.

Mother: True, home values are important, yet they can differ from family to family. They can even differ within families, as is our case. School curriculum should account for that.

Father: But should it also account for books containing the essence of secular humanism, which stresses faith in human beings instead of primarily a faith in a supreme being and absolute values? Secular humanism also emphasizes the use of situation ethics, which should not be forced upon students who disagree with such views. After all, this is a nation whose government is founded on the Judeo-Christian ethic. As US Supreme Court Justice David Brewer said, "This is a Christian nation," or as Mel Gabler noted, "with no absolute values considered, a seed of doubt about the firmness and validity of traditional values is planted each time a choice of alternatives is made. Value clarification programs are based on the anti-Judeo-Christian ethic of humanistic relativism. It places students adrift with no fixed moral values or guidelines."

Mother: Humanists, in the best Renaissance tradition, stress using one's own reasoning faculties to identify and attempt to solve problems. Humanists believe that if people are to learn by developing their knowledge and intellect, they must be allowed to debate, to differ, and to make choices. Humanists, following the footsteps of such individuals of the Enlightenment as Thomas Jefferson, Benjamin Franklin, James Madison, James Monroe, John Adams, John Quincy Adams, and Thomas Paine, believe in freedom and a pluralistic, secular society like ours, as opposed to any authoritarian effort to impose any one certain viewpoint on a society. It is true that Christianity is the majority religion in

Point-Counterpoint Dialogue

our country, with the Roman Catholic religion having the largest Christian religious denomination. But it is not the only religion of Americans, and any reading of the debates at the Constitutional Convention of 1787, the Constitution, and First Amendment, or the *Federalist Papers* by James Madison, Alexander Hamilton, and John Jay, will show that the founding fathers deliberately created a secular and not a Christian government.

Father: But school boards and the State Board of Education should represent the wishes of the majority of voters who elected them to office. This is how our civil governments function, and if a majority of voters do not want something studied in their schools, it should not be taught. Schools should conform to and transmit the majority values of the community. And, if a majority want the textbooks to reflect their views—say conservative ones—that is the way it should be. Without this, anarchy would prevail.

Mother: It is true we govern ourselves by majority rule, but school personnel must also protect the rights and preferences of the minority, and if you allow only what the majority wants, it could happen that the minority might someday become the majority and do its own censoring. What would you say if the majority was a liberal one and wanted the textbooks to reflect that viewpoint? As Alexis de Tocqueville warned in *Democracy in America*, the stressing of mass conformity or indoctrination can stifle minority dissent and individualism. On that same subject, historian Henry Steele Commager noted that only totalitarian governments insist on mass conformity, and part of the American tradition is non-conformist. Schools thereby have a duty to let students responsibly examine many viewpoints. Remember, Thomas Jefferson wrote that if "a nation expects to be ignorant and free, it expects what never was and never will be," or as Lyndon Baines Johnson said, "books and ideas are the most effective weapons against intolerance and ignorance."

Father: But which viewpoints or topics are we talking about here, and for what grade levels? Can you think of certain television programs, movies, or information on the internet or in books you would not want a student to see or read? Is there anything you would not let a child read or view? If so, is that not censorship? Students should not be exposed to content if it is in violation of their beliefs, or if it causes them embarrassment, or if they do not possess the experience or maturity to responsibility deal with it, no matter whether they be in the majority or minority. That would concur with your argument about minority rights. People concerned about students' feelings should practice what Harper Lee wrote in *To Kill a Mockingbird*, stressing that one could never really know someone else unless you stood in that person's shoes and walked around in them.

Mother: But if students are to develop intellectually, they must be allowed to study something thoroughly in the context of its time. That would be in agreement with Harper Lee. As poet Robert Frost said, "Education is the ability to listen to or consider anything without losing your temper or your self-confidence," or as Christopher Morley observed, the "real purpose of books is to trap the mind into doing its own thinking." Students today also can cope well and are not as immature as they may seem to older people.

Father: It is true that students today are more sophisticated about some things, but as historian J. Evetts Haley has noted, stressing opposing sides of issues often confuses the young, even if it does not embarrass them, and results in hasty judgments. Examining conflicting viewpoints should be left until students are more experienced and better equipped with additional knowledge so that they are less prone to brain washing. Even the extent of that knowledge available in schools today is restricted, since teachers and librarians indirectly or directly ban materials by the very act of limited selection, if nothing else.

Mother: That's professional choice. By making informed choices, teachers and librarians recommend a selection of materials in a public and professional manner and do so based on school board and state policies, what is available, and what tax dollars permit to be purchased. Dedicated and educated teachers are the most suitable ones to ultimately focus on the extent to which their pupils can as thoroughly, objectively, or analytically as possible deal effectively with the study of history or other social studies disciplines. For the Texas situation, I would even have a committee of experienced and master social studies teachers from the State Council for the Social Studies, with advice from university academics, be responsible for the state adoption of social studies textbooks, in addition to setting the social studies standards, thereby omitting involvement like a state board of education.

Father: But would that be democratic? Your suggestion would violate the democratic process of electing members of a state board of education, who now set the textbook standards and have final say on what should be adopted. Without that, what happens to majority rule and the voice of citizens who pay the taxes so the state can purchase the textbooks?

Author's Note: What do you think? Considering the foreign and domestic situations in 1961–62, would you have thought the same at that time?

Appendix D

Recommended Readings on the Topic of History Education

THE FOLLOWING references offer a variety of opinions on improving the teaching, learning, and writing of history.

Edwin Fenton, *The New Social Studies* (Holt, Rinehart and Winston, 1967). Main argument: A rationale by the most prominent leader of the New Social Studies movement for an inquiry-oriented approach to the study of social studies, whereby students, through an inductive approach by using primary sources, form conclusions via analytical reasoning with teacher guidance.

Richard H. Brown, Director, Committee on the Study of History, Amherst College, preface to Allan O. Kownslar and Donald B. Frizzle, *Discovering American History* (Holt, Rinehart, and Winston, 1970, 1974). Main argument: When using original sources in a history course, the teacher should "ask students to play the role of the scholar, discovering for themselves the relationships which form the basic structure of the discipline, sharing the excitement of inquiry and learning, in the process, methods of inquiry which will serve them through life." Other related and later works on the topics stressed in *Discovering American History* include Sam Wineburg, *Historical Thinking and Other Unnatural Acts: Charting the Future of Teaching the Past* (Temple University Press, 2001), and Sam Wineburg, Daisy Martin, and Chauncey Monte-Sano, *Reading Like a Historian* (Teachers College Press, Columbia University, 2013).

Allan O. Kownslar, editor, *Teaching American History: The Quest for Relevancy* (National Council for the Social Studies, 1974). Main argument: The old traditional history and the new inquiry-oriented inductive history can be used together to enhance student learning, but the main focus should be to utilize the inquiry process to have students analyze original sources in order for lasting learning to occur. Using the inquiry method when analyzing original sources allows students to develop concepts, empathize with the past, clarify values, learn to evaluate suspected myths or stereotypes, and, most importantly, ask critical questions.

Gilbert T. Sewell, *Necessary Lessons: Decline and Renewal in American Schools* (Free Press, 1983), along with his review of American history textbooks for the National Excellence Network. Main argument: "Textbooks should be written by teachers and historians, not by social studies professionals, ghost writers and committees that lack any sense of history and are often antagonistic to it. Textbooks must face historical conflicts and tensions squarely, not shrink from class, ideological, religious, racial and gender controversies. Selection committees should abandon readability formulas that 'dumb materials down.' Instead, they should welcome complex sentences and challenging vocabulary to spur interest, help comprehension and add to juvenile appreciation of literature, even for less able students."

Theodore R. Sizer, *Horace's Compromise: The Dilemma of the American High School* (Houghton Mifflin, 1985). Main argument: Less is more in education, so that students can analyze and think about certain topics in greater depth.

Allen Bloom, *The Closing of the American Mind: How Higher Education Has Failed Democracy and Impoverished the Souls of Today's Students* (Simon and Schuster, 1987). Main argument: Our universities have abandoned a coherent curriculum founded on the ideas of great Western thinkers for faddish, shallow courses, teaching a tolerance for all ideas, which is a hindrance to intellectual communication.

Lynne V. Chaney, *American Memory: A Report on the Humanities in the Nation's Public Schools* (National Endowment for the Humanities, 1987). Main argument: "Cultural memory flourishes or declines for many reasons, but among the most important is what happens in our schools. Long relied upon to transmit knowledge of the past to upcoming generations, our schools today appear to be about a different task. Instead of preserving the past, they more often disregard it, sometimes in the name of 'progress'—the idea that today has little to learn from yesterday. But usually the culprit is 'progress'—the belief that we can teach our children how to think without troubling them to learn anything worth thinking about, the belief that we can teach them how to understand the world in which they live without conveying to them the events and ideas that have brought it into existence."

Gertrude Himmelfarb, *The New History and the Old: Critical Essays and Reappraisals*, (Harvard University Press, 1987). Main argument: "A mode of history that belittles politics and ideas denigrates the political institutions and intellectual traditions that have shaped the past, and serves the continuity between past and present, leaving little that is usable in their place."

E. D. Hirsch Jr., *Cultural Literacy: What Every American Needs to Know* (Houghton Mifflin, 1987). Main argument: "We know instinctively that to understand what somebody is saying, we must understand more than the surface meanings of words; we have to understand the context as well. The need for background information applies all the more to reading and writing. To grasp the words on a page we have to know a lot of information that isn't set down on the page."

Diane Ravitch and Chester E. Finn Jr., *What Do Our 17-Year-Olds Know? A Report on the First National Assessment of History and Literature* (Harper and Row, 1987). Main argument: High school curriculum needs to encourage students to spend more time reading and analyzing original sources in history and other writings, novels, and poems, which once formed the basis for the traditional humanities curriculum.

Barry K. Beyer, *Improving Student Thinking: A Comprehensive Approach* (Allyn and Bacon, 1997), *Developing a Thinking Skills Program* (Allyn and Bacon, 1988), and *Practical Strategies for the Teaching of Thinking* (Allyn and Bacon, 1987). Main argument: "In the teaching of thinking, practice is not enough. Students must be taught how to think on their own." All three books provide elaborate strategies and rationales by utilizing the many aspects of the inquiry process for doing just that.

Ronald W. Evans, *The Social Studies Wars: What Should We Teach the Children?* (Teachers College Press, Columbia University, 2004). Main argument: Education historian Evans depicts a balanced story of the ongoing conflict over social studies programs involving American historiography, beginning with the nineteenth century to the end of the twentieth century, between the (1) teaching of traditional history and (2) teaching of social studies with components of such areas as geography, economics, political science, and anthropology (the problem-solving controversial issues programs of the John Dewey progressive-reconstructionist school of thought). Evans concludes that the "key question haunting social studies remains the issue of its definition and its vision, and of the approaches to the field that will be practiced in schools. For meaningful resolution, the struggles need complete airing in a public forum—shorn of the propaganda, scapegoating, and interest group financing we have seen during the field's recent history—in an effort to advance forms of social studies that will contribute to the goal of meaningful learning."

Geoff Scheurman and Ronald W. Evans, editors, *Constructionism and the New Social Studies: A Collection of Classic Inquiry Lessons* (Information Age Publishing, 2018), with a foreword by noted Harvard University cognitive scientist Jerome Bruner. The volume contains examples of the best social studies inquiry–oriented lessons to emerge from the New Social Studies movement of the 1960s to 1990s, including those from the Amherst, Harvard, Ohio State, and Carnegie Mellon projects. Beginning with Hilda Taba and Jerome Bruner, the book chronicles the work of leaders in the movement by focusing on their involvement in disciplines that include history, political science, geography, economics, anthropology, and sociology. Main argument: The inquiry approach modeled by inquiry-oriented projects continues to be used by many but not a majority of classroom teachers and university professors today.

Appendix E

Recommended Readings on the Development of American Social Studies and Textbook Wars

SINCE THE EARLY part of the twentieth century, much has been written about the various conflicts over what should be included and emphasized in American social studies textbooks, as well as how that subject should be taught. In addition to the works noted in the preface, introduction, other parts of this manuscript, and appendix D, the following annotated bibliography contains recommended samples of literature available on this topic, along with some historiographical trends from the early 1900s to the present.

Bessie Louise Pierce, *Public Opinion and the Teaching of History in the United States* (Alfred A. Knopf, 1926). Pierce was a pioneer scholar in the study of American school textbooks. Her thorough and well-documented story of attacks on American social studies books and teachers from the 1600s to the late 1920s remains one of the best studies of that era. Aside from her coverage of the emergence of history textbooks from colonial days into the 1920s, she explored nationalism and localism in history legislation, laws requiring the teaching of history, and disloyalty charges against teachers, concluding with a quote from a Dr. Payson Smith of Massachusetts, who wrote in the November 1921, edition of the *Christian Science Monitor* (under the byline "Schools Should Be Uninfluenced") that the "public school does not owe to business interests or to special interests or to labor interests of any kind that there shall be constructed in the minds of young people attitude and opinions designed to be definitely and specifically

266 Appendix E

helpful to those interests. . . . It is not a legitimate part of the public school program to deal in any phase of propaganda. Let the doors of the school-house once be opened to the appeals of those who want . . . any subject taught from the special viewpoints of a group of people and they must remain open until the schools will be so crowded with the teachings of the propagandists that there will be no time or opportunity left for doing the work which is the primary responsibility of the schools."

Bessie Louise Pierce, *Civic Attitudes in American School Textbooks* (University of Chicago Press, 1930; reissued by Arno Press and the *New York Times*, 1971). Pierce examined civic attitudes in ninety-seven histories; sixty-seven books in civic, sociological, and economic problems; and forty-five geographies used in American public schools through the 1920s. She focused mostly on negative comments about Germany, Spain, England, Russia, China, Japan, Latin America, and America, and general political concepts and racist ideology that appeared in the books. Pierce concluded that in view of the upcoming decade of the 1930s, "in which most of these books are read by the child, the question, however, arises as to the character of ideals and attitudes which should be established in this plastic stage of development when many impressions become indelibly fixed. 'The chief part of man's life is remembering,' said [historian] James Harvey Robinson. What do the American people wish their children to remember?" Her study compliments the work she did in her 1926 publication of *Public Opinion and the Teaching of History*.

Howard K. Beale, *Are American Teachers Free? An Analysis of Restraints upon the Freedom of Teaching in American Schools* (Charles Scribner's Sons, 1936), and *A History of Freedom of Teaching in American Schools* (Charles Scribner's Sons, 1941). Combined, these two studies compliment the work of Bessie Pierce, covering topics from colonial days to 1939 dealing with major American protests of social studies textbooks, reasons for the protests, and why more teachers have or have not exercised their freedoms in regard to what they should be teaching. Issues include limits on teacher expression, patriotism, sectional prejudices, teacher tenure, racially segregated schools, and religious influences on the school curriculum. Beale concluded (1) the "challenging result of this study is the discovery that competent teachers must use texts chosen not by themselves but by others who are not teachers—all too often by politicians—who must make their choice in such ways to please, at least not offend, numerous powerful groups in the community who know little about educational processes or the subjects involved," and (2) "that this choice must be made from texts themselves either compromises forced upon scholars by an uninformed public opinion or products made in accordance with public prejudice by men willing to write whatever will pay best." Beale felt the real question is whether children are taught the facts of history based on careful research, or whether they are given, under the guise of history, "an account of persons and events arranged and distorted to serve the purpose of whichever group at the moment is powerful enough to control the teachers and their texts. . . . Thus, teachers in each century and locality have been allowed freedom to discuss subjects that did not seem to matter and denied freedom on issues about which men did seriously care."

Mel and Norma Gabler with James C. Hefley, *Are Textbooks Harming Your Children? Norma and Mel Gabler Take Action and Show You How!* (Mott Media, 1979), and Mel and Norma Gabler with James C. Hefley, *What Are They Teaching Our Children? What You Can Do about Humanism and Textbooks in Today's Public Schools* (Victor Books, 1985). These texts present a defense of the Gablers' approach to evaluating textbooks. The first book is a revised edition of their *Textbooks on Trial* and contains biographical information about the Gablers and why they began their quest to evaluate textbook programs. Both books focus on topics the Gablers regarded as appropriate for public school education, such as the promotion of the Christian religion, free enterprise capitalism, and Biblical Creationism, with opposition to sex education, values clarification, secular humanism, and big government. The Gablers offer their rationale for either opposing or supporting such topics, along with specific suggestions for ways to protest parts of textbooks deemed unsatisfactory. Over the years, many conservative protestors have used these two books by the Gablers as guides, alongside the Bible, for their own critiques of textbooks. The publisher's foreword to *Are Textbooks*

268   Appendix E

Harming Your Children? notes that the "message of this book is that today's textbooks have sacrificed teaching to opinion shaping, basic skills to personality molding, and factual content to ideological propaganda of a kind that the majority of American parents would find totally unacceptable if they but knew of it." The Gabler books can also be read in conjunction with three books whose authors agreed with them: Jerry Falwell, *Listen America!* (Bantam Books, 1981); Cal Thomas, *Book Burning* (Crossway Books, 1983); and Tim LaHaye, *The Battle of the Mind* (Fleming H. Revell Company, 1980), the latter of which deals primarily with criticisms of humanism. A counterpoint to the Gabler, Falwell, Thomas, and LaHaye discussions regarding Creationism and humanism can be found in Henry Reichman, *Censorship and Selection: Issues and Answers for Schools* (American Library Association and American Association of School Administrators, 1988).

More about the Gablers appears in James Moffett, *Storm in the Mountains: A Case Study of Censorship, Conflict, and Consciousness* (Southern Illinois University Press, 1988). Moffett features the prominent role played by Mel and Norma Gabler in the Kanawha County, West Virginia, schoolbook controversy of the 1970s. Additionally, see Edward B. Jenkinson, *Censors in the Classroom: The Mind Benders* (Southern Illinois University Press, 1979). Jenkinson, former chair of the National Council of Teachers of English Committee against Censorship, includes a chapter on Mel and Norma Gabler, focusing on their successes in making changes to textbooks or having textbooks eliminated for adoption in Texas and elsewhere; the roles played by left-wing groups such as the National Organization for Women and their complaints about content or lack thereof in textbooks and dictionaries; and summaries of major textbook battles in the nation's school districts through the 1970s. This should also be read in conjunction with Jenkinson's *The Schoolbook Protest Movement: 40 Questions and Answers* (Phi Delta Kappa Educational Foundation, 1986). See also Joan DelFattore, *What Johnny Shouldn't Read: Textbook Censorship in America* (Yale University Press, 1992). DelFattore offers a summary of textbook protests from 1963 to 1990, with a special focus on six federal court cases involving textbook censorship:

(1) *Mozert v. Hawkins County Public Schools*, (2) *McLean v. Arkansas Board of Education*, (3) *Aguillard v. Edwards*, (4) *Smith v. Board of School Commissioners*, (5) *Farreo v. Hall*, and (6) *Vigil v. Columbia County School Board*. She includes a discussion of the role of Mel and Norma Gabler in textbook criticisms, with an overall focus on issues involving communism, capitalism, religion, evolution, race relations, sex education, values clarification, globalism, and environmentalism.

Howard D. Mehlinger and O. L. Davis Jr., *The Social Studies: Eightieth Yearbook of the National Society for the Study of Education* (University of Chicago Press, 1981). For those interested in a history of the development of the social studies and the role of changes in historiography, consult this text by Mehlinger and Davis Jr., editors and leading experts in the field of social studies curriculum and instruction. It contains essays by teachers of curriculum instruction, history, economics, and political science. Especially useful for social studies teachers and school librarians are discussions about the social studies war in chapter 1, "Understanding the History of the Social Studies," and chapter 13, "Social Studies: Some Gulfs and Priorities," where the authors discusses problems with censorship in social studies programs.

Michael W. Apple and Linda K. Christian-Smith, *The Politics of the Textbook* (Routledge, 1991). The book contains a detailed chapter on the Texas textbook adoption process of the 1980s, based on data from three adoption years of the early 1980s, and "looks at the relationships between those who made decisions within this system and the textbook publishers and protestors who wished to influence those decisions."

Robert Lerner, Althea K. Hagal, and Stanley Rothman, *Molding the Good Citizen: The Politics of High School History Texts* (Prager, 1995). Lerner and colleagues present a preview of the controversy that would eventually lead to the 2010 Texas History Standards. More recent studies of the Far Right include Jill Lepore, *The Whites of Their Eyes: The Tea Party's Revolution and the Battle for American History* (Princeton University Press, 2010), and Frances Fitzgerald, *The Evangelicals: The Struggle to Shape America* (Simon and Schuster, 2017).

270   Appendix E

Diane Ravitch and Maris A. Vinovskis, editors, *Learning from the Past: What History Teaches Us about School Reform* (Johns Hopkins University Press, 1995). This volume contains a chapter by Gary B. Nash, American historian at UCLA, entitled "American History Reconsidered: Asking New Questions about the Past." Nash includes a survey of the dominant white, male, racist, Eurocentric bias in early American histories, including the ones by David Saville Muzzey, whose American histories were among the nation's best sellers. Nash also deals with the late twentieth century trends in multiculturalism. The following titles also elaborate on the Eurocentric theme and the failure of some to teach controversial historical topics in order to make the subject matter come to life for students: James W. Loewen, *Lies My Teacher Never Told Me* (New Press, 1995), and *Teaching What Really Happened: How to Avoid the Tyranny of Textbooks and Get Students Excited about Doing History* (Teachers College Press, 2009). For further reading on related controversies in history instruction and curriculum, a lengthy critique of Loewen's work appears in David Warren Saxe, "Lies and History," in *The New Social Studies: People, Projects, and Perspectives*, edited by Barbara Slater Stern (Information Age Publishing, 2010).

Other works on the topic of history textbook battles by Diane Ravitch include *The Troubled Crusade: American Education 1945–1980* (Basic Books, 1983), and *The Schools We Deserve: Reflections on the Educational Crises of Our Time* (Basic Books, 1985). Those books could also be compared with Frances Fitzgerald, *America Revised: History Schoolbooks in the Twentieth Century* (Random House, 1979). Fitzgerald claims the social unrest of the 1960s influenced the writing of American history textbooks of the 1970s and depicts how cultural trends have affected the writing of history textbooks since 1900, resulting in what she describes in textbooks that are simplistic and dull. A lengthy critique of Fitzgerald's book appears in Joseph Moreau, *Schoolbook Nation: Conflicts over American History Textbooks from the Civil War to the Present* (University of Michigan Press, 2003).

Gary B. Nash, Charlotte Crabtree, and Ross Dunn, *History on Trial: Culture Wars and the Teaching of the Past* (Knopf, 1997). Nash, Professor of History at UCLA; Crabtree, Professor of Curriculum Stud-

Recommended Readings, American Social Studies 271

ies at UCLA; and Ross Dunn, Professor of History at San Diego State University, offer an account of how the culture wars of the late twentieth century spread to the teaching and content of history by the late 1990s, especially after conservatives, including Lynne Cheney, Newt Gingerich, and Rush Limbaugh, offered numerous criticisms of the controversial 1994 *National Standards for United States History*. Nash, Dunn, and Crabtree, who were the main authors of those standards, present rebuttals to those criticisms. A related book, Edward T. Linenthal and Tom Engelhardt, editors, *History Wars: The Enola Gay and Other Battles for the American Past* (Henry Holt, 1996), contains a chapter by historian Mike Wallace, entitled "Culture War: History Front," which also includes an examination of the roles played by critics such as Limbaugh, Gingerich, and Chaney, in the fight against what they called the "counter culture, liberal elitists," who they claimed had taken control of "the arts, the press, the entertainment industry, the universities, the libraries, the foundations, etc." The arguments presented by Nash, Crabtree, Dunn, and Wallace echo those presented in the 1961–62 Texas war.

Joseph Moreau, *Schoolbook Nation: Conflicts over American History Textbooks from the Civil War to the Present* (University of Michigan Press, 2003). Moreau presents a sweeping survey of major concerns about American history textbooks from Reconstruction to the late 1980s, with special emphasis on the roles played by textbook authors, their critics, and local and state educational authorities. Coverage includes Moreau's extensive coverage of the more progressive-multicultural history textbooks that began to appear in the 1960s, with critical responses through the 1980s by conservative, traditional-oriented historians and others, including Lynne Cheney, Arthur Schlesinger, Allan Bloom, Diane Ravitch, E. D. Hirsch, Allan Bloom, and Newt Gingerich; parochial schools; various conservative individuals, including Rush Limbaugh and Phyllis Schlafly; and a mixture of other groups, such as those from business groups, patriotic organizations, ethnic and minority groups, segregationists, labor groups, as well as Moreau's discussion of roles played by such progressive social studies reconstructionists in the tradition of Harold Rugg, such as Charlotte Crabtree and Gary Nash, Ross Dunn, and professional organizations,

272   Appendix E

including the American Historical Association. Moreau especially has a lengthy survey of the differences of opinions about what should be emphasized in the development of American historiography from the nineteenth century to the latter part of the twentieth century. Moreau argued that "the meter of our arguments over national character, the steady rising and falling of public interest in questions of race, class, religion, and other markers of identity, continually echoes through the hallways of our schools." He added that this "national soul-searching has always played out through textbooks, especially those purporting to explain the country's past. . . . Writing history is always political. It always reflects the relations of power in the society."

Especially unique is Moreau's extensive explanations of the philosophies underlying the various concerns of all those involved in the issue. Moreau with *Schoolbook Nation*, along with Ronald W. Evans in *The Social Studies Wars: What Should We Teach the Children?* (Teachers College Press, Columbia University, 2004), also deal specifically with the controversy over the 1994 *National Standards for United States History* developed at the National Center for History in the Schools at UCLA. Both Moreau and Evans cover in great detail the arguments and rationales offered on both sides of that historiographical issue.

Diane Ravitch, *The Language Police: How Pressure Groups Restrict What Students Learn* (Alfred A. Knopf, 2003). Historian Ravitch offers an examination of how textbooks have been prepared, along with a look at how textbook censorship from the left and the right occurred after the post–World War I years and into the 1930s, with the introduction of numerous patriotic and ethnic organizations critical of social studies books. The American Legion and Veterans of Foreign Wars wanted history to stress love of country and nationalism. Ethnic societies, such as those representing Irish Americans, German Americans, Jewish Americans, and African Americans, wanted more emphasis on their unique contributions to society. Anything pro-British was suspect to Irish Americans and German Americans, and exploited by such politicians as Mayor "Big Bill" Thompson of Chicago, with the most popular American history textbook by David Saville Muzzy being especially criticized by protestors.

Ronald W. Evans, *This Happened in America: Harold Rugg and the Censure of Social Studies* (Information Age Publishing, 2007). Evans uses the biography of progressive and social reconstructionist Harold Rugg and his social studies *Problems of Democracy* series to show how Rugg encountered and ultimately lost to powerful conservative cultural and political forces by the 1940s. The biography of Rugg also offers the reader an in-depth examination of the rationale and practice of progressive curriculum strategies by combining relevant issues within fused social studies courses.

Ronald W. Evans, *The Tragedy of American School Reform: How Curriculum Politics and Entrenched Dilemmas Have Diverted Us from Democracy* (Palgrave Macmillan, 2011). Evans explores the story of the New Social Studies movement of the 1960s to 1980s, with its emphasis on inquiry-oriented critical thinking and social activism—spin-offs of a type of a John Dewey approach—and how it met with negative reactions from conservative-traditional thinkers, which resulted in a major return to the teaching of tradition history. In *The Hope for American School Reform: The Cold War Pursuit of Inquiry Learning in Social Studies* (Palgrave Macmillan, 2011), Evans chronicles the story of the federally funded social studies curriculum projects that came to be known as the New Social Studies, as a reaction to the Cold War. He explains why the emphasis on critical inquiry and discovery learning never became as widespread as its authors hoped, due to many factors, including opposition from conservative politicians and history traditionalists, with reasons offered by each side for their positions. Evans concluded, "In each case, the reforms had a profound influence on a small but significant number of classroom, teachers, and students. With sustained support and continued development, it is possible that inquiry teaching and learning could be popularized among a significant number of teachers and students again at some point in the future."

A related work is Barbara Slater Stern, editor, *The New Social Studies: People, Projects, and Perspectives* (Information Age Publishing, 2010). The book offers a comprehensive review of the major leaders and projects to emerge with the New Social Studies movement, beginning when the Soviet Union launched *Sputnik* to the 1980s, with

274 Appendix E

explanations of the philosophies and teaching inherent in the movement, as well as reasons for its decline in popularity, even when many teachers still use the approach.

For other works about the Texas textbook situation of 1961–62, consult Jack Nelson and Gene Roberts Jr., *The Censors and the Schools* (Little, Brown and Company, 1963). The Nelson and Roberts study covers some major textbook controversies during 1961–62, with an emphasis on hearings conducted by the Texas House of Representatives Textbook Investigating Committee. Hillel Black, in *The American Schoolbook* (William Morrow and Company, 1967), has a survey on the history of the development of American textbooks and a special chapter on Texas textbook critics during the 1960s.

For other histories of the emergence of social studies into American schools, see R. M. Elson, *Guardians of Tradition: American Schoolbooks of the 19th Century* (University of Nebraska Press, 1964). Elson deals with early traditional coverage in textbooks, utilizing the McGuffy Readers and Parson Mason Weems type of approach. Those works can be read in conjunction with Thomas S. Popkewitz, editor, *The Formation of the School Subjects: The Struggle for Creating an American Institution* (Falmer Press, 1987); Will S. Monroe, "Early American School Books: A Brief Historic Survey," *The Library*, December 1935; and Richard D. Brown, *Knowledge Is Power: The Diffusion of Information in Early America, 1700–1865* (Oxford University Press, 1989).

Other reforms calling for more emphasis on rigorous critical thinking, among other things, in history courses by the mid-twentieth century appear in Arthur Bestor, *Educational Wastelands* (University of Illinois Press, 1953), and Joel Spring, *The American School, 1642–1985* (Longman, 1986). John G. Herlihy, editor, *The Textbook Controversy: Issues, Aspects and Perspectives* (Ablex, 1992), also contains several chapters on how conflicting priorities from pressure groups and academics led to issues about what should or should not be included in social studies textbooks. Arthur Woodward, David L. Elliott, and Kathleen Carter Nagel, *Textbooks in School and Society: An Annotated Bibliography and Guide to Research* (Garland Publishing, 1988), includes a detailed annotated bibliography of books and articles on such topics as

Recommended Readings, American Social Studies 275

the teaching of social studies, as well as controversies over ideology, censorship, and evolution in textbook selection to the late 1980s.

Finally, Robert Wuthnow's *Rough Country: How Texas Became America's Most Powerful Bible-Belt State* (Princeton University Press, 2014), and Gail Collins's *As Texas Goes . . . How the Lone Star State Hijacked the American Agenda* (Liveright Publishing, 2012) should also be read, along with James Ivy's, *No Saloon in the Valley: The Southern Strategy of Texas Prohibitionists in the 1880s* (Baylor University Press, 2003), as well as and Lawrence Wright, *God Save Texas: A Journey into the Soul of the Lone Star State* (Knopf, 2018).

Appendix F

State-Adopted History Textbooks for 1961

THE FOLLOWING textbooks were recommended by the Texas State Textbook Committee for adoption and approved by the Texas State Board of Education. Others were recommended but not approved, voted down by the board.

Grade Eight American History

Book Title	Publisher	Opposed by Texans for America	Opposed by the Texas Society of the Daughters of the American Revolution	Approved for State Adoption
Story of the American Nation	Harcourt, Brace and World	X	X	Yes
This Is America's Story	Houghton Mifflin	X	X	Yes
Our United States	Laidlaw Brothers		X	Yes
Freedom's Frontier	Lyons and Carnahan	X	X	Yes
Our Free Nation	Macmillan	X	X	Yes
The Story of Our Country	Allyn and Bacon	X	X	No
America: Land of Freedom	D. C. Heath and Company	X	X	No

278 Appendix F

Book Title	Publisher	Opposed by Texans for America	Opposed by the Texas Society of the Daughters of the American Revolution	Approved for State Adoption
Story of Our Land and People	Holt, Rinehart and Winston	X	X	No
Complete History of Our United States	Noble and Noble	X	X	No

High School American History

Book Title	Publisher	Opposed by Texans for America	Opposed by the Texas Society of the Daughters of the American Revolution	Approved for State Adoption
Rise of the American Nation	Harcourt, Brace and World	X	X	Yes
This Is Our Nation	Webster Publishing	X	X	Yes
American History	Ginn and Company	X	X	Yes
History of a Free People	Macmillan	X	X	Yes
The American People: Their History	Row, Peterson and Company	X	X	Yes
A History of the Unites States	American Book Company	X	X	No
United States History	D. C. Heath and Company	X	X	No
Story of America	Holt, Rinehart and Winson	X	X	No

State-Adopted History Textbooks, 1961

Book Title	Publisher	Opposed by Texans for America	Opposed by the Texas Society of the Daughters of the American Revolution	Approved for State Adoption
The United States: A History	Prentice-Hall	X		No
The Making of Modern America	Houghton Mifflin	X	X	No
The Adventure of the American People	Rand McNally	X		No

World History

Book Title	Publisher	Opposed by Texans for America	Opposed by the Texas Society of the Daughters of the American Revolution	Approved for State Adoption
Men and Nations: A World History	Harcourt, Brace and World	X	X	Yes
Story of Nations	D. C. Heath and Company	X	X	Yes
The History of Our World	Houghton Mifflin	X	X	Yes
Our Widening World	Rand McNally	X	X	Yes
The Record of Mankind	D. C. Heath and Company	X	X	Yes
The Making of Today's World	Allyn and Bacon	X		No
A History of the World	American Book Company	X		No

Book Title	Publisher	Opposed by Texans for America	Opposed by the Texas Society of the Daughters of the American Revolution	Approved for State Adoption
Our World History	Ginn and Company	X		No
Past to Present: A World History	Macmillan	X		No
Our World through the Ages	Prentice Hall	X		No
Living World History	Scott, Foresman and Company	X	X	No

Notes

Chapter 1

1. *Major Speeches of Senator Joseph McCarthy*, US Government Printing Office, 1952.

2. Ray Cohn, *McCarthy*, New American Library, 1968, pp. 276–77. For more about the Cold War, Joseph McCarthy, and the McCarthy Era, consult the selected bibliography.

3. *Public Papers of President Harry S. Truman*, US Government Printing Office, 1963, pp. 489–91.

4. Also consult Theodore draper, *The Roots of American Communism*, Viking, 1957; and Harvey Klehr et al., *The Secret World of American Communism*, Yale University Press, 1995. For more about the American Communist Party, consult the bibliography in appendix F.

Chapter 2

1. Overview summaries by Green and Carleton are from George Norris Green, *The Establishment in Texas Politics: The Primitive Years, 1938–1957*, University of Oklahoma Press, 1979, p. 17; and Don E. Carleton, *Red Scare! Right-Wing Hysteria, Fifties Fanaticism, and Their Legacy in Texas*, Texas Monthly Press, 1985, pp. 4, 5, 308, 309, 96–97.

2. Green, *The Establishment in Texas Politics*, p. 134; Maury Maverick Jr., interview with Robert Davis, April 30, 1985.

3. Ronald W. Evans, *The Social Studies Wars: What Should We Teach the Children?*, Teachers College, Columbia University, 2004, pp. 96, 119; Joseph Moreau, *Schoolbook Nation: Conflicts over American History Textbooks from the Civil War to the Present*, University of Michigan Press, 2003, p. 16; Allan O. Kownslar, *Texas Iconoclast: Maury Maverick, Jr.*, Texas Christian University Press, 1997, pp. 60–63; Randolph B. Campbell, *Gone to Texas: A History of the Lone Star State*, Oxford University Press, 2012, pp. 412–13; Green, *The Establishment in Texas Politics*, pp. 72–73, 83–84, 86–89, 102, 150, 184. For an excellent overview of the hunt for alleged communists associated with the New Deal and those employed in higher education in Texas, consult Green's chapter 6,

282   Notes to Pages 37–48

"The Martin Dies Story," chapter 7, "The Coke Stevenson Period," and chapter 12, "Turning Points, 1956–1957," in Green, *The Establishment in Texas Politics*. Another excellent analysis of the Texas hunt for alleged subversives in the field of public education appears in chapter 6, "The Red Scare and the Schools," and chapter 7, "The Victim Is a Symbol: The George W. Ebey Affair," in Carleton, *Red Scare!*.

4. Carleton, *Red Scare!*, pp. 155–56.

5. Carleton, *Red Scare!*, pp. 112, 161, 172–73, and 243; Green, *The Establishment in Texas Politics*, pp. 123–24.

6. Green, *The Establishment in Texas Politics*, p. 129.

7. Green, *The Establishment in Texas Politics*, p. 130.

8. Green, *The Establishment in Texas Politics*, p. 131–32.

9. Maury Maverick Sr., speech to Town Hall Meeting, February 25,1954, Maverick Papers, Speeches, 1952–1954, Dolph Briscoe Center for American Studies, University of Texas at Austin.

10. Green, *The Establishment in Texas Politics*, p. 132.

11. Carleton, *Red Scare!*, pp. 221, 219, 223; and Kownslar, *Texas Iconoclast*, p. 65.

12. Green, *The Establishment in Texas Politics*, p. 123.

13. Carleton, *Red Scare!*, pp. 165–66.

14. *Houston Post*, October 24, 1956; "Berti and the Board," *Time*, August 15,1960; and Carleton, *Red Scare!*, p. 286.

15. Carleton, *Red Scare!*, pp. 288–89.

16. Carleton, *Red Scare!*, pp. 289–95.

17. Carleton, *Red Scare!*, pp. 289–95. For more about the role of the Minute Women's anti-Communist and anti-UN campaign in Houston, consult Diane Ravich's personal story about Nelda Davis, her high school world history teacher who stood up to the Minute Women. See Diane Ravitch, *The Language Police: How Pressure Groups Restrict What Students Learn*, Knopf, 2003, pp. 64–68.

Chapter 3

1. Hillel Black, *American Schoolbook*, William Morrow and Company, 1967, pp. 16–17.

2. Because of the controversies over the conservative-oriented 2010 social studies standards enacted by the Texas State Board of Education, standards which received unfavorable national and international publicity, the Texas legislature in 2011 provided state reimbursement to allow public school districts to adopt textbooks or to purchase other programs on their own. When Texas chose not to use the national Common Core curriculum standards, a state and *not* federally oriented campaign to increase learning standards for the nation's schoolchildren, the Texas legislature granted its public school districts more choices in adopting printed and digital materials, but only on the condition that any materials purchased and reimbursed by the state also meet

the standards set by the Texas State Board of Education, requiring that all the Texas standards, called the Texas Essential Knowledge and Skills (TEKS), are taught by teachers. Meanwhile, publishers continued to develop materials to meet the national Common Core standards, which will not apply to those of Texas. Next, Texas abolished the State Textbook Committee, which had been in existence since 1960, and replaced it with a State Review Panel. According to 19 Texas Administrative Code 66.30, in effect for 2013–17, membership on the State Review Panel "is appointed by the Commissioner of Education from nominations submitted by educational organizations across the state, educators, academic experts, or parents." The job of the State Review Panel was to review instructional materials to determine if they met 50 percent of the TEKS and 100 percent of the English Proficiency Standards, and to look for factual errors. The State Review Panel was not allowed to hold public hearings. It could only report its findings to the Commissioner of Education, who passed those on to the State Board of Education. Any Texas resident can send written comments about instructional materials submitted for adoption. The State Board of Education must also allow citizens the opportunity to also offer public testimony about the standards. For more about this, consult Morgan Smith, "Schools, Textbook Publishers Adjust to Power Shift," *Texas Tribune*, September 29, 2011; Lauren McGaughy, "Texas No Longer Dictates Textbooks, *San Antonio Express-News*, November 28, 2014, pp. 1, 10A; "GOP's Common Core Criticisms Rings Hollow," Associated Press, March 20, 2016. For a review of the current Texas textbook adoption process, consult adoption@tea.texas.gov.

3. Joan Delfattore, *What Johnny Shouldn't Read: Textbook Censorship in America*, Yale University Press, 1992, p. 140.

4. Black, *American Schoolbook*, pp. 148–49.

5. Delfattore, *What Johnny Shouldn't Read*, p. 154. Later, in 1985, the Texas State Board of Education required publishers to "footnote known factual political affiliations of those people who are quoted directly in the textbook. That changed in 1988 to 'verified political affiliations.'"

6. Jonathan Elliot, editor, *The Debates, Resolution, and Other Proceedings in Convention, on the Adoption of the Federal Constitution*, Washington, DC, 1827, volume I, pp. 222–25, 202–3, 93–94, 156–59, 195, 203–5; and vol II, pp. 71–72, 90–97, 30–31, 108–9, 208–9. For an overview of the American colonial Christian tradition, see Allan O. Kownslar and Terry L. Smart, chapter 3, "Political Ideas from the Thirteen Colonies," *American Government*, McGraw-Hill, 1983; and Lea Sinclair Filson, "How Magna Charta, the Mayflower Compact, and Declaration of Independence Shaped America," *Mayflower Quarterly*, September 2015.

7. Also consult, for example, the debates of the Constitutional Convention; Alan Wolfe, "Keeping the Faith at Arm's Length," *New York Times Book Review*, May 7, 2006; Jill Lepore, "Prior Convictions: Did the Founders Want Us to Be Faithful to Their Faith?," *The New Yorker*, April 14, 2008; and Gregg L. Frazer, *The Religious Beliefs of America's Founders: Reason, Revelation, and Resolution*,

University of Kansas Press, 2012; Edwin S. Gaustad, *Faith of the Founders: Religion and the New Nation, 1776–1826*, Baylor University Press, 2003; Frank Lambert, *The Founding Fathers and the Place of Religion in America*, Princeton University Press, 2003; and Daniel L. Dreisbach, Mark D. Hall, and Jeffry H. Morrison, editors, *The Founders on God and Government*, Rowman and Littlefield, 2004; and compare those with two of the works by David Barton, a pastor, conservative radio host, and a former vice chairman of the Texas Republican Party: *The Myth of Separation: What Is the Correct Relationship between Church and State?*, Wallbuilder Press, 1989, and *America's Godly Heritage*, Wallbuilder Press, 2007.

8. *The Works of John Adams, Second President of the United States: With a Life of the Author, by His Grandson Charles Francis Adams*, volume X, Little Brown and Company, 1856, pp. 45–46.

9. Kownslar and Smart, *American Government*, pp. 386–87.

10. Delfattore, *What Johnny Shouldn't Read*, p. 78.

11. Prayer by Honorable T. W. Ogg of Crockett, Texas, and member of the Texas State Textbook Committee, State Textbook Committee Hearing Held in the Conference Room, Texas Education Agency, Austin, Texas, September 14, 1961, p. 2.

12. Delfattore, *What Johnny Shouldn't Read*, p. 87. For a detailed point-counterpoint discussion about this controversy, consult Edward B. Jenkinson, *Censors in the Classroom: The Mind Benders*, Southern Illinois University Press, 1979, pp. 95–107, and compare that with Mel Gabler, "Religion Is Back in School," in Mel and Norma Gabler, *What Are They Teaching Our Children?*, Victor Books, 1985, pp. 33–46. For further reading, consult Paul Kurtz, *In Defense of Secular Humanism*, Prometheus Books, 1983, and Roger E. Greeley, editor, *The Best of Humanism*, Prometheus Books, 1988, and compare those with Tim LaHaye, *The Battle for the Public Schools: Humanism's Threat to Our Children*, Fleming H. Revell, 1983. For more about Darwinism, creationism, and secular humanism, consult the selected bibliography.

13. Don E. Carleton, *Red Scare! Right-Wing Hysteria, Fifties Fanaticism, and Their Legacy in Texas*, Texas Monthly Press, 1985, p. 100.

14. Sean P. Cunningham, "The Paranoid Style and Its Limits: The Power, Influence, and Failure of the Postwar Texas Far Right," and Nancy E. Baker, "Focus on the Family: Twentieth-Century Conservation Texas Women and the Lone Star Right," in David O' Donald Cullen and Kyle G. Wilkison, editors, *The Texas Right: The Radical Roots of Lone Star Conservativism*, Texas A&M University Press, 2014, pp. 104, 105, 131; and Sean P. Cunningham, *Cowboy Conservatism: Texas and the Rise of the Modern Right*, University Press of Kentucky, 2010, p. 58.

15. Ronald W. Evans, *The Social Studies Wars: What Should We Teach the Children?*, Teachers College, Columbia University, 2004, pp. 22–24, 27; and Edgar B Wesley and Stanley P. Wronski, *Teaching Secondary Social Studies in a World*

Notes to Pages 68–74

Society, D.C. Health, 1973, pp. 86, 342. For more about John Dewey, consult Larry Hickman and Thomas Alexander, editors, *The Essential Dewey*, Indiana University Press, 1998; John J. McDermott, editor, *The Philosophy of John Dewey*, University of Chicago Press, 1981; and Thomas D. Fallace, *Race and the Origins of Progressive Education, 1880–1929*, Teachers College Press, Columbia University, 2015.

16. Evans, *The Social Studies Wars*, pp. 59–65. For more about Harold Rugg, consult Peter F. Carbone Jr., *The Social and Educational Thought of Harold Rugg*, Duke University Press, 1977, and Anne Lyon Haight and Chandler B. Grannis, *Banned Books: 387 B.C. to 1978 A. D.*, R. R. Bowker Company, 1978.

17. Evans, *The Social Studies Wars*, pp. 52–53; Joseph Moreau, *Schoolbook Nation: Conflicts over American History Textbooks from the Civil War to the Present*, University of Michigan Press, 2003, pp. 219, 221.

18. George S. Counts, *The American Road to Culture in Howard K. Beale: A History of Freedom of Teaching in American Schools*, Scribner's Sons, 1941, p. 83.

19. For more about George S. Counts, consult chapter 4, "Social Reconstruction," in Ronald W. Evans *This Happened in America: Harold Rugg and the Censure of Social Studies*, Information Age Publishing, 2007.

20. Evans, *The Social Studies Wars*, pp. 2, 21, 48, 98.

21. Evans, *The Social Studies Wars*, pp. 62–63, 93.

22. Diane Ravitch, *The Language Police: How Pressure Groups Restrict What Students Learn*, Alfred A. Knopf, 2003, p. 69.

23. Moreau, *Schoolbook Nation*, p. 244.

24. H. O. Rugg, "Study in Censorship: Good Concepts and Bad Words," *Social Education*, March 1941.

25. Evans, *The Social Studies Wars*, p. 121.

26. John A. Nietz, *Old Textbook as Taught in the Common Schools from Colonial Days to 1900*, University of Pittsburgh Press, 1961, pp. 267–68.

27. Eugene Kinkead, *In Every War but One*, W. W. Norton, 1959, pp. 208–9. In a similar vein, textbook critics could have also read E. Merrill Root's *Brainwashing in the High Schools*, Devin-Adair, 1958, where he argued that those Korean War American POWs were susceptible to such communist brain washing techniques because they had not been taught to know "American politics, American economics, American history and American ideals."

Chapter 4

1. For limited media coverage of those hearings, consult Richard M. Moreland, "SMU Professor's Textbook under Fire at State Hearing," *Dallas Morning News*, September 15, 1961; "45 Books Approved by Panel," *Austin American Statesman*, October 6, 1961; "Four Texts Turned Down," *Austin American Statesman*, November 5, 1961; and "46 Texts Adopted by Panel," *Austin American Statesman*, November 14, 1961.

286 Notes to Pages 75–83

2. Richard Stewart, "J. Evetts Haley: He Was a Promising Writer of Texas Range History Until He Made the Mistake of Taking on Lyndon B. Johnson," *Houston Chronicle*, November 11, 1990.

3. Bob Sherrill, "Freedom and Fatheads," *The Texas Observer*, February 3, 1962.

4. For an in-depth examination of J. Evetts Haley's early philosophy of life, consult Stacey Spague, "James Evetts Haley and the New Deal: Laying the Foundations from the Modern Republican Party in Texas," MA thesis, University of North Texas, 2004.

5. James Evetts Haley, speech to the Texas State Democratic Executive Committee, June 1956; Stewart, "J. Evetts Haley"; B. Byron Price, "James Evetts Haley, Sr.," *The Handbook of Texas*, volume 3, Texas State Historical Society, 1996, pp. 410–11; Robert Wuthnow, *Rough Country: How Texas Became America's Most Bible-Belt State*, Princeton University Press, 2014, pp. 285–89, 295; and Lynn Landrum, "Thinking Out Loud," *Dallas Morning News*, June 10, 1956.

6. Bill Modisett, *J. Evetts Haley: A True Texas Legend*, Staked Plains Press, 1996, p. 67.

7. Jack Nelson and Gene Roberts Jr., *The Censors and the Schools*, Little Brown and Company, 1963, p. 121; Stewart, "J. Evetts Haley"; Price, "James Evetts Haley, Sr.," pp. 410–11; and Landrum, "Thinking Out Loud."

8. Stewart, "J. Evetts Haley."

9. Stewart, "J. Evetts Haley"; Appendix A, Minutes of the Texas State Board of Education, November 13, 1961, p. 5; and "Dobie Says Censors Bigots," *San Antonio Light*, February 1, 1962.

10. Stewart, "J. Evetts Haley."

11. Sherrill, "Freedom and Fatheads."

12. "J. Evetts Haley Leads Attack on School Texts," *Lubbock Avalanche Journal*, October 6, 1960; Richard M, Morehead, "SMU Professor's Textbook under Fire at State Hearing," *Dallas Morning News*, September 15, 1961; and "Textbook Attacks Feared as Criticism of System," *Galveston Daily News*, September 14, 1962.

13. J. Evetts Haley, Statement on September 14, 1961, State Texas State Textbook Committee Transcript, State Textbook Committee Hearing, Texas Education Agency, p. 5.

14. Lucile Evelyn La Ganke, "The National Society of the Daughters of the American Revolution: Its History Politics, and Influence, 1890–1949," PhD diss., Western Reserve University, 1951, pp. 208, 219; Textbook Studies, 1958–1959, National Defense Committee, National Society of the Daughters of the American Revolution.

15. J. Evetts Haley, "Public Testimony," State Textbook Committee Hearing Held in the Conference Room, Texas Education Agency, Austin, Texas, September 14, 1961, pp. 5–8.

Notes to Pages 83–91 287

16. "Textbook Study 1958–1956, National Defense Committee, National Society, Daughters of the American Revolution"; and "School Textbooks Face Increasing Censorship," *San Antonio Express*, February 25, 1963.

17. A. A. Jimmie Jenkins Forester, Public Testimony, Report to Speaker Byron Tunnell and Members of the House Textbook Investigating Committee of the 57th Legislature, pp. 217–25.

18. Public Testimonies by Representatives of Texans for America and the Texas Society of the Daughters of the American Revolution, State Textbook Committee Hearing Held in the Conference Room, Texas Education Agency, Austin, Texas, September 14, 1961, pp. 25, 63, 64, 66, 67–68, 70, 71–72, 73, 75, 76, 77, 78, 80, 83–84, 93–95, 97–115, and Public Testimony before the Texas House of Representatives Textbook Investigating Committee, pp. 217–25; Public Testimony of A. A. Forester, submitted by Rep. Bob Bass, who allowed Forester to update the earlier testimony she gave to the House Textbook Investigating Committee on January 31, 1962, Report to Speaker Byron Tunnell and Members of the House Investigating Committee of the 57th Legislature, pp. 218–19, 225, 228; "Dobie Says Censors Bigots," *San Antonio Light*, February 2, 1962; Joan Delfattore, *What Johnny Shouldn't Read: Textbook Censorship in America*, Yale University Press, 1992, p 157; and Joseph Moreau, *Schoolbook Nation: Conflicts over American History Textbooks for the Civil War to the Present*, University of Michigan Press, 2006, pp. 197–221, 253–64, 321, 373.

Chapter 5

1. While the topic of social studies programs dominated the concerns of the Texas State Textbook Committee, the anti-Communist issue went on to affect the committee's take on music books. As a result, the State Textbook Committee voted to delete the names of folksinger Pete Seeger and poet Langston Hughes "wherever they appear in the [vocal] music books." Award-winning author Langston Hughes, an African American, was a civil rights activist. He was never a member of the Communist Party USA, but prior to World War II, he did support Communist-led groups such as the League of Struggle for Negro Rights. Award-winning Pete Seeger was a civil rights, labor union, and environmental activist, as well as a famous folk singer and composer. While performing with The Weavers, for example, Seeger and Lee Hayes wrote the now famous "Hammer Song." For a brief time during the early 1940s, Seeger was a member of the Communist Party USA, but he left the group because he felt Joseph Stalin was a brutal dictator. Seeger's refusal in 1955 to reveal his political views to the US House Un-American Activities Committee got him jailed for contempt, a conviction overturned on appeal a year later. For more about Langston Hughes, consult Laurie F. Leach, *Langston Hughes: A Biography*, Greenwood Press, 2004; Arnold Rampersad, *The Life of Langston Hughes*, Oxford University Press, 2 vols., 1986–88; and Arnold Rampersad et al., editors, *Selected Letters of Langston*

Notes to Pages 91–102

Hughes, Alfred A. Knopf, 2015. For Pete Seeger, consult Alec Wilkinson, *The Protest Signer: An Intimate Portrait of Pete Seeger*, Knopf, 2009; and Pete Seeger, *The Incomplete Folksinger*, Simon and Schuster, 1972.

2. See appendix A.

3. Jack Nelson and Gene Roberts Jr., *The Censors and the Schools*, Little, Brown, 1963, pp. 130–32, and Hillel Black, *The American School Book*, William Morrow and Company, 1967, pp. 149–50.

4. Report of the Commissioner of Education on Textbooks, November 13, 1961, pp. 1–2; "Geography Books: Four Texts Turned Down," *Austin American Statesman*, November 5, 1961; and Report of the State Textbook Committee to the State Commissioner of Education, Minutes of the State Textbook Committee, May 5, 1961, p. ix.

5. "Textbook Study 1958–1959," National Defense Committee, National Society, Daughters of the American Revolution, p. 5.

6. Official Agenda, State Board of Education, May 7, 1962, p. 2.

7. Don E. Carleton, *Red Scare! Right-Wing Hysteria, Fifties Fanaticism, and Their Legacy in Texas*, Texas Monthly Press, 1985, pp. 288–89.

8. A. A. Forester, Public Testimony, Submitted by Rep. Bob Bass, who allowed Forester to update the earlier testimony she gave to the House Textbook Investigating Committee of January 31, 1962, Report to Speaker Byron Tunnell and Members of the House Investigating Committee of the 57th Legislature, pp. 218–19, 225, 228.

9. Official Agenda, State Board of Education, May 7, 1962, Minutes of the State Board of Education, Austin, Texas, pp. 61, 87.

10. Nelson Cowles, Interim Report on Textbooks, Report to Speaker Byron Tunnell and Members of the House Textbook Investigating Committee of the 57th Legislature, pp. 34, 38.

11. "Free Enterprise Course Debated," *Abilene Reporter News*, February 12, 1963. From then on, conservative critics of textbooks would insist that the materials stress "the less government regulation the better," along with the positive aspects of a free capitalistic enterprise economic system.

12. "Textbooks Protested," *San Antonio Express*, November 9, 1965, p. 5A.

13. Hillel Black, *The American School*, William Morrow and Company, 1967, pp. 151–52.

14. Report of the State Textbook Committee to the State Commissioner of Education on Books Offered for Adoption, 1961, Texas Education Agency, p. xx.

15. Official Agenda of the Texas State Board of Education, November 13, 1961, p. x.

16. Report of the State Textbook Committee to the State Commissioner of Education on Books Offered for Adoption, 1961, Texas Education Agency, pp. 18, 29, 34; Appendix A, Minutes of the Texas State Board of Education, November 13, 1961, p. 17; Public Testimony before State Textbook Committee Held in the Conference Room, Texas Education Agency, Austin, Texas, September 14,

Notes to Pages 102–107 289

1962, pp. 97–115; Public Testimony of A. A. Forester, January 31, 1962, Report to Speaker Byron Tunnell and Members of the Texas House of Representatives of the 58th Legislature by the House Textbook Investigating Committee of the 57th Legislature, pp. 217–32; "Dobie Says Censors Bigots," *San Antonio Light*, February 1, 1962; Textbook Study, 1958–1959, National Defense Committee, National Society of the Daughters of the American Revolution, pp. 11–12, 13–14, 17–20; Report to Speaker Byron Tunnell and Members of the Texas House of Representatives of the 58th Legislature, Main Committee Room, Texas House of Representatives, Austin, Texas; History books adopted in 1961 and protested by Texans for America, the Daughters of the American Revolution, and those who agreed with them during hearings conducted on January 10, 17, 24, 31, February 9, 26, and April 2–3, 1962, by the Texas House of Representatives Textbook Investigating Committee; and Report to Speaker Byron Tunnell and Members of the Texas House of Representatives Textbook Investigating Committee of the 58th Legislature by the House Textbook Investigating Committee of the 57th Legislature.

17. Jack Nelson and Gene Roberts Jr., *The Censors and the Schools*, Little Brown and Company, 1963, p. 132.

Chapter 6

1. John Howard Griffin, "Current Trends in Censorship," *Southwest Review*, September 1962, p. 199.

2. Information about the Southern Conference for Human Welfare, the Southern Conference Educational Conference, the Southern Educational Welfare, the Southern Educational and Conference Fund, James A. Dombrowski, Carl Braden, Anne Braden and Aubrey Willis Williams Is from Public Testimony of Harris Holmes, Texas State Textbook Committee Hearing Held in the Conference Room, Texas Education Agency, Austin, Texas, September 14, 1961, pp. 130–32; "SMU Professor's Textbook under Fire at State Hearing," *Dallas Morning News*, September 15, 1961; "46 Texts Adopted by Panel," *Austin American Statesman*, November 14, 1961; Bob Sherrill, "A Carnival on Textbooks," *The Texas Observer*, January 19, 1962; "Textbooks 'Pro-Red' Prober Told," *El Paso Herald Post*, June 1, 1962; *Braden v. United States*, 365 U.S. 431, 1961; *Dombrowski v. Pfister*, 380 U.S. 479; *Copper v. Aaron*, 238 U.S. 1, 1965; Paul F. Boller Jr., *Memoirs of an Obscure Professor*, Texas Christian University Press, 1992, pp. 18–28; "Resolution," Texas Library Association, 1962; Taylor Branch, *Parting the Water: America in the King Year, 1954–1963*, Simon and Schuster, 1988, pp. 121–22, 328; Juan Williams, *Eyes on the Prize: America's Civil Rights Years, 1954–1965*, Penguin Books, 1987, pp. 32, 198; Robert Weisbot, *Freedom Found: A History of America's Civil Rights Movement*, A Plume Book, 1991, p. 42; John Howard Griffin, "Current Trends in Censorship," *Southwest Review*, summer 1962, pp. 199–200; Cedric Belfrage, *The American Inquisition 1945–1960*; and *Outside the Magic Circle: The Autobiography of Virginia Foster Durr*, Simon and

290   Notes to Pages 111–120

Schuster and University of Alabama Press, 1985, pp. 120–35, 139, 152–57, 184–87, 195, 225–43, 257–61, 325–26. For more information about those groups and individuals, consult the following: Anne Braden, *The Wall Between*, University of Tennessee Press, 1958; Thomas A. Kruger, *And Promise to Keep: The Southern Conference for Human Welfare, 1938–1948*, Vanderbilt University of Tennessee Press, 1967; John M. Glen, *Highlander: No Ordinary School*, University of Tennessee Press, 1996, Myles Horton, *The Long Haul: An Autobiography*, Columbia Teachers College Press, 1997; and Eliot Wigginton, editor, *Refuse to Stand Silently By: An Oral History of Grass Roots Social Activism in America, 1921–1964*, Doubleday, 1991. This source listing also serves as a bibliography for the emerging civil rights revolution to the early 1960s.

3. J. Evetts Haley, Public Testimony, State Textbook Committee Hearing Held in the Conference Room, Texas Education Agency, Austin, Texas, September 14, 1961, pp. 84–93.

4. Claire C. Galloway, compiler, "Guide to the Paul F. Boller, Jr., Papers," Special Collections, Texas Christian University.

5. Based on the Obituary for Evelyn Jean Tilford Claugus, *Cincinnati Inquirer*, August 18, 1992.

6. Paul Boller Jr., *Memoirs of an Obscure Professor*, Texas Christian University Press, 1992, pp. 2–3.

7. Boller, *Memoirs of an Obscure Professor*, pp. 3–8, 10, 13.

8. Boller, *Memoirs of an Obscure Professor*, pp. 18–28.

9. Report of the State Textbook Committee, October 5, 1961, to the State Commissioner of Education on Books Offered for Adoption, 1961, Texas Education Agency, 1961, pp. 29–30; and Official Agenda, Appendix A, Changes, Corrections, and Deletions Recommended by the State Textbook Committee, November 14, 1961, p. 14.

Chapter 7

1. Letter of J. Evetts Haley to Education Commissioner J. W. Edgar, October 9, 1961, in Minutes of the State Board of Education, May 1, 1961, p. vii; and J. Evetts Haley, "Texans Protest Slanted Textbooks," *Education Report*, volume 8, number 1, p. 6.

2. Letter of Dr. Donald I. Riddle, October 11, 1961, in Minutes of the State Board of Education, May 1, 1961, p. viii.

3. Official Agenda of the State Board of Education, November 13, 1961, pp. ix–x.

4. Quoted in J. Evetts Haley, "Texans Protest Slanted Textbooks," *Education Report*, volume 8, number 1, p. 6.

5. "46 Texts Adopted by Panel," *Austin American Statesmen*, November 14, 1961.

6. "46 Texts Adopted by Panel," *Austin American Statesmen*.

Notes to Pages 120–129   291

7. J. Evetts Haley quoted in Jack Nelson and Gene Roberts Jr., *The Censors and the Schools*, Little, Brown and Company, 1963, p. 121.

8. Appendix A, Minutes of the Texas State Board of Education, November 13, 1961, pp. 3–5.

9. Appendix A, Minutes of the Texas State Board of Education, November 13, 1961, pp. 16–17.

10. Appendix A, Minutes of the Texas State Board of Education, November 13, 1961, p. 17.

11. Paul Boller Jr., *Memoirs of an Obscure Professor*, Texas Christian University Press, 1992, pp. 28–30.

12. Paul Boller Jr., "Essay," *Southwest Review*, summer 1962, p. 218.

13. Appendix A, Minutes of the Texas State Board of Education, November 13, 1961, pp. 3–5; J. Evetts Haley, Public Testimony, January 17 and January 31, 1962, before members of the Texas House of Representatives of the 58th Legislature of the House Textbook Investigating Committee of the 57th Legislature; "46 Texts Approved by Panel," *Austin American Statesman*, November 14, 1961; and Report to Speaker Byron Tunnell and Members of the Texas House of Representatives of the 58th Legislature by the House Textbook Investigating Committee of the 57th Legislature.

Chapter 8

1. "Dobie and Haley at Odds in Hearing on Textbooks," *Amarillo Globe News*, February 2, 1962; and "Dobie Says Censors Bigots," *San Antonio Light*, February 2, 1962.

2. Texas H.S.R. 205, Interim Report, 57th RS, 1961.

3. Appendix B, Minutes of the State Board of Education, September 4, 1961, p. 40.

4. Report to Speaker Byron Tunnell and Members of the Texas House of Representatives of the 58th Legislature by the House Textbook Investigating Committee of the 57th Legislature, pp. vi–x.

5. History books adopted in 1961 and protested by Texans for America, the Texas Society of the Daughters of the American Revolution, and those who agreed with them during hearings conducted on January 10, 17, 24, 31, February 9, 26, and April 2–3, 1962, by the Texas House of Representatives Textbook Investigating Committee; Report to Speaker Byron Tunnell and Members of the Texas House of Representatives of the 58th Legislature by the House Textbook Investigating Committee of the 57th Legislature.

6. Public Testimonies by Representatives of Texans for America and the Texas Daughters of the American Revolution, State Textbook Committee Hearing Held in the Conference Room, Texas Education Agency, Austin, Texas, September 14, 1961, 25, 63, 64, 66, 67–68, 70, 71–72, 73, 75, 76, 77, 78, 80, 83–84, 93–95, 97–115, Public Testimony before the Texas House of Representatives

Textbook Investigating Committee, pp. 217–25; Public Testimonies before the Texas House of Representatives Textbook Investigating Committee on January 10, 17, 24, 31, February 9, 26, April 2, 3, 1962; Public Testimony of A. A. Forester, submitted by Rep. Bob Bass, who allowed Forester to update the earlier testimony she gave to the House Textbook Investigating Committee on January 31, 1962; and Report to Speaker Byron Tunnell and Members of the House Investigating Committee of the 57th Legislature, pp. 218–19, 225, 228.

7. Public Testimony of the Reverend Brandoch Lovely, February 9, 1962, before the House Textbook Investigating Committee, Austin, Texas, House Hearing Room.

8. Public Testimony of Dr. William E. Roth, February 9, 1962, before the House Textbook Investigating Committee, Austin, Texas, House Hearing Room.

9. Public Testimony of State Senator Franklin Spears, April 3, 1962, before the House Textbook Investigating Committee, Sidney Lanier High School Auditorium, San Antonio, Texas.

10. Public Testimony of Julius Grossenbacher, April 3, 1962, before the House Textbook Investigating Committee, Sidney Lanier High School Auditorium, San Antonio, Texas, Report to Speaker Byron Tunnell to Members of the Texas House of Representatives of the 58th Legislature by the House Textbook Investigating Committee, pp. 13–20.

11. "In Memoriam: Ernest C. Mossner," The University of Texas at Austin Faculty Council, December 20, 2000.

12. Public Testimony of Dr. Ernest Mosser, January 31, 1962, Report to Speaker Byron Tunnell and Members of the Texas House of Representatives of the 58th Legislature by the House Textbook Investigating Committee of the 57th Legislature, Main Committee Room, Texas House of Representatives, Austin, Texas, pp. 279–82.

13. Maury Maverick, Jr., Public Testimony before the House of Representatives Textbook Investigating Committee, April 2, 1962, Sidney Lanier High School Auditorium, San Antonio, Texas, Report to Speaker Byron Tunnell to Members of the Texas House of Representatives of the 58th Legislature by the House Textbook Investigating Committee, pp. 5–8.

Chapter 9

1. Dr. Don I. Riddle, Public Testimony, State Textbook Committee Hearing Held in the Conference Room, Texas Education Agency, Austin, Texas, September 14, 1961, pp. 8–10.

2. Public Testimony of Lewis C. Gilbert of Amarillo, Texas, before the Texas House of Representatives Textbook Investigating Committee, Amarillo, Texas, February 26, 1962, p. 259.

3. Jim Clark, "Schools, AC Pull Ten Books: Obscene Content Studied," *Amarillo Globe Times*, January 26, 1962; and Report to Speaker Byron Tunnell to Members of the Texas House of Representatives of the 58th Legislature by the House Textbook Investigating Committee, p. 259.

Notes to Pages 142–159   293

4. Jim Clark, "Schools, AC Pull Ten Books: Obscene Content Studied," *Amarillo Globe Times*, January 26, 1962.

5. Jim Clark, "Schools, AC Pull Ten Books: Obscene Content Studied."

6. Jack Nelson and Gene Roberts Jr., *The Censors and the Schools*, Little, Brown and Company, 1963, p. 133.

7. Anita Brewer, "Books Selection Hit," *Austin American Statesman*, January 18, 1962.

8. Public Testimony of Dr. W. D. Kelly, January 17, 1962, Report to Speaker Byron Tunnell and Members of the Texas House of Representatives of the 58th Legislature by the House Textbook Investigating Committee of the 57th Legislature, Main Committee Room, Texas House of Representatives, Austin, Texas, pp. 157–64.

9. Public Testimony of Douglas Morgan, before the House Textbook Investigating Committee, Austin, Texas, House Hearing Room, January 24, 1962.

10. Public Testimony of the Reverend Lee Freeman, January 24, 1962, Report to Speaker Byron Tunnell and Members of the Texas House of Representatives of the 58th Legislature by the House Textbook Investigating Committee of the 57th Legislature, Main Committee Room, Texas House of Representatives, Austin, Texas, pp. 282–84.

Chapter 10

1. J. Evetts Haley from a comment of which he endorsed, Public Testimony before Members of the Texas House of Representatives of the 59th Legislature of the House Textbook Committee of the 57th Legislature, January 17, 1962.

2. For more about Lon Tinkle, consult Evelyn Oppenheimer, *A Book Lover in Texas*, University of North Texas Press, 1995; and "Something about the Author," volume 36, Vertical Files, Dolph Briscoe Center for American History, University of Texas at Austin.

3. Lon Tinkle, Public Testimony before Members of the Texas House of Representatives of the 58th Legislature of the House Textbook Investigating Committee of the 57th Legislature, January 31, 1962, pp. 21–23.

4. Frank Wardlaw, Public Testimony before Members of the Texas House of Representatives of the 58th Legislature of the House Textbook Investigating Committee of the 57th Legislature, January 31, 1962, also published in *Southwest Review*, summer 1962, pp. 211–13.

5. Public Testimony of Dr. Frank E. Vandiver, President of the Texas Institute of Letters, Professor of History, Rice University, January 24, 1962, Report to Speaker Byron Tunnell and Members of the Texas House of Representatives of the 58th Legislature by the House Textbook Investigating Committee of the 57th Legislature, Main Committee Room, Texas House of Representatives, Austin, Texas, pp. 279–82.

6. Summarized from C. Allyn Russell, "J. Frank Norris: Violent Fundamentalist," *Southwestern Historical Quarterly*, January 1972; Robert Wuthnow, *Rough Country: How Texas Became America's Most Powerful Bible-Belt State,*

294   Notes to Pages 164–167

Princeton University Press, 2014, pp. 140–53; and Samuel K. Tullock, "He, Being Dead, Yet, Speaketh: J. Frank Norris and the Texas Religious Right at Mid Century," in David O'Donald and Kyle G. Wilkison, *The Texas Right: The Radical Roots of Lone Star State Conservatism*, Texas A&M University Press, 2014, pp. 51–67. For more about Darwinism and Creationism, consult the bibliography in appendix F.

7. Public Testimony of Dr. Joseph M. Dawson, January 31, 1962, Report to Speaker Byron Tunnell and Members of the Texas House of Representatives of the 58th Legislature by the House Textbook Investigating Committee of the 57th Legislature, Main Committee Room, Texas House of Representatives, Austin, Texas, pp. 274–79.

8. Public Testimony of Dr. Joseph M. Dawson, January 31, 1962, Report to Speaker Byron Tunnell and Members of the Texas House of Representatives of the 58th Legislature by the House Textbook Investigating Committee of the 57th Legislature, Main Committee Room, Texas House of Representatives, Austin, Texas; and Anita Brewer, "Stars Aplenty in Censor Hassle," *Austin American Statesman*, February 1, 1962.

9. Based on "James Frank Dobie," *The New Handbook of Texas*, volume 2, Texas State Historical Association, 1996, p. 663.

10. "James Frank Dobie," *The New Handbook of Texas*. See also J. Frank Dobie, quoted in "Dobie Says Censors Bigots," *San Antonio Light*, February 1, 1962. For some books by J. Frank Dobie, consult the following: *Cow People*, Little, Brown, 1964; *The Flavor of Texas*, Jenkins Publishing, 1975; *The Longhorns*, reprint by Little, Brown, 1951; *Guide to Life and Literature of the Southwest*, Southern Methodist University Press, 1952; *My Rambles as East Texas Cowboy, Hunter, Fisherman, Tie-Cutter*, Texas Folklore Society, 1942; *On the Open Range*, Southwest Press, 1931; *Some Part of Myself*, Little, Brown and Company, 1953; *Tales of Old-Time Texas*, Little, Brown and Company, 1995; and *A Vaquero of the Brush Country*, Grosset and Dunlap, 1929. For works on the life of J. Frank Dobie, consult Francis Edward Abernethy, *J. Frank Dobie*, Steck-Vaughn, 1967; Winston Bode, *A Portrait of Pancho: The Life of a Great Texan*, Pemberton Press, 1965; John Henry Faulk, "The Best Name I Know," *Texas Observer*, July 24, 1964; Don Graham, "J. Frank Dobie: A Reappraisal," *Southwestern Historical Quarterly*, July 1988; William A. Owens, *Three Friends: Roy Bedichek, J. Frank Dobie, Walter Prescott Webb*, University of Texas Press, 1975; Joe B. Frantz, *The Forty-Acre Follies: An Opinionated History of the University of Texas*, Texas Monthly Press, 1983; and Lon Tinkle, *An American Original: The Life of J. Frank Dobie*, Little, Brown, 1978. For an excellent summary of the criticisms and praises of J. Frank Dobie's works, consult Steven L. Davis, *J. Frank Dobie: A Liberated Mind*, University of Texas Press, 2009.

11. J. Frank Dobie, Public Testimony before Members of the Texas House of Representatives of the 58th Legislature of the House Textbook Investigat-

ing Committee of the 57th Legislature, Report to Speaker Byron Tunnell and Members of the Texas House of Representatives of the 59th Legislature by the House Textbook Investigating Committee of the 57th Legislature, pp. 9–12.

12. Public Testimony of James Donovan, January 17, 1962, Report to Speaker Byron Tunnell and Members of the Texas House of Representatives of the 58th Legislature by the House Textbook Investigating Committee of the 57th Legislature, Main Committee Room, Texas House of Representatives, Austin, Texas, pp. 94–98.

13. J. Evetts Haley, Public Testimony before Members of the Texas House of Representatives of the 58th Legislature of the House Textbook Investigating Committee of the 57th Legislature, January 31, 1962.

14. Bob Sherrill, "A Carnival of Textbooks," *The Texas Observer*, January 19, 1962.

15. Haley quoted in "Textbooks 'Pro-Red' Probe Told," *El Paso Herald Post*, June 1, 1962.

16. Anita Brewer, "Stars Aplenty in Censor Hassle," *Austin American Statesman*, February 1, 1962.

17. Dawson Dugan, "Charges on Dallas Hearing Mark End of Textbook Probe," *Dallas Morning News*, June 26, 1962; Jerry Pillard, "Textbook Panel Drops Testimony at Dallas Hearing from Record," *Corsicana Daily Sun*, June 25, 1962; Jerry Pillard, "State Textbooks Panel in Secret Session Votes to Halt Work until November," *Galveston News*, June 26, 1962. On the same topic, also consult *Corsicana Daily Sun*, June 26, 1962; *San Antonio Light*, June 26, 1962; *Abilene Reporter News*, June 26, 1962.

18. Bob Bass, Report to Speaker Byron Tunnell and Members of the Texas House of Representatives of the 58th Legislature by the House Textbook Investigating Committee of the 57th Legislature, pp. 210–12.

19. Bob Bass, Report to Speaker Byron Tunnell and Members of the Texas House of Representatives of the 58th Legislature by the House Textbook Investigating Committee of the 57th Legislature, pp. 218–19.

20. Resolution passed by the American Studies Association of Texas, December 2, 1961, reprinted in *Southwest Review*, summer 1962, p. 219.

21. Resolution by the Texas Library Association, reprinted in *Southwest Review*, summer 1962, p. 219.

22. John Howard Griffin, "Current Trends in Censorship," *Southwest Review*, summer 1962, pp. 199–200.

23. "Dungan Goes Astray," *Corpus Christi Caller Times*, March 18, 1962.

Chapter 11

1. Mel and Norma Gabler, Report to Speaker Byron Tunnell and Members of the Texas House of Representatives of the 58th Legislature by the House Textbook Investigating Committee of the 57th Legislature, pp. 39–56.

2. Mel and Norma Gabler, Report to Speaker Byron Tunnell and Members of the Texas House of Representatives of the 58th Legislature by the House Textbook Investigating Committee of the 57th Legislature, pp. 39–65.

3. William Martin, "The Guardians Who Slumberth Not," *Texas Monthly*, November, 1982, p. 264; Mel Gabler, Public Testimony before the Texas House of Representatives Textbook Investigating Committee, January 31, 1962; and Mel and Norma Gabler, Report to Speaker Byron Tunnell and Members of the Texas House of Representatives of the 58th Legislature by the House Textbook Investigating Committee of the 57th Legislature, pp. 51–59.

4. William Martin, "The Guardians Who Slumberth Not," *Texas Monthly*, November, 1982, p. 150, 151, 261, 262, 264, 266; House Report, p. 51; Public Testimony of Norma Gabler, Texas House of Representatives Textbook Investigating Committee, January 24, 1962; Public Testimony of Mel Gabler, Texas House of Representatives Textbook Investigating Committee, January 31, 1962; "Parents Urged to Take Active Interest in Textbook Content," *Pampa Daily News*, May 19, 1963; Mel Gabler, "Values Clarification—To Build or Destroy Basic Values," in James C. Hefley, *Are Textbooks Harming Your Children?*, Mott Media, 1979, pp. 213–14; Mel Gabler, quoted in Melissa Marie Deckman, *School Board Battles: The Christian Right in Local Politics*, Georgetown University Press, 2004, p. 13; Edward Jenkinson, *The Schoolbook Protest Movement*, Phi Delta Kappa Educational Foundation, 1986, pp. 108–23; Joan DelFattore, *What Johnny Shouldn't Read: Textbook Censorship in America*, Yale University Press, pp. 139–44, 72–74; Joseph Moreau, *Schoolbook Nation: Conflicts over American History Textbooks from the Civil War to the Present*, University of Michigan Press, 2006, p. 321; William Martin, "The Guardians Who Slumberth Not," *Texas Monthly*, November, 1982, p. 264; Mel Gabler, Public Testimony before the Texas House of Representatives Textbook Investigating Committee, January 31, 1962; Mel and Norma Gabler, Report to Speaker Byron Tunnell and Members of the Texas House of Representatives of the 58th Legislature by the House Textbook Investigating Committee of the 57th Legislature, pp. 51–59; Edward B. Jenkinson, *Censors in the Classroom: The Mind Benders*, Southern Illinois University Press, 1979, p. 108–23; Gil Sewall, D. Lee, and Ron Henkoff, "The Textbook Debate," *Newsweek*, December 17, 1070, p. 103; Jerry Falwell, *Listen, America!*, Doubleday and Company, 1980, pp. 211–12; James C. Hefley, *Are Textbooks Harming Your Children?*, Mott Media, 1979, p. 26; Robert Wuthnow, *Rough Country: How Texas Became America's Most Powerful Bible-Belt State*, Princeton University Press, 2014, p. 286; and Gene B. Powers, "As Texas Goes, So Goes the Nation: Conservatism and Culture Wars in the Lone Star State," in Keith Erekson, *Politics and the History Curriculum: The Struggle Over Standards in Texas and the Nation*, Palgrave Macmillan, 2012, p. 28.

5. For what the Gablers regarded as effective strategies when criticizing textbooks, consult Mel and Norma Gabler, *What Are They Teaching Our Children? What You Can Do About Humanism and Textbooks in Today's Public Schools*, Victor Books, 1985, pp. 171–74.

Notes to Pages 184–203

6. Gail Collins, *As Texas Goes . . . How the Lone Star State Hijacked the American Agenda*, Liveright Publishing, 2012, p. 109.

7. Paula Allen, "The Great Textbook Fiasco," *San Antonio Express-News*, May 3, 1992.

8. Michael W. Apple and Linda K. Christian-Smith, "The Politics of the Textbook," in J. Dan Marshall, *With a Little Help from Some Friends: Publishers, Protestors, and Texas Textbook Decisions*, Routledge, Chapman, and Hall, 1991, p. 69.

9. Edward B. Jenkinson, *Censors in the Classroom: The Mind Benders*, Southern Illinois University Press, 1979, pp. 115–16.

10. See, for example, Edward B. Jenkinson, *The Schoolbook Protest Movement*, Phi Delta Kappa Educational Foundation, 1986, p. 56.

11. For more about the Gablers, consult Frank Edward Piasecki, "Norma and Mel Gabler: The Development and Causes of Their Involvement Concerning the Curricular Appropriateness of School Textbook Content," PhD diss., University of North Texas, 1982.

12. Public Testimony of Mel Gabler and report of Mel and Norma Gabler in their written report to the Texas House of Representatives Textbook Investigating Committee, January 31, 1962, p. 59.

13. Public Testimony of Mel Gabler before the Texas House of Representatives Textbook Investigating Committee, January 31, 1962.

14. Public Testimony of Mel Gabler before the Texas House of Representatives Textbook Investigating Committee, January 31, 1962.

15. Source obtained from the Rice University website, http://www.rice.edu.

16. William Martin, "The Guardians Who Slumberth Not," *Texas Monthly*, November, 1982, pp. 267–71.

Chapter 12

1. "One Man Hearing on Un-American Textbooks," *Brownsville Herald*, May 31, 1962; "Textbook Panel's Members to Submit Separate Reports," *Dallas Morning News*, November 13, 1962; Jerry Pillard, "State Textbook Panel in Secret Session Votes to Halt Work until November," *Galveston Daily News*, June 26, 1962; and Robert Wuthnow, *Rough Country: How Texas Became America's Most Powerful Bible-Belt State*, Princeton University Press, 2014, pp. 284–86.

2. For a full text of Representative Bass's final report, consult Report to Speaker Byron Tunnell and Members of the Texas House of Representatives of the 58th Legislature by the House Textbook Investigating Committee of the 57th Legislature, pp. 209–60.

3. John C. Alaniz, Report to Speaker Byron Tunnell and Members of the Texas House of Representatives of the 58th Legislature by the House Textbook Investigating Committee of the 57th Legislature, pp. 1–4.

4. Nelson Cowles, Report to Speaker Byron Tunnell and Members of the Texas House of Representatives of the 58th Legislature by the House Textbook Investigating Committee of the 57th Legislature, pp. 32–37, 127–28.

298 Notes to Pages 206–217

5. Bill Dungan, Report to Speaker Byron Tunnell and Members of the Texas House of Representatives of the 58th Legislature by the House Textbook Investigating Committee of the 57th Legislature, pp. 130–42.

6. Ronald E. Roberts, Report to Speaker Byron Tunnell and Members of the Texas House of Representatives of the 58th Legislature by the House Textbook Investigating Committee of the 57th Legislature, pp. 144–56.

Chapter 13

1. Billie Frances Boots, Public Testimony before the Texas House of Representatives Textbook Investigating Committee, Amarillo, Texas, February 26, 1962.

2. Billie Frances Boots, Public Testimony before the Texas House of Representatives Textbook Investigating Committee, Amarillo, Texas, February 26, 1962.

3. David Roberts, "Solons Clash at Book Probe," *San Antonio Light*, April 3, 1962; and "Words over Communism Enliven Textbook Hearing," *Big Spring Herald*, April 4, 1962.

4. Larry Williams, Testimony before the Texas House of Representatives Textbook Investigating Committee, Amarillo, Texas, February 26, 1962.

5. "Legislator Files Suit for 'Communist' Label," *El Paso Times*, April 19, 1962; and Clyde Walter, "Slander Suit Answer Filed," *Amarillo Globe Times*, April 19, 1962.

6. "Speaker Turman Disturbed by Trend in Textbook Probe," *Dallas Morning News*, February 25, 1962; "Book Probe Is Asked for in San Antonio," *San Antonio News*, February 17, 1962; "Books Blasted in Panhandle," *Austin American Statesman*, February 27, 1962; "San Antonio Colon Criticizes Book Hearing Witness," *Amarillo Globe Times*, February 27, 1962; "Textbook Hearing: Probe Delay Urged," *San Antonio Light*, February 27, 1962; "Book Witness Hurls Red Slur," *El Paso Herald Post*, February 27, 1962; "Hearings Termed 'Political Football,'" *Abilene Reporter News*, February 27, 1961; "Legislator Files Suit for 'Communist' Label," *El Paso Times*, April 19, 1962; and Clyde Walter, "Slander Suit Answer Filed," *Amarillo Globe Times*, April 19, 1962.

7. Jack Nelson and Gene Roberts Jr., *The Censors and the Schools*, Little, Brown and Company, 1962, p. 144.

8. Willie Morris of *The Texas Observer*, quoted in Jack Nelson and Gene Roberts Jr., *The Censors and the Schools*, Little, Brown and Company, 1963, p. 144.

9. The full text of the lawsuit can be found in *Ronald Roberts, Plaintiff, v. Mrs. Billie Frances Boots et al., Defendants*, 66th Judicial District Court of Hill County, Texas, Case Number 21730.

10. Email to Allan O. Kownslar, from Stephanie Soward, Deputy Clerk, Hill County, Texas.

Notes to Pages 218–220

11. "One-Man Hearing on Un-American Textbooks," *Brownsville Herald*, May 3, 1962; Jerry Pillard, "State Textbook Panel in Secret Session Votes to Halt Work until November," *Galveston Daily News*, June 26, 1962.

12. Dawson Dungan, "Charges on Dallas Hearing Mark End of Textbook Probe," *Dallas Morning News*, June 26, 1962; Jerry Pillard, "Textbook Study Bars Spectators," *Abilene Reporter News*, June 26, 1962; "One-Man Hearing on Un-American Textbooks," *Brownsville Herald*, May 31, 1962; "Textbook Group of Legislature Refuses Petition," *San Antonio Express*, December 25, 1962.

13. "Textbook Panel Drops Testimony at Dallas Hearing from Record," *Corsicana Daily Sun*, June 25, 1962; "State Textbook Panel in Secret Session Votes to Halt Work until November," *Galveston Daily News*, June 26, 1962; Jerry Pillard, "Walker Textbook Testimony Nixed," *The Abilene Reporter News*, June 25, 1962; Jan Reid, *Let the People In: The Life and Times of Ann Richards*, University of Texas Press, 2012, p. 30; Carlos Conde, "Textbooks Ripped Apart," *Dallas Morning News*, June 1, 1962; "Walker Says Schoolbooks Anti-Christian," *El Paso Herald-Post*, May 31, 1962; "One Man Hearing on Un-American Textbooks," *Brownsville Herald*, May 31, 1962; "Textbooks 'Pro-Red' Prober Told," *El Paso Herald Post*, June 1, 1962; Robert Wuthnow, *Rough Country: How Texas Became America's Most Powerful Bible-Belt State*, Princeton University Press, 2014, pp. 284–86; and Sean P. Cunningham, "The Paranoid Style and Its Limits: The Power, Influence, and Failure of the Postwar Texas Far Right," in David O'Donald Cullen and Kyle G. Wilkison, editors, *The Texas Right: The Radical Roots of Lone Star State Conservatism*, Texas A&M University Press, 2014, pp. 110–11.

14. "Textbooks Ripped Apart at Dallas Meeting," *Dallas Morning News*, June 1, 1962; and "Textbooks 'Pro-Red' Prober Told," *El Paso Herald Post*, June 1, 1962.

15. "Both Sides in Textbook Controversy Tell Story," *Galveston Daily News*, March 5, 1963; "Dungan Defends Using State Funds," *The Denton Record Chronicle*, March 5, 1963; "Legislator Asks Probe in Sales of Transcript," *Dallas Morning News*, March 2, 1963; and "Report Sale Probe Asked," *Dallas Morning News*, March 5, 1963.

16. Appointed by Speaker, Texas House of Representatives, March 13, 1963, pursuant to H.S.R. 236.

17. House of Representatives, May 24, 1963, Report of Investigating Committee Pursuant to H.S.R. 236, *House Journal*, pp. 2630–31.

18. *House Journal*, May 24, 1963, p. 2633.

19. *House Journal*, May 24, 1963, p. 2633–34. The full text of the defenses made by Roberts and Dungan on March 4, 1963, in regard to the charges against them, appear in the Journal of the House of Representatives of the Regular Session of the Fifty-Eighth Legislature of the State of Texas, *House Journal*, pp. 450–56.

Chapter 14

1. Petition from Reverend W. S. Arms to the House of Representatives Textbook Investigating Committee, December 24, 1962; and Richard M. Moorehead, "Text Panel Member Raps Ultra-Rightists," *Dallas Morning News*, December 28, 1962.

2. Petition from Reverend W. S. Arms to the Texas House of Representatives Textbook Investigating Committee, December 24, 1962.

3. Petition from Reverend W. S. Arms to the Texas House of Representatives Textbook Investigating Committee, December 24, 1962.

4. "Textbook Group of Legislature Refuses Petition," *San Antonio Express*, December 25, 1962; "Textbook Committee Feuds over Politics," *Brownsville Herald*, December 27, 1962; "Background Check Urged for Textbook Witnesses," *Abilene Reporter News*, December 27, 1962; "Investigation of Witnesses in Textbook Hearings Is Asked," *Mexia Daily News*, December 28, 1962; "Austin Man Asks Look into Backgrounds of Witnesses," *Denton Record Chronicle*, December 28, 1962; and "Textbook Panel Spurns Scattergun Petition," *Big Spring Daily Herald*, December 28, 1962.

5. Public Testimony before Texas House of Representatives Textbook Investigating Committee, December 24, 1962; "Textbook Group of Legislature Refuses Petition," *San Antonio Express*, December 25, 1962; "Textbook Committee Feuds Over Politics," *Brownsville Herald*, December 27, 1962; "Background Check Urged for Textbook Witnesses," *Abilene Reporter News*, December 27, 1962; "Investigation of Witnesses in Textbook Hearings Is Asked," *Mexia Daily News*, December 28, 1962; "Austin Man Asks Look into Backgrounds of Witnesses," *Denton Record Chronicle*, December 28, 1962; and "Textbook Panel Spurns Scattergun Petition," *Big Spring Daily Herald*, December 28, 1962.

6. Report to Speaker Byron Tunnell and Members of the Texas House of Representatives of the 58th Legislature by the House Textbook Investigating Committee of the 57th Legislature, p. xi.

7. "Two Legislative Issues Lukewarm," *Big Spring Herald*, December 30, 1962. For recent major changes in the Texas textbook adoption process, see footnote 2 in chapter 3.

8. "Textbook Hearing," *Corpus Christi Caller Times*, April 5, 1962.

Selected Bibliography

The Cold War, the American Communist Party, Joseph McCarthy, the McCarthy Era, Darwinism, and Creationism

The Cold War

Beschloss, Michael R., and Strobe Talbott. *At the Highest Levels: The Inside Story of the End of the Cold War*. Little, Brown, 1992.

Brands, H. W. *The Devil We Knew: Americans and the Cold War: 1945–1990*. Oxford University Press, 1993.

Critchlow, Donald T. *Phyllis Schlafly and Grassroots Conservatism: A Woman's Crusade*. Princeton University Press, 2005.

Gaddis, John Lewis. *We Now Know: Rethinking the Cold War*. Clarendon Press, 1997.

Gleason, Abbott. *Totalitarianism: The Inner History of the Cold War*. Oxford University Press, 1996.

Halberstam, David. *The Fifties*. Villard Books, 1993.

Hogan, Michael, editor. *The End of the Cold War: Its Meaning and Implications*. Cambridge University Press, 1992.

Holloway, David. *Stalin and the Bomb: The Soviet Union and Atomic Energy, 1939–1956*. Yale University Press, 1994.

Kolko, Gabriel. *Confronting the Third World: United States Foreign Policy, 1945–1980*. Pantheon Books, 1988.

La Feber, Walter. *America, Russia and the Cold War, 1945–1990*. McGraw-Hill, 1985.

Lebow, Richard Ned, and Janice Gross Stein. *We All Lost the Cold War*. Princeton University Press, 1994.

302   Selected Bibliography

Leffler, Melvyn P. *A Preponderance of Power: National Security, the Truman Administration, and the Cold War.* Stanford University Press, 1992.

Lukacs, John, and George Kennan. *A Study in Character.* Yale University Press, 2006.

Paterson, Thomas G. *Meeting the Communist Threat: Truman to Reagan.* Oxford University Press, 1988.

Thomas, Evan, and Walter Issacs. *The Wise Men: Architects of the American Century.* Simon and Schuster, 1986.

Thompson, Nicholas. *The Hawk and the Dove: Paul Nitze, George Kennan, and the History of the Cold War.* Henry Holt, 2009.

Walker, Martin. *The Cold War: A History.* Henry Holt, 1994.

Williams, William Appleman. *The Tragedy of American Diplomacy.* Dell, 1962.

Woods, Randall B., and Howard Jones. *Dawning of the Cold War: The United States' Quest for Order.* University of Georgia Press, 1991.

Zubok, Vladislar, and Constantine Pleshakov. *Inside the Kremlin's Cold War: From Stalin to Khrushchev.* Harvard University Press, 1996.

The American Communist Party

Buhle, Paul. *Marxism in the United States: Remapping the History of the American Left.* Verso, 1991.

Feklisov, Alexander, and Sergei Kostin. *The Man behind the Rosenbergs.* Enigma Books, 2001.

Gornick, Vivian. *The Romance of American Communism.* Basic Books, 1977.

Haynes, John Earl, et al. *Spies: The Rise and Fall of the KGB in America.* Yale University Press, 2009.

Haynes, John Earl, and Harvey Klehr. *Decoding Soviet Espionage in America.* Yale University Press, 1998.

Jacoby, Susan. *Alger Hiss and the Battle of History.* Yale University Press, 2009.

Klehr, Harvey, John Earl Haynes, and Fridrikh I. Firsov. *The Secret World of American Communism.* Yale University Press, 1995.

Lewy, Guenter. *The Cause That Failed: Communism in American Political Life.* Oxford University Press, 1990.

Moss, Norman. *Klaus Fuchs: The Man Who Stole the Atomic Bomb*. St. Martin's Press, 1987.

Pincher, Chapman. *Treachery: Betrayals, Blunders, and Cover-Ups: Six Decades of Espionage against America and Great Britain*. Random House, 2009.

Roberts, Sam. *The Brother: The Untold Story of Atomic Spy David Greenglass and How He Sent His Sister, Ethel Rosenberg, to the Electric Chair*. Random House, 2001.

Schmeir, Walter. *Final Verdict: What Really Happened in the Rosenberg Case*. Melville House, 2010.

Tanenhaus, Sam. *Whittaker Chambers*. Random House, 1997.

Weinstein, Allen. *Perjury: The Hiss-Chambers Case*, rev. edition. Random House, 1997.

Weinstein, Allen, and Alexander Vassiliev. *The Haunted Wood: Soviet Espionage in America—The Soviet Era*. Random House, 1998.

Williams, Robert Chadwell. *Klaus Fuchs, Atom Spy*. Harvard University Press, 1987.

Joseph McCarthy

Adams, John G. *Without Precedent: The Story of the Death of McCarthyism*. Norton, 1983.

Anderson, Jack, and Ronald W. May. *McCarthy: The Man, the Senator and the "Ism."* Beacon, 1952.

Bayler, Edwin R. *Joe McCarthy and the Press*. University of Wisconsin Press, 1981.

Bennett, David H. *The Party of Fear: From Nativist Movements to the New Right in American History*. University of North Carolina Press, 1988.

Bragg Ewald, William, Jr. *Who Killed Joe McCarthy?* Simon and Schuster, 1984.

Buckley, William F., Jr. *The Red Hunter: A Novel on the Life of Joe McCarthy*. Little, Brown, 1999.

Buckley, William F., Jr., and L. Brent Bozell. *McCarthy and His Enemies: The Record and Its Meaning*. Henry Regnery Company, 1954.

Cohn, Roy. *McCarthy*. New American Library, 1968.

Selected Bibliography

Crosby, Donald F. *God, Church, and Flag: Senator Joseph McCarthy and the Catholic Church, 1950–1957*. University of North Carolina Press, 1978.

Curry, Richard O., and Thomas M. Brown, editors. *Conspiracy: The Fear of Subversion in American History*. Holt, Rinehart and Winston, 1972.

Fried, Richard M. *Nightmare in Red: The McCarthy Era in Perspective*. Oxford University Press, 1990.

Graebner, Norman A., editor. *The Cold War: A Conflict of Ideology*, 2nd edition. D. C. Heath, 1976.

Griffin, Robert. *The Politics of Fear: Joseph R. McCarthy and the Senate*, 2nd edition. University of Massachusetts Press, 1987.

Herman, Arthur. *Joseph McCarthy: Reexamining the Life and Legacy of America's Most Hated Senator*. Free Press, 2000.

Hofstadter, Richard. *The Paranoid Style in American Politics*. Knopf, 1965.

Ingalls, Robert. *Point of Order: A Profile of Senator Joe McCarthy*. Putnam's Sons, 1981.

Landis, Mark. *Joseph McCarthy: The Politics of Chaos*. Susquehanna University Press, 1987.

Latham, Earl, editor. *The Meaning of McCarthyism*. D. C. Heath, 1973.

Lipset, Seymour, and Earl Raab, *The Politics of Unknown: Right Wing Extremism in America, 1790–1970*. Harper and Row, 1970.

Major Speeches and Debates of Senator Joe McCarthy Delivered in the United States Senate 1950–1951. US Government Printing Office, 1952.

Matusow, Allen J., editor. *Joseph McCarthy*. Prentice-Hall, 1970.

McCarthy, Joseph. *McCarthyism: The Fight for America*. The Devin-Adair Company, 1952.

Morgan, Ted. *Reds: McCarthyism in Twentieth-Century America*. Random House, 2003.

Oshinsky, David M. *A Conspiracy So Immense: The Cold War of Joe McCarthy*. Free Press, 1983.

Reeves, Thomas C., editor. *McCarthyism*, 3rd edition. Robert E. Krieger, 1989.

Reeves, Thomas C. *The Life and Times of Joe McCarthy: A Biography*. Stein and Day, 1982.

Wicker, Tom. *Shooting Star: The Brief Career of Joe McCarthy*. Harcourt, 2006.

The McCarthy Era

Belfrage, Cedric. *The American Inquisition, 1945–1960.* Bobbs-Merrill, 1973.

Belfrage, Sally. *Un-American Activities: A Memoir of the Fifties.* Harper-Collins, 1994.

Bender, David L., editor. *What Is True Patriotism?* Greenhaven Press, 1984.

Bentley, Eric, editor. *Thirty Years of Treason: Excerpts from Hearings before the House Committee on Un-American Activities, 1938–1968.* Viking, 1971.

Carleton, Don E. *Red Scare: Right-Wing Hysteria, Fifties Fanaticism and Their Legacy in Texas.* Texas Monthly Press, 1985.

Diamond, Sigmund. *Compromised Campus: The Collaboration of Universities with the Intelligence Community, 1945–1955.* Oxford University Press, 1992.

Donner, Frank J. *The Age of Surveillance: The Aims and Methods of America's Political Intelligence System.* Knopf, 1980.

Donohue, William A. *The Politics of the American Civil Liberties Union.* Transaction Books, 1985.

Friendly, Fred. *The Good Guys, the Bad Guys and the First Amendment.* Random House, 1976.

Goldstein, Robert Justin. *American Blacklist: The Attorney General's List of Subversive Organizations.* University of Kansas Press, 2008.

Heale, M. J. *American Anticommunism: Combating the Enemy Within.* Johns Hopkins University Press, 1990.

Kovel, Joel. *Red Hunting in the Promised Land: Anticommunism and the Making of America.* Basic Books, 1994.

Kutler, Stanley I. *The American Inquisition: Justice and Injustice in the Cold War.* Hill and Wang, 1982.

Lewis, Lionel S. *Cold War on Campus: A Study of the Politics of Organizational Control.* Transaction Books, 1988.

Mandelbaum, Seymour J., editor. *The Social Settings of Intolerance: The Know-Nothings, the Red Scare, and McCarthyism.* Scott, Foresman, 1964.

McGilligan, Patrick, and Paul Buhle, editors. *Tender Comrades: A Backstory of the Blacklist.* St. Martin's Press, 1997.

Selected Bibliography

Mitgang, Herbert. *Dangerous Dossiers: Exposing the Secret War against America's Greatest Authors*. Donald I. Fine, 1988.

Newman, Robert P. *Owen Lattimore and the "Loss" of China*. University of California Press, 1992.

Powers, Richard Gid. *Not without Honor: The History of Anticommunism*. Free Press, 1995.

Sanders, Jane. *Cold War on the Campus: Academic Freedom at the University of Washington, 1946–1964*. University of Washington Press, 1979.

Schrecker, Ellen W. *The Age of McCarthyism: A Brief History with Documents*. St. Martin's Press, 1994.

Schrecker, Ellen W. *Many Are the Crimes: McCarthyism in America*. Little, Brown, 1998.

Schrecker, Ellen W. *No Ivory Tower: McCarthyism and the Universities*. Oxford University Press, 1986.

Tudda, Chris. *The Truth Is Our Weapon: The Rhetorical Diplomacy of Dwight D. Eisenhower and John Foster Dulles*. Louisiana State University Press, 2006.

Whitfield, Stephen J. *The Culture of the Cold War*. Johns Hopkins University Press, 1990.

Ybarra, Michael J. *Washington Gone Crazy: Senator Pat McCarran and the Great American Communist Hunt*. Steerforth, 2004.

Darwinism

Bowlby, John. *Charles Darwin: A Life*. Norton, 1991.

Browne, Janet. *Charles Darwin: The Power of Place*. Knopf, 2003.

Browne, Janet. *Charles Darwin: Voyaging*. Knopf, 1995.

Browne, Janet. *Darwin's Origin of Species: A Biography*. Grove, 2008.

Clark, Ronald W. *The Survival of Charles Darwin: A Biography of a Man and an Idea*. Random House, 1984.

Coyne, Jerry A. *Why Evolution Is True*. Viking, 2008.

Degler, Carl N. *In Search of Human Nature: The Decline and Revival of Darwinism in American Social Thought*. Oxford University Press, 1991.

Denett, Daniel C. *Darwin's Dangerous Idea: Evolution and the Meanings of Life*. Simon and Schuster, 1994.

Desmond, Adrian. *Huxley: From Devil's Disciple to Evolution's High Priest*. Addison-Wesley, 1997.

Selected Bibliography

Desmond, Adrian, and James Moore. *Darwin.* Warner Books, 1992.

Dupre, John. *Darwin's Legacy.* Oxford University Press, 2004.

Eldredge, Niles. *Reinventing Darwin: The Great Debate at the High Table of Evolutionary Theory.* John Wiley and Sons, 1994.

Ford, Alan. *James Ussher: Theology, History, and Politics in Early-Modern Ireland and England.* Oxford University Press, 2007.

Forrest, Barbara, and Paul R. Gross. *Creationism's Trojan Horse.* Oxford University Press, 2004.

Gould, Stephen Jay. *Full House: The Spread of Excellence from Plato to Darwin.* Harmony Books, 1996.

Kaesok Yoon, Carol. *Naming Nature: The Clash between Instinct and Science.* Norton, 2009.

Lane, Nick. *Life Ascending: The Great Inventions of Evolution.* Norton, 2009.

Mayr, Ernst. *One Long Argument: Charles Darwin and the Genesis of Modern Evolutionary Thought.* Harvard University Press, 1992.

McCalman, Iain. *Darwin's Armanda: Four Voyages and the Battle for the Theory of Evolution.* Norton, 2009.

Moyer, Wayne A. *Scopes Revisited: Evolution vs. Biblical Creationism.* People for the American Way, 1983.

Quammen, David. "The Real Darwin," *Newsweek,* November 28, 2005.

Quammen, David. *The Reluctant Mr. Darwin.* Atlas/Norton, 2006.

Quammen, David. "Was Darwin Wrong? No. The Evidence Is Overwhelming," *National Geographic,* November 2004.

Shanks, Niall. *God, the Devil, and Darwin.* Oxford University Press, 2004.

Shermer, Michael. *In Darwin's Shadow: The Life and Science of Alfred Russell Wallace.* Oxford University Press, 2003.

Shermer, Michael. *Why Darwin Matters.* Times, 2006.

Sulloway, Frank J. "The Evolution of Charles Darwin," *Smithsonian,* December, 2005.

Tudge, Colin, with Josh Young. *The Link: Uncovering Our Earliest Ancestor.* Little, Brown, 2009.

Vanderpool, Harold Y., editor. *Darwin and Darwinism: Revolutionary Insights Concerning Man, Nature, Religion, and Society.* D. C. Heath, 1973.

Witham, Larry A. *Where Darwin Meets the Bible.* Oxford University Press, 2004.

308 Selected Bibliography

Creationism

Bowden, M. *The Rise of the Evolution Fraud: An Exposure of Its Roots.* Creation-Life Publishers, 1982.

Dworkin, Ronald. "Three Questions for America," *The New York Review*, September 21, 2006.

Hiebert, Henry. *Evolution: Its Collapse in View?* Horizon House, 1979.

Humes, Edward. *Monkey Girl: Evolution, Education, Religion, and the Battle for America's Soul.* Ecco, 2007.

Keith, Bill. *Scopes II: The Great Debate.* Huntington House, 1982.

Kitcher, Philip. *Living with Darwin: Evolution, Design, and the Future of Faith.* Oxford University Press, 2007.

La Haye, Tim. *The Battle for the Public Schools: Humanism's Threat to Our Children.* Fleming H. Revell, 1983.

Lebo, Lauri. *The Devil in Dover: An Insider's Story of Dogma v. Darwin in Small-Town America.* New Press, 2008.

Lewontin, Richard. "The Wars over Evolution," *The New York Review*, October 20, 2005.

Morris, Henry M. *Education for the Real World.* Creation Life Publishers, 1978.

Morris, Henry M. *History of Modern Creationism.* Master Books, 1984.

Richerson, Peter J. *Not by Genes Alone: How Culture Transformed Human Evolution.* University of Chicago Press, 2005.

Ruse, Michael. *The Evolution-Creation Struggle.* Harvard University Press, 2005.

Steve Kemper, "Evolution," *Smithsonian*, April 2005.

Sunderland, Luther D. *Darwin's Enigma: Fossils and Other Problems.* Master Books, 1984.

Whitcomb, John. *The Early Earth.* Baker Book House, 1972.

Wilder-Smith, E. *The Natural Sciences Know Nothing of Evolution.* Master Books, 1981.

Index

Page numbers in *italics* refer to illustrations.

Abernathy, Francis, 164
Abernathy, Ralph, 29, 106
Acheson, Dean, 218
ACLU. *See* American Civil Liberties Union
Adams, John, 54, 55, 56, 130, 256
AGLOSO. *See* Attorney General's List of Subversive Organizations
Aikin, A. M., 48
the Alamo, 137
Alaniz, John C., *xx*, 127, 174, 189–90, 197–201, 212, 218, 219, 229
Alien Contract Labor Law, 51–52
Allen, Bill, 63
Amarillo College, 142–43
Amarillo high schools, 142–43
American Civil Liberties Union, 3–4, 129–30, 202, 204
American Communist Party. *See* Communist Party USA
American Federation of Labor Teachers Union, 232
American Federation of Teachers, 46
American GI Forum, 233
American Government, by Frank Magruder, x, 1, 41–42. *See also* Magruder, Frank A.
American Historical Association, ix, x
American History (Ginn Publishing), 99, 117, 179
American Legion, 73, 74, 204
American Library Association, 195
The American People (Row Peterson), 179

American Revolution, 130, 166
American Studies Association, 3–4, 129, 175–76, 228
Americans for Prosperity, 232
Ames, Bill, xi
Anderson, Maxwell, 142, 229
Anderson, Sherwood, 142
Andersonville, by McKinley Kantor, 142, 175, 202, 203
Antidefamation League of B'nai B'rith, 233
antimiscegenation laws, 26, 31
anti-Semitism, 113, 114, 149
Arms, W. S., 221–22
Ashworth, Robert, 142
Attorney General's List of Subversive Organizations, 19
Attucks, Crispus, 104
Austin, Stephen F., 157–58
Averys, Clarence, 36

Barnes Primary History of the United States, 71–72, 90, 178–79
Barnett, Ross, 27
Bass, Robert Wilton "Bob," *xx*, 87, 126–27, 130, 148, 174–75, 197–98, 217–18, 222, 229, 231
Bauer, Marion, 101
Bay of Pigs, 13
Baylor University, 158, 160–61
Beard, Charles, 78
Bedichek, Roy, 164
Benet, Stephen Vincent, 142
The Big Sky, by A. B. Guthrie, 142, 202, 203
Binion, Jack, 119, 120, 121, 123

Index

blacklisting (of alleged communists), 15–16, 154. *See also* Red Scare, McCarthyism
Boatright, Mody, 164
Boller, Paul F., 2, 103, 104–17, 118, 176, 230
Boots, Billie Frances, 212–220
Boston Massacre, 104
Braden, Anne, 105–6
Braden, Carl, 105–6
Brandeis, Louis D., 210–11
Brave New World, by Aldous Huxley, 142
Brewer, David Josiah, 51–52
Brewer, J. Mason, 164
Brooks, Chet, 223
Brown v. the Board of Education of Topeka, Kansas, 24–25, 31–32, 46, 76, 114, 218. *See also* civil rights movement; integration; racism; segregation
Buck, Pearl S., 78, 229
Bunche, Ralph, 142
Burke, Edmund, 166

California social studies textbook wars, 2
Canfield Fisher, Dorothy, 101
capitalism: as portrayed in textbooks, 95–96, 198. *See also* economics textbooks
Carleton, Don E., 33, 65
Carr, Waggoner, 220
Carter, Jimmy, 60
Castro, Fidel, 13
Cather, Willa, 142, 229
Catholicism, 97–98, 212–14, 257. *See also* separation of church and state
Censorship Committee of the Texas Institute of Letters. *See* Texas Institute of Letters
censorship: as a form of bigotry, 165, 225–26; generally defined, 255–56; in libraries, 140–51; of textbooks, 67, 132–34
Chambers, Robert, 62
Chambers, Whittaker, 14
Chaney, Lynne, 234
Chavez, Cesar, 182
Christian values. *See* Judeo-Christian values

Church of Christ, 97–98
Church of the Holy Trinity v. United States, 51–52
church vs. state. *See* separation of church and state
Churchill, Winston, 12, 225
Civil Rights Act of 1866, 23. *See also* civil rights movement
Civil Rights Congress, 174. *See also* civil rights movement
civil rights movement, 2, 21–30, 65–66, 78, 105, 114, 182–83, 218, 226–27. *See also* integration; racism; segregation
Civil War era textbook protests, ix, 2, 225
Cleveland, Grover, 88
Cold War, 4, 6, 11–22, 31, 226. *See also* communism; McCarthyism; Red Scare; socialism; Soviet Union
Collins, Gail, xi
Commissioner of Education (Texas). *See* Texas State Commissioner of Education
Common Core Educational Standards, 233, 235
communism: accusations regarding, 212–20; alleged influence in textbooks, 84–85, 104, 108–11, 120–21, 129, 145, 207–8, 221–22; and the civil rights movement, 65–66; post-WWII threat of, 1–2; sympathizers, 14–15. *See also* blacklisting; Cold War; McCarthyism; Red Scare; Soviet Union
Communist Control Act of 1954, 13
Communist Party USA, 21–22, 65–66, 90, 108–9, 124
Congress of Freedom Award, 185
Connor, Theophilus Eugene, 27
conservatives vs. liberals, 4–5, 31, 33–34, 65–66, 151, 152–77, 227–28, 231–33
Constitution. *See* US Constitution
Cooper v. Aaron, 106
Copeland, Aaron, 78, 104, 142, 229
Counts, George S., 67, 68–69, 204–5
Cowles, Nelson, 95–96, 127, 138, 198, 201–3, 229
CPUSA. *See* Communist Party USA
Crabtree, Charlotte, 233–34
creationism, 62, 63–64, 183, 193–94, 236
Cullen, David O'Donald, xii

Index

311

Cunningham, Sean P., 65
Curti, Merle, 123–24

Dallas Civil Liberties Union, 114
Daniel, Price, 32, 76, 77, 213
Darwin, Charles, 62–63
Darwinism, 62–64, 129, 158, 193–94
Daughters of the American Revolution, 3–4, 41–42, 47, 50, 73–74, 78, 81–83, 85–86, 88, 93–95, 102, 119, 126, 128, 140, 152, 177, 179, 198, 203, 228, 229, 230–31
Dawson, Joseph E., 152, 158–64, 228
De Voto, Bernard, 142
Dean, Vera M., 99
Delgado v. Bastrop ISD, 22
Dennis v. United States, 13
Dewey, John, 66–67, 69, 78, 88, 89, 116, 128, 183, 204–5, 230
Dies, Martin Jr., 15–16
District of Columbia v. John R. Thompson Company, 24
Dobie, J. Frank, *ii*, v, 2, 78, 80, 138, 142, 152, 164–67, 171, 174–76, 225–26, 228–29
Dombrowski, James A., 105, 106–7, 109
Donovan, James P., 152, 167–70
Dreiser, Theodore, 142
dress codes in schools, 183
Dungan, William "Bill" Taylor, *xx*, 96, 127, 130, 164, 197–98, 203–6, 208, 211, 213, 216–20, 229, 231
Dunn, Ross, 233–34
Durr, Clifford, 106
Durr, Virginia, 106

East Texas Chamber of Commerce, 95
Eastland, Donald, 217
Ebey, George, 40–41
economics textbooks: criticism of, 94–98, 198. *See also under* textbook publishing
Edgar, J. W., 37, 93–95, 118–19
Education Research Analysts, 159, 184, 186, 194, 232. *See also* Gabler, Mel; Gabler, Nora
education: and multiculturalism, 2; and patriotism, 70–72, 89, 90, 178–79, 199; political nature of, 35; as subversive,

36, 38, 88, 121, 183; as progressive, 66–71, 89; and the Korean War, 72–73, 85; loyalty oaths for teachers, 36–37
Einstein, Albert, 78, 104, 142, 229
Eisenhower, Dwight D., 12, 13, 20–21
Endangered Species Act, 45
Equality Texas, 232
Erekson, Keith, xi
Evans, Ronald W., 1–2, 35, 67, 69
Everson v. Board of Education, 59. *See also* separation of church and state
evolution. *See* Darwinism
Executive Order 9835, 19–20

Fair Deal: criticism of, 4, 12, 31, 88, 128, 181, 226; support for, 46, 129, 180. *See also* Truman, Harry S.
Falwell, Jerry, 185
Faulkner, William, 78, 104, 142, 229
Federal Bureau of Investigation: investigation of textbook authors, 70
First Amendment. *See under* US Constitution
Fischer, Fritz, xii–xiii
Ford, Alan, 62
Forester, A. A., 82–88, 94–95, 126–27, 148, 198, 222–23, 228, 229. *See also* Daughters of the American Revolution
founding fathers, 54–55, 130, 155
Fourteenth Amendment. *See under* US Constitution
Franklin, Benjamin, 116
free enterprise system, 89, 95–96, 129, 188, 230. *See also* capitalism
Free Market Foundation, 232
Freedom Riders, 28, 29
Freedom's Frontier (Lyons and Carnahan), 98–99
Freeman, Lee, 148–50, 228
Frost, Robert, 258
Fuchs, Klaus, 15

Gabler, Mel, 50, 177, 178–96, 228, 230, 236. *See also* Education Research Analysts
Gabler, Norma, 50, 96–97, 177, 178–96, 228, 230, 236. *See also* Education Research Analysts
Gaines v. S. W. Canada, 22

Index

gay marriage. *See* same-sex marriage
geography textbooks: criticism of, 91–93, 229–30. *See also under* textbook publishing
GI Bill, 45
Gilbert, Lewis C., 141–42
Gilmer-Aikin Law, 48
Gingrich, Newt, 234
Golden, J. B., 49, 74
Gonzales, Henry B., 46
Gonzales, Jovita, 164
The Grapes of Wrath, by John Steinbeck, xv, 142, 202, 203
Great Depression, 83, 89, 133, 181–82, 226
the Great Society, 28, 45, 78. *See also* Johnson, Lyndon B.
Green, A. C., 78–79
Green, George Norris, 33, 38
Greenglass, David, 15
Greenwood, Paul G., 121–22
Grossenbacher, Julius, 131–32
Guthrie, A. B., 142

Haley, J. Evetts, *ii*, v, 74–84, 103, 104–17, 118–125, 152–53, 170–75, 222–23, 225–26, 228, 258. *See also* Texans for America
Hall, Theodore, 14
Hamilton, Alexander, 209
Harte, Houston, 65
Harvey, Richard, 96–97
Hearst, William Randolph, 70
Hemingway, Ernest, 78, 104, 142, 229
the Heritage Foundation, xii
Hernandez v. Texas, 24
Hindu American Foundation, 233
Hiss, Alger, 14
History of a Free People (Macmillan), 99, 179
The History of Our World (Houghton Mifflin), 179
history textbooks: criticism of, 98–103. *See also under* textbook publishing
history traditionalists, 69
Hitler, Adolf, 149, 215
Holbrook, C. Ray Jr., 120–21
home schooling, 183
Hoover, J. Edgar, 20, 16, 85, 108

House Un-American Activities Committee, 15–16, 39, 85, 106, 116, 214–15. *See also* McCarthyism; Red Scare
Howard, John, 176–77
HUAC. *See* House Un-American Activities Committee
Hughes, Bob, 219
Hughston, T. R., 123
humanism, 64–65, 191–92, 256–57
Hume, David, 132
Huxley, Aldous, 142

integration, 32, 45–46, 114, 170, 218. See also *Brown v. the Board of Education of Topeka, Kansas*; civil rights movement; racism; segregation
Isaacs, Maude, 97

Jefferson, Thomas, 53–54, 56, 116, 124, 143, 157, 209
Jewish Community Relations Council, 233
John Birch Society, 3–4, 21, 73, 74, 78, 95, 128, 209, 212, 215
Johnson, Lyndon B., 4, 12, 27–28, 45–46, 78, 106, 226. *See also* Great Society
Judeo-Christian values, 180–81, 182, 187, 203, 218–19. *See also* separation of church and state

Kantor, McKinley, 142, 229
Kellogg, W. H., 222
Kelly, W. D., 142–48
Kennedy, John F., 4, 12, 13, 45, 181, 209, 218, 226
Khrushchev, Nikita, 12, 84
King, Martin Luther Jr., 22, 25–26, 65–66, 106
Kinkead, Eugene, 72
Korean War, 12–13, 20, 72–73, 85, 184, 226; American POWs, 72–73, 85

labor unions: opposition to, 95
Labor-Management Act of 1947, 95
LaFarge, Oliver, 142
Landon, Alf, 76
Landrum-Griffin Act of 1959, 95
Laughing Boy, by Oliver LaFarge, 142, 202, 203

Index

313

League of United Latin American Citizens, 233
Lee, Harper, 28
Legette Yelvington McCallum, Jane, 36
Lenin, Vladimir, 84, 145
Lewis, Sinclair, 78, 104, 142
liberals vs. conservatives. *See* conservatives vs. liberals
Liberty Institute, xi, 232
libraries: censorship of, 140–51
Limbaugh, Rush, 234
Little Rock nine, 27
Lomax, John, 164
London, Jack, 78, 142, 229
Lovely, Brandoch, 129–30
loyalty oaths: for authors, 88; for individuals noted in textbooks, 98–99, 101; for publishers, 49; for teachers, 36–37. *See also* McCarthyism; Red Scare

Magruder, Frank A., x, 1, 41–42
Man and His Changing Society, by Harold B. Rugg, 68
Marjorie Morningstar, by Herman Wouk, 142, 202, 203
Marsh v. Chambers, 57–58
Martin, A. B., 142
Martin, William, 190–96
Marx, Karl, 84
Maryland Toleration Act, 51
Masters, B. E., 97, 123
Maughmer, Bertie, 42–43, 44, 94
Maughmer, Earl, 43
Maverick, Maury Jr., 2, 34–35, 39–40, 134–38, 228
Mayer, William E., 85
McCarran Internal Security Act of 1950, 18–19
McCarran-Walter Immigration and Nationality Act of 1952, 19
McCarthy, Joseph, 16–18, 39. *See also* Cold War, McCarthyism, Red Scare
McCarthyism, 4, 11, 18, 112, 123–24, 226
McFarland, John, 43
McGuffey Readers, 179
Men and Nations (Harcourt, Brace and World), 100, 179
Mexican American Legal Defense Fund, 233

Mexican American Legislative Caucus, xi, 233
Mexican American School Board Members Association, 233
Mexican American Studies, 235–36
Michigan social studies textbook wars, 2
Midland high schools, 142, 146–47
Milton, John, 132, 159–60, 209
Minute Women, 3–4, 21, 37–44, 47, 73, 74, 94
Minutemen Militia, xi
Modisett, Bill, 77
Montgomery bus boycott, 25–26. *See also* civil rights movement; King, Martin Luther Jr.; Parks, Rosa
The Moral Majority, 185, 194, 232
Moreau, Joseph, 1–2, 35, 70
Moreland, Bill, 42–43
Morgan, Douglas, 148–49
Morgan, Irene, 25
Morris, Willie, 213–14
Mossner, Ernest C., 132–34
Multicultural Alliance for Social Studies Advocacy, 232

Nash, Gary B., 233–34
Nation, Carry, 182
National Association for the Advancement of Colored People, 24, 25, 29, 77, 233
National Council for History Education, 232
National Council for Social Studies, 112
National Defense Act of 1958, 2–3
National Defense Act of 1961, 2–3
National Education Association, 38, 205
National Geographic, 63
National Japanese-American Memorial Federation, 232
National Organization of Women, 232
National Rifle Association, xii
National Standards for United States History, 233–34
New Deal, 12; criticism of, 1, 4, 31, 75–76, 81, 88, 128, 226; support for, 46, 112, 106, 116–17, 129. *See also* Roosevelt, Franklin D.
New Math, 181
New Social Studies, 3, 227

New York social studies textbook wars, 2

Nineteen Eighty-Four, by George Orwell, 142, 203, 225

Nita Stewart Haley Memorial Library and History Center, 79

Norris, J. Frank, 158–59, 183

O'Daniel, W. Lee "Pappy," 76

O'Neill, Eugene, 142

obscenity. *See under* textbook publishing

Of Time and the River, by Thomas Wolfe, 142

On the Origin of Species, 62–63. *See also* Darwin, Charles; Darwinism

Organization of American Historians, 232

Orwell, George, 142, 225, 229

Our Nation's Story (Laidlaw Brothers), 178–79

Our United States History (Laidlaw Brothers), 101

Our Widening World, by Ethel Ewing, 135–38

Panhandle Plains Historical Society, 75, 76

Paredes, Americo, 164

Parks, Rosa, 25–26, 182–83

patriotism, 71–72, 199: and Korean War POWs, 72–73, 85; in textbooks, 89, 90, 129, 178–79, 199

PBS. *See* Public Broadcasting Service

Pearl Harbor, 188

People for the American Way, 232

Perez, Soledad, 164

Perry, Rick 185

Peterson, Henry, 41

phonics, 182

Pilgrims, 50–51

poll tax, 31

pornography. *See under* textbook publishing

post–World War II social conflicts: in America, 11–30; in Texas, 31–44

prayer in schools, 59–60. *See also* separation of church and state

Price, Rayford, 223

Primary History of the United States. See Barnes Primary History of the United States

Problems of Democracy series, by Harold B. Rugg, x, 1, 70. *See also* Rugg, Harold B.

Project Social Studies, 2–3, 227

Public Broadcasting Service, 37, 39

Puritan worldview, 225

racism: in America, 27–28, 32; in Texas, 32–33; biological "evidence" for, 76. *See also* civil rights movement; segregation

Rainey, Homent, 36

Ravitch, Diane, 70

Rayburn, Sam, 45–46

Red Scare, 4, 34, 35–37, 39, 13–22, 129, 207. *See also* McCarthyism

religion. *See* separation of church and state

religious Right, influence of, xii, 180, 192

Riddle, Donald I., 81, 115–16, 118–20, 140–41

Rio Grande Valley Coalition for Mexican American Culture, 233

Rise of the American Nation (Harcourt, Brace and World), 99, 117, 119, 123–24, 179

Roberts, Ronald E., *xx*, 97, 127, 197–98, 207–10, 211, 212–20, 218, 219–20, 229, 231

Robinson, Jo Ann, 26

Roman Catholicism. *See* Catholicism

Roosevelt, Eleanor, 23, 106, 218

Roosevelt, Franklin D., 4, 12, 75, 113, 114, 116–17, 161, 181, 199, 226. *See also* New Deal

Roosevelt, Theodore, 56, 57–58, 88, 137

Rosenberg, Julius and Ethel, 14–15

Roth, William E., 130

Rugg, Harold B., x, 1, 67–68, 69–71, 112, 204

same-sex marriage, 182

San Antonio, 136–37

San Antonio Missions National Park, 60–61

Sandburg, Carl, 142, 229

Save Our History, 232

Sax, Saville, 14

Scarborough, G. C., 43

Schlafly, Phyllis, xii, 185

Index

secular humanism. *See* humanism
segregation, 22–30, 32, 42, 76, 105
separation of church and state, 52–62, 88–89, 128, 158–64, 256–57; in the Constitution, 55–56, 163–64, 171, 225; and the founding fathers, 53, 54–56, 130; and "In God We Trust," 56–57, 171; and prayer in legislature, 57–58; religious tax exemption, 57; the US "Christian Nation," 52–53, 171–72, 182, 187, 203, 225, 256–57
Separatists, 50–51
Shelley v. Kraemer, 22
Shivers, Allan, 32, 34, 45
Sinclair, Upton, 116, 142
slavery: as depicted in textbooks, 104–5, 182
Slay, John, 119–20
Smart, Terry, x
Smith, Preston, 197, 218
Smith Act of 1940, 13
socialism: criticism of, 11, 21, 37, 66, 78, 86–87; in textbooks, 101, 175, 181, 188. *See also* communism; McCarthyism; Red Scare
Sons of the American Revolution, 185
Southern Conference Education Fund, 105, 114
Southern Conference for Human Welfare, 105
Southern Manifesto, 26–27, 32, 46
Southern Methodist University, 113
Southern Regional Conference, 105
southwestern folklore, 164–65
Soviet Union, 4, 12, 13, 99, 226. *See also* Cold War; McCarthyism
Space Race, 13
Spears, Franklin, 131
Spiuel v. Board of Regents of the University of Oklahoma, 23
Stalin, Josef, 12, 109, 113
State Board of Education (Texas). *See* Texas State Board of Education
State Secrets Privilege Surveillance Program, 21
State Textbook Committee. *See* Texas State Textbook Committee
states' rights, 76–77, 78, 89, 128, 181, 206
Steele, Joel Dorman, 72
Steele Commager, Henry, 78

Stees, Wally, 115
Steffens, Lincoln, 116, 142, 229
Steinbeck, John, xv, 142, 229
Sterne, Ann, 101
Stevenson, Suzanne, 37
Stone, Emerson Sr., 122–23
Story of Nations (Holt, Rinehart and Winston), 100, 179
Sutton, Garlington J., 46
Sweatt, Herman Marion, 23–24. See also *Sweatt v. Painter*
Sweatt v. Painter, 23

Talmadge, Eugene, 27
Tarbell, Ida M., 116, 142, 229
Ten Commandments, 50, 57, 60, 63, 182. *See* separation of church and state
Texans for America, 3–4, 47, 50, 73, 74–75, 78, 81–83, 88, 93, 95, 98–99, 102, 103, 104–17, 118–125, 126, 128, 140, 151, 152–77, 179, 204, 209, 228, 229
Texas A&M University, 157
Texas Attorney General, 217
Texas Christian University, 111, 230
Texas Commissioner of Education. *See* Texas State Commissioner of Education
Texas Communist Control Law of 1951, 34
Texas Conservative Coalition, xi, 232
Texas Eagle Forum, 232
Texas Education Agency, 49, 73, 126
Texas Education Service Centers Curriculum Collaborative, 234
Texas Essential Knowledge and Skills, 234–35, 236–37
Texas Folklore Society, 164
Texas Freedom Forum, 185
Texas Freedom Network, x, 232
Texas Good Citizenship Medal, 185
Texas Historical Records Survey, 75
Texas history from 1945–61 (overview), 31–44
Texas House of Representatives Textbook Investigating Committee, *ii*, v, 125, 126–39, 178–79, 184, 186–90, 197–224, 229; intense nature of hearings, 197–221; internal conflicts, 217–20; and library censorship, 140–51

Texas Institute of Letters, 3–4, 80, 129, 151, 152–77, 173, 204, 228, 229
Texas Jefferson Democrats, 76
Texas Latino Education Coalition, 233
Texas Library Association, 3–4, 129, 176, 228
Texas Public Policy Foundation, 232
Texas Senate Awards of Appreciation, 185
Texas Social Studies Standards of 2010, xi–xii
Texas Society of the Daughters of the American Revolution. *See* Daughters of the American Revolution
Texas State Board of Education, 74, 91–103, 126, 179, 184–86, 229; conservatism within, 185–86; and the Textbook Committee, 48–49, 229; and the textbook election process, 87, 88; textbook proclamation, 48, 93; recommendations to, 91–103, 118–25, 229
Texas State Commissioner of Education, 198, 229; and critics of textbook programs, 49; recommendations to, 91–103, 118–25; and textbook selection, 48–49, 87
Texas State Historical Association, 232
Texas State Teachers Association, 232
Texas State Textbook Committee, 179, 198, 229; background of, 48–49, 101, 122; and library censorship, 140–51; November 1961 recommendations to the Texas State Commissioner of Education, 90, 91–103, 119, 123, 126, 241–49; September 1961 hearings, 61, 73, 74–90
Texas Tea Party, 232
Texas Tech University, 76
Texas textbook hearings. *See* Texas State Textbook Committee
Texas Values Action, 232
Texas Veterans Land Program, 32
textbook hearings. *See* Texas State Textbook Committee
textbook proclamation. *See under* Texas State Board of Education
textbook publishing: and censorship, 67, 132–34, 165, 185–86, 195–96, 198, 225–26; economics textbooks, 94–98; geography textbooks, 91–93; history

textbooks, 91, 98–103; influence on students, 87, 132, 180–81; loyalty oaths, 49; and pornographic/obscene content, 8, 150, 161–62, 192, 202–3, 205; protesting process, 49, 102; Texas as a national leader for, 47–48; textbook adoption process in Texas, 48–49
theory of evolution. *See* Darwinism
This Is America's Story (Houghton Mifflin), 100, 179
This Is Our Nation, by Paul Boller Jr. and Jean Tilford, 103, 104–17, 118, 123, 124, 179. *See also* Boller, Paul Jr., and Tilford, Jean
Thurmond, Strom, 27
Tilford, Jean, 103, 112, 118, 230
Till, Emmett, 26
Tillman, Benjamin Ryann, 27
Tinkle, Lon, 152, 153, 228
Todd, Paul, 123–24
To Kill a Mockingbird, by Harper Lee, 28, 258
Trace, Arthur S., 87
Truman, Harry S., 4, 18–20, 23, 113, 181, 184, 218, 226. *See also* Executive Order 9835; Fair Deal
Trump, Donald, 57
Truth in Texas Textbooks Coalition, 232
Tunnell, Byron, 219–20
Turman, James A., 197, 218

UN Educational, Scientific and Cultural Organization (UNESCO), 37, 89, 129, 205
Uncle Tom's Cabin, 181
UNESCO. *See* UN Educational, Scientific and Cultural Organization
United Nations, 4, 23, 89, 104; criticism of, 21, 40, 76, 88–89, 129, 181, 188–89, 199, 226; support for, 135–36
Universal Declaration of Human Rights, 23
University of Texas, 75, 129, 148, 154, 164, 171, 172–74, 175, 218–19, 228
US Constitution: as a secular document: 51–52; and separation of church and state, 55–56, 158–64; First Amendment, 59, 61; Ninth Amendment, 89,

129, 181; Tenth Amendment, 89, 129, 181; Fourteenth Amendment, 22–25, 47, 59, 61
Ussher, James, 62

Vandiver, Frank E., 152, 157–58, 228
Vardaman, James K., 27
Vietnam War, 182
Vincent Benet, Stephen, 229

Walker, Edwin A., 197, 218–19, 228
Wallace, Russell, 62
Wallbuilders, 232
War on Poverty, 45
Ward, Nathaniel, 225
Wardlaw, Frank, 152, 154–55, 228
Warren, Earl, 25, 218
Washington, George, 116, 129, 178
Watergate, 182
The Way West, by A. B. Guthrie, 142, 202
Webb, Walter Prescott, 164
Weems, Parson, 179

Weis, William A., 14
Werlein, Ewing, 41–42
West Texas A&M University, 80–81
White, Hattie Mae, 46
White, Jack, 39
White Citizens Council, 43
Wilkison, Kyle G., xii
Williams, Aubrey Willis, 105–6, 109
Williams, Larry, 213
Wilson, Woodrow, 88, 209
Wolfe, Alan, 54
Wolfe, Thomas, 142, 229
Women on the Wall, 232
women's rights movement, 2, 31, 36, 182, 227
Wouk, Herman, 142
Wuthnow, Robert, xiii

Yarborough, Ralph, 45–46, 76
Yates v. United States, 13
Yezierska, Anzia, 116